The Pen Makes a Good Sword

The Pen Makes a Good Sword

John Forsyth of the *Mobile Register*

Lonnie A. Burnett

THE UNIVERSITY OF ALABAMA PRESS

Tuscaloosa

Typeface: AGaramond

∞

The paper on which this book is printed meets the minimum requirements of American
National Standard for Information Sciences-Permanence of Paper for Printed Library
Materials, ANSI Z39.48–1984.

Library of Congress Cataloging-in-Publication Data

Burnett, Lonnie A. (Lonnie Alexander), 1958–
  The pen makes a good sword : John Forsyth of the Mobile register / Lonnie A. Burnett.
    p. cm.
  Includes bibliographical references and index.
  ISBN-13: 978-0-8173-1524-5 (cloth : alk. paper)
  ISBN-10: 0-8173-1524-1
  1. Forsyth, John, 1812–1877. 2. Newspaper editors—United States—Biography.
3. Journalism—Political aspects—Alabama—Mobile—History—19th century. 4. United
States—Politics and government—19th century. 5. Daily register (Mobile, Ala.) I. Title.
  PN4874.F5725B87 2006
  070.4'1092—dc22

                                                              2006007284

Contents

Acknowledgments

The idea for this book came during a 1993 Ph.D. seminar course at the University of Southern Mississippi. Over the last twelve years, I have amassed many debts of gratitude which, although they can never be adequately repaid, must, at the very least, be acknowledged. My highest expression of thanks goes to Charles C. Bolton whose comments and suggestions were always valuable and whose encouragement always treasured. William K. Scarborough, John D. W. Guice, Jürgen Buchenau, and Margaret Barnett provided valuable counsel and instruction. Many other individuals played significant roles in this project and deserve special mention: Edward Forsyth of Lockport, New York, provided genealogical information on the Forsyth family; Betty Brandon helped secure visiting researcher status for me at the University of South Alabama; Michael Thomason of the University of South Alabama was never too busy to answer questions; Michael Fitzgerald of St. Olaf College met with me on several occasions and gave valuable advice and encouragement; and Eric Foner of Columbia University read the chapter on Reconstruction and offered valuable comments. Lynne Thomas Burnett read several versions of the manuscript and offered editorial comments. Lauren Ashley Burnett, before she became old enough to realize it was not cool to do so, ran many copies and pulled many books and reels of microfilm.

I had the wonderful opportunity to work in some of the best libraries and archives in the southeastern United States. I found extremely professional and courteous people at every stop. My sincere appreciation is expressed to the research staffs of the Alabama State Department of Archives and History, Gorgas Library and the W. S. Hoole Special Collections Library at The University of Alabama, University of South Alabama Archives, Mobile Public Library, Historic Mobile Preservation Society, Museum of the City of Mobile, Mobile Municipal Archives, Mobile Probate Court Archives, Cook Library at the University of Southern Mississippi, Hill Memorial Library at Louisiana State University, Georgia State Department of Archives, Hargrett Rare Book and Manuscript Library at the University of Georgia, Perkins Library at Duke University, and Wilson Library (Southern Historical Collection) at the University of North Carolina. I was especially impressed with the assistance I received at the Library of Congress Manuscript and Rare Books Divisions as well as at the National Archives in both Washington, D.C., and College Park, Maryland. The gracious people at the University of Chicago provided photocopies of material in the Stephen A. Douglas Papers.

Finally, the editors at The University of Alabama Press have been immensely helpful during this process. The staff has shown the utmost degree of professionalism, patience, and wisdom. I am also grateful to the anonymous readers assigned by the Press, who obviously took their tasks seriously and provided valuable suggestions. Any remaining shortcomings are mine alone.

In a project of this long duration, one is bound to experience many mountains and valleys. The highs were indeed very high. One cannot forget afternoon discussions with Mike Fitzgerald over key lime pie, studying Reconstruction history with Eric Foner during a summer week in Manhattan, the first time entering the main reading room at the Library of Congress, or springtime on the campus at the University of Georgia. However, life is not spent on the mountaintop and when valleys come, they can be very deep. One week before I signed a contract with The University of Alabama Press to publish this book, I lost my father, Robert Kennedy Burnett. My dad grew up during the Great Depression and was a member of the 101st Airborne Division during World War II. He was in the snow at Bastogne and received the Purple Heart for wounds sustained in the Battle of the Bulge. He died on 18 February 2004. I have missed him every day since, and it is to him that I dedicate this book.

Introduction

"The Pen Makes a Good Sword"

In December of 1837, a twenty-five year-old John Forsyth Jr. published his first editorial as co-owner of the *Mobile Daily Commercial Register*. The young Forsyth, perhaps with (at least in this early stage of his career) an exaggerated sense of his own importance, assured his readers that "the great concerns which demand the advocacy, and should inspire the pens of Southern editors, will not be neglected." During the next four decades, Forsyth wrote about, and often played an active role in, many of the most important "concerns" of the emotionally and, later, politically divided nation. Described, after his death in 1877, by the *New York Times* as "the leading Democratic editor of the South," Forsyth commanded an important platform. As the brash Georgia native and long-time Mobilian embarked on his journalistic career, he conceded that one could not "make proselytes by fire and the sword." Nonetheless, personifying the old adage that held "the pen is mightier than the sword," Forsyth, through the *Register*, set out to "steadily pursue the maxim so strongly recommended, and so admirably adapted to wordly intercourse." This initial offering began what would be a remarkable career in the world of both newspapers and politics. From 1837 through 1877, during what one historian referred to as the "age of personal journalism," John Forsyth used his pen as his personal sword for the Democracy.[1]

Investigating the career of John Forsyth sheds light on many of the most important issues and events concerning nineteenth-century Alabama and national history. During Forsyth's earliest (and often ignored) stint at the *Register*, his major writings dealt with the emergence of a viable two-party system in Alabama as well as in Mobile. The competition between the Whigs and the Democrats provided reams of material. His twelve-year return to Georgia provides a firsthand account of a soldier's life in the Mexican War and later reveals the battles in a political war—the move to form a Southern Rights party. During the early 1850s, the Southern reaction to the passage of the Kansas-

Nebraska Act took center stage. His brief tenure as United States' Minister to Mexico demonstrates the delicate nature of foreign relations as well as internal political party relations. Forsyth's support of Stephen A. Douglas in the crucial presidential election of 1860 may have been his most controversial (at least among his fellow Alabamians) stance. After four years of loyal service to the Confederacy, Forsyth assumed the role he is perhaps best remembered for—that of vocal Reconstruction critic. In each of these cases, a study of Forsyth's writings and actions proves the validity of J. Mills Thornton's assertion that Alabama state politics consistently reflected larger national issues.[2]

During Forsyth's long journalistic tenure, several major themes emerged—all of which will be examined in this book. The first theme involves his role as a Southern editor and just what such a role encompassed. John Forsyth Jr. was a key figure in the golden age of partisan newspapers—a time when the journals were devoted to "politics and quarrels, not necessarily in that order." As historian Avery Craven noted, "The best product of the Southern press was always the newspaper. Its editor, more than any other person, spoke to and for the people of the section. Only the clergyman rivaled him in influence." It is difficult today in the age of twenty-four hour electronic media to grasp the importance of the nineteenth-century newspaper and its spokesman. For example, a small community, such as Vicksburg, Mississippi (population 4,500), had six independent newspapers in 1861. As an editor during this period, John Forsyth was a "leader of men and . . . as prominent in shaping the politics of the South as either Toombs, or Wise, or Rhett." It is also difficult for modern students to understand the partisan nature of the mid nineteenth-century newspaper. During the presidential election of 2004, national television news figure Dan Rather had criticism heaped on him for just the suggestion that he favored one side over the other. In the nineteenth century, just the opposite was true. As one historian has noted, during those days, "no southern editor rose to the top of his profession by being non-committed." Editors could be attacked for *not* taking a strong stand for their chosen and professed party. To support such partisanship, editors often had to "manufacture facts or give coloring to those already established."[3] The only unpardonable sin for the party editor was *impartiality*. Partisan advertisers and subscribers paid for partisan views.

A second theme involves the parallel nature of John Forsyth's career with that of his father. Both father and son grew up in the shadow of a notable parent. Both were educated in the North (at Princeton) before returning home to become active in local and state concerns. Each man faced probably the most frustrating times of his life at a foreign diplomatic post. Perhaps most interesting is that both Forsyths often found themselves at odds with the political establishments of their own state. Each man often had to defend himself from charges of political "treason." Forsyth Sr. argued against nullification in the 1830s while his son fought against immediate secession in the 1860s. In both instances, the men departed from what had been their earlier avowed positions—leading to charges of political inconsistency, if not outright treachery. The final similarity deals with how each man survived political storms and emerged respected, if not completely vindicated. There were, however, two major differences between the men. The father, famous as an orator, fought with the spoken word while the son, gifted with the pen, attacked with the written word. Additionally, the father was eminently successful in the political arena, rising to some of the highest national offices. The son was elected to only two positions, both times in the lower house of the state legislature.

Another theme involves Forsyth's changing, sometimes out-of-step views on several important issues. In his own national Democratic party, he often seemed to be going against the majority current. For example, in the early 1850s, he left his beloved Democracy as an advocate of the Southern Rights movement. He eventually came back into the mainstream and actually won a diplomatic appointment because of his party loyalty. During the debates of 1859–60, when the majority of the Southern Democracy appeared to be leaning toward secession, Forsyth chose to anchor himself firmly in the moderate camp. After his strong support for Stephen A. Douglas in the election of 1860, he baffled his Northern friends by becoming a secessionist and strong supporter of the Confederacy. After being hailed by postwar Republicans as a good example of a "reconstructed" citizen, he became one of the nation's most rabid (and quoted) Reconstruction critics. Forsyth also seemed to find a way to be on the losing side of a variety of causes. From 1840 until his death in 1877, he backed the winning presidential candidate only three times—and in one of those three cases, he had supported another candidate to be the party's nominee. In Mexico, he backed the losing side in a revolution. He staked his political reputation on the losing candidacy of Douglas. He abandoned his moderate position to back the losing side in the American Civil War. Finally, he used the last years of his life to fight in a losing effort to deny freedmen their newfound rights.

The final theme involves Forsyth's motivation. What prompted him to take the often unorthodox views he championed? Was his motivation based on political or economic factors? Since politics was a consuming passion in Forsyth's life, this book could easily (and perhaps justifiably) take the form of a political biography. However, recent scholarship has highlighted the extent to which economic factors also affected the editor's positions.[4] It is actually difficult to separate political and economic factors when looking at a nineteenth-century newspaper enterprise. Party patronage was certainly a source of income that helped defray the high cost of sustaining such a venture. The goal of the partisan press was obviously political victory for the chosen party, but along with such victory came lucrative party spoils. During Forsyth's adult life, only five Democrats (excluding Andrew Johnson during Reconstruction) held the nation's highest office. In each of the five terms, he reaped personal financial rewards through party patronage. Andrew Jackson appointed him as United States Attorney for the Southern District of Alabama; James Polk named him as postmaster of Columbus, Georgia; Franklin Pierce selected him as minister to Mexico; and James Buchanan awarded him large government printing contracts.

Before embarking on this exploration into the career of one of the South's most outstanding journalistic stalwarts, a couple of points should be made about sources and style. To my knowledge, no large single collection of John Forsyth's personal papers exists. Fortunately, a large number of his personal letters are found in various collections scattered throughout the South and Northeast. Almost all of these records are of a political or economic nature. Letters of a personal nature to his wife and children are practically nonexistent. Obviously, his editorials, composed over a period of nearly forty years, are the most abundant source of his personal writings. When using these records, one must realize that they were intended for a public (partisan) audience and thus must always face historical scrutiny. A second point pertains to the use of quotes in this work. The language of the nineteenth century indeed seems somewhat stuffy when compared with our own. However, John Forsyth took great pride in his use of the language. Words were his weapon of choice. Therefore, I have chosen to let his words speak for themselves in many cases where the reader might feel he would have been better served by a paraphrased version.

Return now to Forsyth's already mentioned maiden editorial. The novice editor closed his first column by stating: "We trust in Providence for the duration and prosperity of our voyage—for its faithful navigation, we must rely upon ourselves, believing that in the sunshine of peace, and in the storm of political war, rising or sinking upon the undulations of party change, we shall never lose sight of the true interests of our State, abandon those of our City, or 'give up the ship of American Democracy.'"[5] The illustration of a ship serves as an appropriate metaphor for Forsyth's career. For four decades, the fiery penman steered an active, sometimes veering, often controversial, but persistent course.

I

"The Great Son of a Noble Sire"

By the time John Forsyth Jr. penned his first editorial, five generations of his ancestors had already lived in America. Members of the Forsyth family first crossed the Atlantic in the late seventeenth century. James Forsyth, the first of the clan to immigrate to America, arrived from Scotland in 1680. In 1688 he received a land grant in Amelia County, Virginia. Scant evidence remains of the next two generations. However, James had at least one son (also named James) who, in turn, had a son named Matthew. Matthew's youngest son Robert (the grandfather of John Forsyth Jr.) began the more "distinctive" line of the Forsyth family. Born in Scotland in 1754, Robert came with his family to New England and, sometime before 1774, relocated to Fredericksburg, Virginia. At the outbreak of the American Revolution, Robert joined the Continental Army, serving briefly as a captain in Colonel Henry ("Light-Horse Harry") Lee's Battalion of Light Dragoons. He eventually attained the rank of major and assumed responsibility for purchasing food for the Revolutionary Southern Army.[1]

One of the more interesting notes to Robert Forsyth's Revolutionary War career involved a court martial proceeding against Lee. In September of 1779, Lee faced charges relating to his conduct during a march to Powles Hook. The eight specific counts ranged from "disorder and confusion" to "behaving in a manner unbecoming an officer and a Gentleman." In charge four, Lee was accused of placing Robert Forsyth in charge of a column instead of another office of senior rank. The court found that Lee acted properly as his action was "in consequence of Captain Forsythe's [*sic*] being well acquainted with the situation of the enemy." Forsyth soon resigned from Lee's battalion to take his place in the Virginia Militia. He received a personal letter from General Washington stating that he was "always sorry to lose a good officer."[2]

After the war, Robert Forsyth returned to Fredericksburg. Around this time he married Fanny Johnston Houston (an aunt of Joseph E. Johnston of later

Civil War fame). On 22 October 1780, Mrs. Forsyth gave birth to her second son—John, the father of John Forsyth Jr. In 1784 the family moved to Charleston and, the following year, claiming a land grant given in appreciation for his Revolutionary War service, Robert relocated to Augusta, Georgia. In 1786 local authorities named Robert to the board of commissioners for Augusta. After the formation of the new federal government, President George Washington, in the same communication in which he nominated John Jay as the nation's first chief justice, submitted Forsyth's name to the United States Senate for the position of marshal for the District of Georgia. Some of the responsibilities of this position included the apprehension of criminals, the conduct of public sales of seized property (including slaves), the direction of the first state census in the District of Georgia, and process serving. While performing the supposedly mundane latter duty, one Beverly Allen—a Methodist minister—on 11 January 1794, murdered Robert Forsyth. Convicted of the crime, Allen, while awaiting his punishment in jail, gained his freedom thanks to a group of armed men. The party fled to Texas, with Allen escaping justice. Congress, in another appreciative gesture, passed a bill entitled "An act to make provision for the widow and orphan children of Robert Forsyth, who was killed in the service of the United States." This legislation appropriated two thousand dollars for the education and support of the Forsyth family.[3]

Only thirteen years of age when his father died, John Forsyth Sr. rose to be one of the most notable figures in the early history of the state of Georgia.[4] The first known schooling of the future career-politician took place at Springer Academy in Wilkes County. Forsyth studied under John Springer, a Presbyterian minister. One of his classmates was William Harris Crawford, a future U.S. senator, secretary of the treasury under President James Monroe, and one of the four candidates in the presidential election of 1824. In 1799 Forsyth graduated from the College of New Jersey (now Princeton University). Forsyth returned to Georgia, where, after being admitted to the bar in 1802, he married Clara Meigs. Miss Meigs was the oldest daughter of Josiah Meigs, the first president of Franklin College (now the University of Georgia). The marriage produced eight children: Julia (1802), Mary (1807), Clara (1810), John Jr. (1812), Virginia (1818), Rosa and Anna (twins—1823), and Robert (1826).[5]

John Forsyth Sr.'s first public office came in 1808 when both houses of the state legislature elected him attorney general. By 1810, the senior Forsyth's ambitions led him to seek higher office. He launched an unsuccessful bid for election to the United States House of Representatives. In the campaign, his political opponents questioned Forsyth's loyalty to Jeffersonian republicanism.

Apparently, Forsyth at one time had given the impression that he supported the Federalist policies of John Adams. This accusation, a curse in much of the antebellum South, resurfaced from time to time throughout Forsyth's career.[6] When Howell Cobb resigned his seat in Congress, Forsyth tried once more (unsuccessfully) to enter the national body. After the 1810 census increased Georgia's representation from four to six members, Forsyth Sr. eventually won election to the body in October 1812. His national career actually began a few months earlier than planned because of a special session of Congress called for the purpose of addressing problems associated with international relations.

In 1818 the Georgia legislature promoted the young congressman to the U.S. Senate. Forsyth's first stint in the upper chamber lasted only a few months. Having served as the chairman of the House Committee of Foreign Relations, and being an unwavering supporter of the administration, President James Monroe named Forsyth as United States minister to Spain. Under the best of circumstances, this appointment was probably not a well-suited assignment for the Georgian. As one diplomatic historian noted, "His temperament and prejudices unfitted him for this mission." As a member of Congress, Forsyth had been a bitter critic of Spain and, like many Southerners, advocated military occupation of Florida.[7] The domestic situation in Spain further complicated the nature of the mission. King Ferdinand VII faced a struggle with liberal factions in his nation and had to deal with increasing revolutions in the Spanish colonies. Obviously both sides lacked patience. On one occasion, Forsyth sent a written rebuke to the king, lecturing the monarch regarding duty to his own nation and to the world. This communication evoked a strong denunciation from Spain's foreign office and prompted demands for Forsyth's recall. In perhaps the senior Forsyth's only achievement of note during this period, the U.S. minister secured ratification of the Adams-Onis Treaty, which ceded Florida to the United States (1819). In an understatement, one historian noted that Forsyth "had not yet developed the suavity and tact for which he was later known." His biographer referred to this period as the "nadir of his career."[8]

John Forsyth Sr.'s foreign assignment mercifully came to a close with his resignation—tendered after receiving the news that his state had returned him to Congress. From 1823 through 1827, Forsyth served in the lower chamber. In 1827, his legislative career was again interrupted—this time by his election as governor of Georgia. When Governor George M. Troup chose not to run for a third term in 1827, his party selected Forsyth as its candidate. His opponent in this race was Matthew Talbot, who died just days before Election Day. Probably the most significant issue during his tenure in the state capitol concerned relations with the Native Americans of the region. Forsyth, in his 1828 message to the state legislature protested the federal government's failure to remove them from Georgia. He urged the legislators to extend the state's authority over the Cherokee nation. The governor also found time to work on improvements in prisons, transportation, and education.[9]

After one uneventful two-year term in the statehouse, the public servant returned to the Senate. Serving here continuously from 9 November 1829 to 27 June 1834, Forsyth played an active role in the most important debates of the "Age of Jackson." Much like his son years later, the senior Forsyth appeared, to his critics, to waiver on certain important issues. He was first sent to Congress as a strong champion of states' rights. For example, he had openly denounced the "tariff of abominations" in 1828 and had supported a challenge to the federal government in connection with removal of Native Americans from Georgia. Much to the dismay of many of his constituents, however, Forsyth took a strong unionist stance during the nullification crisis of 1832. One of the more notable debates in Georgia history took place at a tariff convention held in Milledgeville in 1832. One hundred and thirty-one delegates from sixty of the state's eighty counties met to discuss the tariff and nullification. Leading the nullifiers were prominent Georgians such as John M. Berrien and William H. Crawford. Fearing such a move would lead to a bloody civil war, Forsyth led the antinullification forces. For three days the two men—both known as fluent debaters—locked horns. After Forsyth's resolutions were rejected, he and fifty likeminded supporters walked out of the meeting. The remaining delegates passed resolutions against the tariff but stopped short of nullification. While Forsyth did vote against the Tariff Act of 1832—feeling that it did not bring needed relief to the South—he led the opposition to nullification in Georgia and voted in favor of the compromise tariff of 1833 and was one of only two Southern senators to vote aye on the subsequent Force Bill. For these latter actions, he was denounced frequently and, on at least one occasion, burned in effigy. Forsyth defended his votes by stating, "I gave my aid to a great evil to avert the greatest of all evils—civil war."[10]

Louis McLane resigned as President Jackson's secretary of state in 1834. Most likely as a reward for Forsyth's faithful support, Jackson appointed the Georgian to fill the post. Jackson's successor, Martin Van Buren, kept Forsyth on board for his full four-year term. Several events and issues highlighted Forsyth's relatively uneventful cabinet years. The first of these involved the settlement of American claims against France. In an 1831 agreement, France had agreed to pay five million dollars to the United States as payment for damages sustained by American vessels during the Napoleonic wars. In return, the United States agreed to lower the import duties on French wines. The French leadership reneged on their obligation—feeling that the United States was too weak to press its grievance. Forsyth was instrumental in insisting on and securing the promised payments.[11]

The second diplomatic issue centered on the admission of Texas into the union. This situation proved to be among the most controversial of the elder Forsyth's career. After the successful revolt against Mexico, representatives of the Lone Star Republic frequently sounded out the administration in Washington (including Secretary Forsyth) on the possibility of U.S. recognition and annexation. Much as he did in the aforementioned nullification controversy, Forsyth took a position contrary to the Southern mainstream. Although many in the South saw the acquisition of Texas as a chance to spread the slave economy, Forsyth consistently opposed both recognition and annexation. Due in part to his objections, the annexation issue was not resolved during his tenure as secretary of state.[12]

A third issue related to sensitive negotiations with Spain over the resolution of the *Amistad* case. In June of 1839, while en route between two Cuban ports, the Spanish schooner *Amistad* was commandeered by its African slave passengers. The ship ended up off the shore of New York and eventually in New London, Connecticut. A controversy over possession of the ship and, more important, the status of the slave mutineers, soon ensued. John Forsyth Sr. found himself in the middle of competing interests—the Spanish officials who claimed the status of the ship and its passengers had not changed versus American factions (such as the abolitionists) who held that the slaves should now be freed. Forsyth, siding with the Spanish, felt that the United States had no legal authority over the disposition of the affair. A lengthy legal battle commenced, which would not be settled until after Forsyth left office. Forsyth had strong views regarding the institution of slavery. As a slaveholder, he saw a sinister plot in the abolition of the domestic slave trade. In his view, such a move would lead to three steps. First, Congress would prohibit slave transportation by land or sea from one state to another. The next step would involve a ban on the selling of slaves from one man to another within the same state, and finally, gradually usher in emancipation. The federal government would purchase the slave's freedom using money made from the sale of public lands or the surplus tax revenues.[13]

With William Henry Harrison's defeat of Van Buren in 1840, John Forsyth's service in Washington came to a close. Ironically, criticisms of Forsyth helped the Whigs carry his native state. Forsyth's last public duty was to serve as an honorary pallbearer for Harrison, who died only a few weeks after his inauguration. Back home there was talk of a return to the Senate. Forsyth put out communications expressing his interest in such a course of action. All plans remained idle speculation as Forsyth himself became ill and died soon after on 21 October 1841—one day short of his sixty-first birthday.

John Forsyth Jr. was born on 31 October 1812—only three weeks after his father's first election to Congress. Quite literally, from the day he was born in Augusta, Forsyth found himself associated with public affairs—either through his father's or his own career. One can catch only small glimpses of his earliest years. The young Forsyth benefited from an education gained at the best schools of his home state, the North, as well as abroad. In 1828 he was enrolled in a prestigious boarding school in Amherst, Massachusetts. In a foretaste of the future, Forsyth was selected to edit the school journal. After completion of his studies, he returned to Georgia to enroll in the state university. After a devastating fire in 1830 destroyed much of the small campus, Forsyth followed his father's path to Princeton, where he graduated (as class valedictorian) in 1832. One biographical sketch noted that Forsyth "enjoying unusual advantage, socially and scholastically . . . turned them to great practical benefit."[14] While this account might be somewhat overly romanticized, the writer is essentially correct. For example, at age eight, Forsyth joined his father in Spain, where he remained for two years. Certainly exposure to court life at such an impressionable age had a lasting impact on the young man.

After graduation, Forsyth returned once again to Georgia. He studied law in the office of Augustan Henry Cumming, gaining admittance to the Georgia bar in 1834. On 22 April of the same year, he married Margaret Hull, a native of South Carolina. The new couple moved to Columbus, Georgia, in 1834 and, in the following year, to Mobile, Alabama—there to establish his practice. The union produced two sons—John and Charles. Forsyth's first public position came in 1836 with the help of his influential father. Rumors circulating in the nation's capital held that the senior Forsyth was about to resign his post as secretary of state in protest over President Jackson's appointment of Amos Kendall as postmaster general. Forsyth Sr. flatly denied these reports. One Washington newspaper reported that Forsyth had been consulted before the appointment and had given his approval. Forsyth Sr.'s biographer noted that "a few months later, Jackson publicly showed his esteem for the secretary of state by appointing John Forsyth, Jr. to the office of United States attorney for the Southern District of Alabama."[15]

Beginning in 1837, Forsyth spent a total of nearly thirty years associated with the *Mobile Register* as owner, editor, or both. The *Register* traces its origin back to the founding of the *Mobile Gazette* in 1813. Soon after American troops took over the city from the Spanish, the *Gazette* published its first issue. In 1821 Johnathan Battelle and John W. Townsend founded the *Mobile Commercial Register*. The next year, the upstart *Register* absorbed the *Gazette*. In 1828, Thaddeus Sanford purchased the fledgling journal. Born in Connecticut, Sanford held many local public offices, including a term as president of the Bank of Mobile and United States collector of customs. Sanford soon purchased the *Mobile Patriot* and combined his two ventures into the *Mobile Daily Commercial Register and Patriot*. It was at this stage that the young Forsyth arrived in town. After two years in his U.S. attorney's post, during which time he contributed several letters to the paper, Forsyth, along with partner Epapheas Kibby, bought the business from Sanford and his new partner Samuel F. Wilson.[16]

In addition to his editorial duties, over the next several decades Forsyth served as Mobile city alderman, mayor of the city of Mobile, state legislator, United States minister to Mexico, Confederate peace commissioner to the Lincoln administration, and a field correspondent during the American Civil War. During a twelve-year absence from Mobile (in which he returned to Columbus, Georgia, after the death of his father), Forsyth was a planter, editor of the *Columbus Times*, 1st lieutenant and adjutant in the 1st Georgia Regiment during the Mexican War, local postmaster, and even president of the Columbus Gas Light Association. Along with his political interests, Forsyth was also an untiring proponent of economic development in the South and, more particularly, Mobile. Although the record of Forsyth's formative years is one of relative silence, after 1837, until his death forty years later, few of his deeds or thoughts would remain private. Seldom would anyone have to inquire as to where John Forsyth Jr. stood on an issue.

2

"What Rare Times We New Opposition Editors Will Have"

When John Forsyth Jr. arrived in Mobile, the port city had already survived more than a century of history that included relocation, a period of colonial rule, deadly disease, financial struggles, and several natural as well as man-made disasters. Originally settled by the French at Twenty-Seven-Mile Bluff in present-day north Mobile County, the inhabitants moved the city to its current site in 1711. The outpost was governed successively by the French (1702–63), British (1763–80), and Spanish (1780–1813) before falling under United States' jurisdiction. Mobile entered the Union as part of the new state of Alabama in 1819. After the United States finally obtained possession of the area, the size and makeup of the city's population went through a marked change. By 1839, the city claimed 13,621 residents (8,594 white, 4,470 slaves, and 557 free persons of color). As the cotton kingdom expanded into what was then known as the Old Southwest, Mobile emerged as an important financial and transportation center of the cotton trade. A south Alabama cotton crop of 10,000 bales in 1819 grew, by 1840, to 445,725 bales. When the young Forsyth arrived in Mobile, the town could boast of being second in the United States (to New Orleans) in cotton exports.[1]

Although certainly not as comfortable as several more established southern cities, Mobile, in the 1830s, did offer several amenities. Guests or transient residents of the port could choose from at least five hotels. Three banks, led by the local branch of the State Bank of Alabama (capital $2,000,000) served the needs of commerce and credit. Government business could be transacted at the U.S. Custom House while foreign concerns could be mediated at the consulate offices of Great Britain, France, Spain, Portugal, Mexico, and Columbia. Those in physical need turned to a "new, large, and convenient" 150-bed hospital. Certainly the elite did not suffer from a lack of social and cultural distractions. Religious denominations—Methodist, Presbyterian, Baptist, Episcopal, Catholic, and African—flourished. Those so inclined could participate in any number of civic/social organizations, including the Franklin Society, Typographical Association, St. Andrews Society, Mechanics Association, Hibernian Benevolent Society, and various Fire Department organizations. The proprietors of the Mobile Theatre promised six evenings per week of entertainment (at least from November to May) featuring a "stock company capable of giving effect to tragedy, comedy, opera, farce, and ballet." Of the most interest to this study was the number of newspapers in the city. By 1839, Mobile readers had access to five daily newspapers—the *Register, Mercantile Advertiser, Chronicle, Merchants and Planter's Journal,* and the *Gazette and General Advertiser.* Additionally, the *Mobile Monitor* appeared on a weekly basis.[2]

Apparently the law profession did not hold Forsyth's attention or satisfy his ambition. Thus, when Thaddeus Sanford and Samuel F. Wilson offered the *Mobile Commercial Register and Patriot*—a journal its proprietors claimed had "an extensive circulation and a very lucrative patronage"—for sale in September of 1837, Forsyth abandoned the full-time law practice, never to return. The novice journalist, along with business partner Epapheas Kibby, came up with both capital and, more important, a line of credit with Sanford and Wilson, to make the purchase.[3]

It is not exactly clear why Forsyth gave up his law office to pursue a journalistic calling. Some critics felt the *Register* was just a gift from a distinguished father to a pampered son. A correspondent to the *Mobile Advertiser* claimed that Forsyth, the "son of the premier," became an editor at the behest of the domineering elder statesman. Instead of referring to Forsyth by name, the *Advertiser* routinely labeled him "the son of Mr. Van Buren's Secretary of State." Forsyth Jr. adamantly denied this charge, arguing that, on the contrary, his father had done everything possible to discourage him from acquiring the *Register.* Several decades of public service taught the senior Forsyth to "be suspicious of a profession too often degraded." The father warned the son "never to sink the character of gentleman into that of a partisan editor."[4]

Another possible explanation is simply that the youthful Forsyth needed a steady income. Mobile in the 1830s had an ample supply of legal hirelings. One illustration makes this point. In June of 1837 when Forsyth was still active in the world of jurisprudence, it was common for the *Register* to print legal advertisements (known as "cards") on page one. In looking at the first six cards in one issue, one notices that, in addition to Forsyth, one could find attorneys John Bragg, a future state legislator; John A. Gayle, a future governor of Alabama; and John A. Campbell, a future United States Supreme Court justice. Indeed the competition was stiff—even for the son of the U.S. secretary of state. Perhaps the most plausible explanation is that the high-strung Forsyth was bored with the mundane nature of his legal occupation. Certainly a young man who had grown up around the trappings of power and had experienced at various times some of the world's most lavish settings saw little hope for fame and advancement in—as his legal card stated—"land titles, foreign and domestic, and claims before the General Land Office, or either of the Departments of the Government at Washington."[5] Forsyth's first stint as editor of the *Register* coincided with the single presidential term of Martin Van Buren. The emergence of a strong two-party political system, the Panic of 1837, the continuing controversy over the relationship between the federal government and banks, the presidential election of 1840, and the Alabama "general ticket" fiasco all provided plenty of fodder for the young journalist.

The emergence and strengthening of the Whig party provided Forsyth the first of many future chances to serve in the capacity of an opposition editor. Casual political observers tend to erroneously project the image of the post–Civil War "solid South" backward to the antebellum period. When, for example, in the 1980s, the citizens of Alabama elected their first Republican governor since Reconstruction, many claimed that, at last, Alabama had a true two-party system. This traditional view—labeled by one historian as part of "the hoary myth of cavalier aristocracies, monolithic sectionalism, and Confederate chauvinism"—placed all antebellum Southerners into a unified political category. Charles Grier Sellers Jr. blamed such "geographical sectionalism" on historians of the Frederick Jackson Turner School, in that they "fostered the further myth that political strife within the Old South was confined largely to struggles over intrastate sectional issues between upcountry and low country, hill country and black belt."[6]

Quantitative studies bear out the reality of rigid political divisions in antebellum Alabama and document the strong showing of an emerging Whig party. Statistical evidence shows that the South had a vigorous (or, in Forsyth's mind, "menacing") two-party system. For example, in the 1836 presidential election, of 425,629 votes cast in the slave states, the Whigs had a total majority of only 243 popular votes. In the four presidential elections held between (and including) 1836 and 1848, the Whigs won a total of twenty-seven Southern states and the Democrats twenty-six. In the five congressional elections held between 1832 and 1842, the Southern Democrats won 234 seats while their opponents (usually Whigs) took 263.[7]

The numbers for Alabama during the same period also point to active competition between the two parties. Although the Whigs never carried the state in a presidential election, they lost by only 5 percent in 1840 and only 1 percent in 1848. While they never won the governor's seat, the Whigs did manage to twice capture a majority of the state senate. The Whigs could count on consistently strong support from certain areas. Much to the chagrin of Forsyth, the Whigs considered the city of Mobile a safe stronghold. Likewise, Montgomery, site of the future capital, usually fell in the Whig column. The 1841 state legislature contained fifty-five Democrats and forty-five Whigs. In the governor's race of 1841, Benjamin Fitzpatrick (Democrat) won over James McClung (Whig) with 57 percent of the vote. Since the Whigs could usually count on 40 to 45 percent of the statewide vote, both of these examples are fairly typical. In Mobile County, although the Whigs won more often than not, the results could never be taken for granted. In the governor's race of August 1840, Mobile County Whigs outvoted their Democratic counterparts by a close margin of 1,191 to 1,100.[8]

To ascertain the origins and nature of this political division, one must go back to Van Buren's predecessor—Andrew Jackson. Clement Eaton, in his magisterial study *A History of the Old South,* stated that "Jackson's autocratic measures as president and his violent partisanship produced a strong coalition against him, the Whig party." The Whigs took their name from the English party opposed to the king. On 14 March 1834, Kentucky Senator Henry Clay used the term in a speech. As early as 1832, however, nullifiers in Georgia and South Carolina applied the moniker to their cause. In any event, by 1836, there was no doubt that the term meant anti-Jackson. Whig cartoons portrayed Jackson as "King Andrew I" trampling over the United States Constitution. Jackson's war against the Second Bank of the United States proved to be the defining issue between the two parties. Van Buren's presidency only aggravated the political rift.[9]

In Mobile, John Forsyth traced a consistent political division back to the early days of the republic. In a lengthy 1838 editorial, Forsyth stated that "under all the names and types assumed by political parties in this country, since the adoption of the Federal Constitution, there has been but one great dividing line of principle running between them. American politicians have been either Federalists or Republicans." Linking the Whigs of the late 1830s with the "schemes" of Alexander Hamilton and the Federalists of the 1790s, Forsyth concluded that "the objects of the two parties have been the same. The Federalists, nationals, or Whigs, by whatever different names called, have always distrusted the people, and had no faith in Republicanism."[10] Regardless of when the actual division occurred, one cannot disagree with Richard L. McCormick's conclusion that "by the 1840s, the dual forces of commercial development and Jackson's personality had profoundly altered the country's political culture from what it had been before 1820."[11] Above all, it was now a partisan political culture.

Although Forsyth routinely referred to the Whigs as the party of "moneyed aristocracy" and "kingly government," at least five (sometimes ill-fitting) groups combined to form the antebellum Whiggery. The first group consisted of National Republicans—many of whom had voted for Henry Clay in his 1832 presidential bid. A second faction contained disgruntled Democrats. Some hard-line nullifiers bolted from the party in resentment of what they viewed as Jackson's betrayal of the states' rights doctrine. Advocates of federal internal improvement—angry over such Jacksonian decisions as the Maysville Road veto—also found a home in the Whig family. A fourth group resented the influence of the New Yorker Van Buren in the party. All these factions combined with the steady line of Federalists in the Daniel Webster mold to form a credible Southern opposition.[12]

While perhaps relatively easy to identify which groups made up the Whig Party, the task of identifying the party's guiding philosophy is more difficult. Forsyth and most Democrats had no problem with this task. The Whigs, in the opinion of the Democracy, was the party of "broad-cloths and silk stockings" serving the aristocracy at the expense of the people. Whig attacks on Andrew Jackson were, in the minds of most Democrats, an extension of the Hamiltonian, "moneyed interest" attacks on the Jeffersonian/Jacksonian rule of the people. Arthur C. Cole presented this stereotypical view of the Whig Party when he wrote that it "was from its origin, and continued to be throughout its history, the party of the planter and the slave-holder—the aristocrat of the fertile black belt." In contrast, the Democrats "drew upon the opposite side of the social scale—especially upon the small farmer of the back hill country who could always be reached by the party's appeal to the agrarian spirit."[13] Eaton summarized (while not agreeing with) the traditional view: "There was an aphorism concerning the black belt of the lower south to the effect that whenever you found rich soil, there you would find a cotton bale, and sitting on the bale a Negro, and nearby would be a Whig in a silk hat. The great planter joined the Whig party believing it to be the conservative party, careful of property interests—the broad-cloth party."[14]

On closer scrutiny, several factors seem to underscore the fallacy of the traditional views of the two parties—at least in Alabama. After subjecting the membership of antebellum Alabama congressional delegations and state legislatures to a quantitative analysis, Grady McWhiney concluded that "in the state as a whole it may have indeed been true that more large planters were Whigs than Democrats. But if the men they sent to Congress and to state legislatures are any indication, the Whigs were no more exclusively the 'silk stocking' party in Alabama than the Democracy was exclusively the party of the 'common man.'"[15] Additionally, J. Mills Thornton applied simple logic when, after examining the median slaveholdings and property value of Whig and Democratic legislators, he found that the Whigs more than doubled the Democrats in both categories. Thornton, however, understood that the Whigs represented the wealthier counties of the state and that "it would seem reasonable to suppose that their Democratic opponents in those counties were not greatly poorer than they."[16] Finally, even the perceived vision of the Whig Party appears debatable. While many historians agree with Edward Pessen that the party emerged out of a "mixture of hatreds, ambitions, jealousy, and a 'modicum of principles,'" others felt the Whigs "spoke to the explicit hopes of Americans as Jacksonians addressed their diffuse fears and resentments."[17]

When Martin Van Buren took office in March of 1837, he inherited an immense political legacy—both positive and negative. On the positive side, he was the chosen successor of General Jackson. Many Democratic editors such as Forsyth could not fathom a break in the party ranks. This loyalty, however, did not hold true universally. For example, Thomas Ritchie, of the *Richmond Enquirer*, was slow to support many of Van Buren's financial policies. Forsyth often complained about a "schism" among the Democracy. In one instance, when Democrats in Mobile gravitated toward an expressed Whig position, Forsyth admonished them that "if there be a Democrat who has so much of an Arnold in him as to contemplate this course of action, he should hide his head with shame."[18]

Party loyalties aside, the fallout from President Jackson's war against Nicholas Biddle and the Second Bank of the United States, the veto of the bank's recharter, the removal of federal deposits, and the Specie Circular (which made gold and silver the only acceptable payment for public land) made the continuation of the "Era of Good Feelings" impossible.[19] On 4 May 1837, Van Buren, against the advice of many party regulars, decided to retain the Specie Circular. Six days later, the New York Bank suspended specie payments, and within several weeks, all but six of the nation's eight hundred banks followed suit. Thus arrived the Panic of 1837.

The shortage of currency, or, as Forsyth termed it, the "explosion in trade and men's affairs," hit Alabama and specifically Mobile particularly hard. State banks followed the national trend in suspending specie payments. Real estate values fell, manufactured goods could not be sold, and commercial transactions all but ceased. Most speculation during the flush times had been done on borrowed money. As many Americans learned in the 1980s, when the bottom fell out of the real estate market, the inflated debts remained but could not be paid by the debtor nor collected by the creditors. The shortage of currency particularly hurt urban families—such as those in Mobile—since they often had no resources with which to purchase food. Since taxes could not be collected and assessments dropped, the city of Mobile defaulted on its bonded indebtedness. Forsyth poetically described the collapse by writing: "From the apex of a hollow prosperity, the fragile thread which held us over ruin snapped, and down the world came—down, down, nobody knew how deep." The Mobile economy, dependent on trade, suffered greatly. On New Year's Day 1838, Forsyth reported that "the commerce between Great Britain and the United States is, at the moment, almost entirely suspended by the calamity common to both countries."[20]

More than just an abstract issue, the economic downturn greatly affected the proprietors of the *Mobile Register*. People in severe economic straits do not tend to buy newspapers or advertisements. What business came to the *Register* came in the form of credit contracts. Expressing his frustration over the inability to collect on outstanding accounts, Forsyth lamented that "publishers like lovers are generally supposed to be able to live on air." The *Register*, like most other Mobile businesses, suffered from a lack of cash flow. One humorous event typified the problem. In April of 1841, Forsyth complained about a robbery that took place at the *Register* business office. A thief had come in the night and broken into the company's money drawer. The irritated editor did not know if the perpetrator was "most knave or fool." He did conclude that the criminal was a "superlative ass" to think that there would be any cash in the *Register*'s office. The greatest loss in the burglary was the price of a new lock for the drawer.[21]

The newspaper's editors realized that they had to make a change in their liberal credit policy or risk going out of business. In June of 1838, the publishers of several Mobile newspapers, in a rare spirit of cooperation, published a joint statement regarding a new financial policy. Basically, the new plan called for advance payment in cash for all advertisements, subscriptions, and printing orders. Soon this policy appeared on the first page of every issue of the *Register*.[22]

Making matters even worse, the citizens of Mobile suffered an outbreak of both natural and man-made disasters in 1838 and 1839. Yellow fever, always a very present seasonal fear, hit the town and the *Register* particularly hard. In Mobile, most stores were closed, the post office opened only in the morning, and banks were in operation only one or two hours per day. The local newspapers struggled to put out even a weekly edition. The *Register* staff was decimated by the plague. Epapheas Kibby died from the disease in September of 1839 while Forsyth was forced to take a two-month leave of absence. By November, the substitute editor (D. J. Dowling) noted that the bookkeeper was afflicted with congestive fever, the pressman was out with chills and fever, the compositors were down with "some other" disease. Only the foreman and the temporary editor remained to try to put out a suitable product. The *Register* did manage to appear three times a week. Returning to the helm on 9 November 1839, Forsyth mourned the "hundreds of new made graves in our crowded cemeteries, the gaunt chimneys, and toppling walls in various parts of town."[23] Man-made disasters, in the form of arson fires, also hit especially hard in 1839. A series of blazes, peaking in October, devastated a large portion of the city. During this month alone, fires caused more than $1.5 million in damage. The most severe inferno destroyed five hundred buildings over eleven blocks and affected nearly one-third of the downtown area. The *Register* building barely escaped the carnage.[24]

Although Forsyth knew the plague of the fever must be attributed to the "overruling Providence, whose decrees are always directed to some good purpose," and that the fires were the work of the most vile element of society, he was not so fatalistically serene when it came to assigning blame for the economic problems. The economic depression had enormous political impact in at least two areas. First, it raised questions about the overall soundness of federal economic development policy. Second, and more specifically, the downturn prompted disagreements about the proper relationship between the federal treasury and the banking system. Finger-pointing reached new heights. Forsyth lamented that "as usual, nobody took the blame to themselves—their own conduct, their own recklessness and extravagance were not looked to; but every peccadillo or trifle in their neighbors, were magnified into portentous causes producing disastrous effects." The panic probably did more to galvanize the Whig Party than any other event of the antebellum period. The Whig leadership "triumphantly announced the bankruptcy of Jackson's 'experiment' on the currency, tracing backward from the Specie Circular the alternative evils of suspension, contraction, and excess to his veto in 1832 of the bill to re-charter the Bank of the United States." Since urban areas such as Mobile as well as plantation centers were the most adversely affected areas in Alabama, it was only natural that these were the greatest Whig inroads. As Thornton noted, after the panic, both the opposition politicians and a great many of their constituents began seeking some scheme of relief.[25]

The Democracy, clearly on the defensive, refused to take the blame lying down. Finding difficulty in refuting hard economic facts, the Democrats blamed the banks. Hostility to banks—at least for a while—became a unifying issue. As one historian noted, "Money questions at such a moment became moral questions."[26] Forsyth, refusing to place the blame on Jackson or Van Buren, instead attacked the banking community in general. He felt the bank leaders exaggerated the strength of their institutions, causing people to engage in risky business ventures. However, Forsyth claimed that "the truth was that no Bank, or combination of Banks on the face of the earth, could have checked an evil which had become distended to bursting." According to the staunch partisan, the blame for the crash was simple: "When the whole speculating community had run in debt one hundred percent beyond their possible means of paying, there was no virtue in paper magic to save them—and when ten dollars in paper were representing the value of property which in healthier times would have been answered by one, what wonder that the revulsion came, and nine of the ten were lost."[27]

The Panic of 1837 clearly contributed to the polarization of the two-party system in Alabama throughout the administration of Van Buren. The role of banks at both the federal and state level, as well as Van Buren's "sub-treasury" system, provided additional fuel for the political fires. Factions emerged in the Democracy regarding how best to handle the nation's financial woes. Many wanted Van Buren to rescind or revise Jackson's Specie Circular while others favored an unmodified retention. Members of the latter group based their support on one of two arguments. One was pragmatic—retention would help the deposit banks, especially in the West. A second was ideological—retention would enlarge the amount of specie in circulation.[28] Adherents to this point of view (including John Forsyth) believed banks, not government policy, were the root of all problems.

The national aspects of the bank question were crucial. The number of banks in the United States had grown from 330 in 1830 to 788 in 1836. In the same period, the aggregate debt of the nation increased from $74.9 million to $220.3 million. As Charles Sellers noted, except for John C. Calhoun and his (relatively few) followers, "politicians in the South were fighting over the same questions that were agitating the north—mainly questions of banking and financial policy." Jacksonians, such as Forsyth, blamed the bank for "the transgressions committed by the people of their era against the political, social, and economic values of the old Republic." The Whigs, on the other hand, "generally defended the national bank until its doom was sealed, then advocated a liberal chartering of commercial banks by the states, and finally, after the Panic of 1837, demanded a new national bank."[29]

Forsyth, through the pages of the *Register,* consistently spoke out against any form of a national bank. Since he could not argue the economic success of Jackson's financial policies, Forsyth chose to make the matter a constitutional and moral crusade. The editor accused the Whigs of claiming for the banks "power above the constitution—a power to compel both Government and people to make do with a paper currency, when the Constitution has declared that gold and silver shall be the only legal tender." In contrast, the Democratic party felt it more important to "preserve the National faith, and keep up the character of the Government for honesty and punctuality with all the world." In a moralizing tone that would make any Southern minister proud, Forsyth claimed that the Whigs wanted a bank for the sake of convenience while "the Democrats reply, 'Principle before Expediency'—we cannot do evil that good may come—we will adhere to and maintain the Constitution, against all your promises of imaginary benefits, and doubtful expediency!"[30]

At the state level, the question of banks also took center stage. Here a clear distinction in philosophy could be made. If one cannot say with certainty that the Whigs were the party of the aristocracy, there is no doubt that they were the party of banks. In the 1840 Alabama state legislature, the minority Whig members owed almost 80 percent of the total debt due from the legislature to the Bank of Alabama. Whig calls for a new chartered federal bank led several middle-of-the-road Democrats (such as Dixon H. Lewis) to become more closely aligned with the party mainstream. In the 1841 Alabama gubernatorial race, Democrat Benjamin Fitzpatrick (the eventual winner) felt it a plus to boast: "I have never borrowed a dollar from a bank, neither was I ever president or director of one. I am a tiller of the earth and look to that as the only source of prosperity and wealth."[31]

To Forsyth, the problem with the Alabama banking system again went back to philosophical concerns. He defined the credit system as "an unbounded license in speculation, to trifle with the resources of the country, deal in millions of other people's money, without one dollar of solid capital, sport their paper thousands, bank upon the public revenues, the people's money—issue the notes of a defunct corporation, and refuse to redeem them and by a course of extravagance and profligacy do everything within the power of man, to destroy the 'general confidence of mankind in each other's integrity, solvency and resources.'" Forsyth also contended that bank debtors held too much influence in the state legislature. Many apparently shared this view as the state of Alabama published a listing of all legislators who owed debts to the various banks. The *Register* took the position that debtors "wish to go to the legislature in order so to manage and control the appointment of directors that their interests may be protected."[32]

In one of his occasional misjudgments of the public mood, Forsyth proposed what he saw as the obvious solution to the state's debt crisis—a new tax. Realizing the "horror that some politicians have of the word 'taxation,'" Forsyth nevertheless felt that "the people need but to be convinced that it is right and honest to submit to the tax, and they will endure it as cheerfully as they would indignantly spurn it, were it oppressively laid." In 1838, the people of Alabama faced a true debt crisis. At the time of the specie suspension, the people of the state owed nearly $20 million to banks. After the banks gave an extension of terms, the first repayments were to come due in March of 1838. Still facing a currency shortage, doubt remained as to the ability of the people to remain solvent. Forsyth confidently stated that he could "not for a moment imagine that any man will propose as the remedy, a refusal to pay the loans. Honesty and honor scout the idea. The debt must be paid. We have borrowed it, squandered it, and we owe it."[33]

President Van Buren faced two difficult tasks—providing relief for, and preventing future recurrences of, the economic situation. In a special session of Congress, on 5 September 1837, Van Buren asked for new legislation that would make the Treasury independent of the banks. As Van Buren's biographer noted, "Because suspension, for most Jacksonians, seemed to discredit the deposit banks, with which Jackson had replaced the national bank, the clear prescription was to move on to some new arrangement. With the purpose of divorce, Van Buren made his basic response to the Panic of 1837."[34] Forsyth strongly supported the measure. In a January 1838 editorial, he called the plan "the great leading measure of the administration. Another 'grand experiment,' opposition will term it—and in one sense it is an experiment worthy of the statesman who planned it, and one which essentially differs from all its predecessors in Finance—that it is an experiment to return to the Constitution, from which we have been darkly wandering in quest of safety and stability."[35]

The president signed the sub-treasury bill into law on 4 July 1840. The law, which provided for the total divorce of the Treasury from state banks and regulated Treasury practices regarding the distribution and receipt of specie, could not have been presented with more symbolism. Speeches hailed the measure as the "Second Declaration of Independence." Amos Kendall, a prominent member of Jackson's "Kitchen Cabinet," compared the two documents by noting that "the former delivered the American people from the power of the British throne, the latter delivered them from the power of British banks." For Forsyth and many other Democratic stalwarts "the issue was not divorce versus a national bank at all: it was, rather, hard money versus the credit system of banking—a currency that would be permanently deflated or one that would expand in response to the needs of recovery and enterprise."[36] These issues would not go away easily. In fact, they resurfaced with greater strength during the presidential election of 1840.

As early as the spring of 1838, Forsyth handicapped the Whig presidential aspirants. He saw the nomination going to one of three choices—Daniel Webster, Henry Clay, or William Henry Harrison. Forsyth incorrectly predicted the demise of General Harrison's political fortunes. Believing that, through the maneuverings of Clay, Harrison would be "denounced as a renegade and traitor to his party," Forsyth felt the hero of Tippecanoe was "on the high road to political asylum."[37] In December of 1839, however, delegates to the Whig convention in Harrisburg, Pennsylvania, nominated Harrison as their candidate for president along with John Tyler for vice president. Thus was born the famous "Tippecanoe and Tyler too" team.

John Forsyth left Mobile on 9 March 1840, bound for the nation's capital. The purpose of his journey was twofold. He went to cover the Democratic National Convention, which was to be held in Baltimore in May, as well as to observe the dealings of the United States Congress while both houses debated important parts of Van Buren's proposed financial plan. A side benefit would be to spend time with his father for (unbeknownst to both) one of the last times. The national party meeting convened at noon on 5 May. Forsyth's report of the convention presented a glowing (and obviously slanted) tone. After being "appropriately and solemnly opened by an address to the [no doubt Democrat-occupied] throne of grace," the delegates conducted themselves in such a manner that the visiting editor could claim he had "never witnessed a finer spirit of harmony, good feeling, and devotion to the cause of Democratic principles."[38]

The delegates to the convention renominated Van Buren. Strangely, the body made no decision on a vice-presidential nominee. Richard M. Johnson, the incumbent vice president, appeared ready to relinquish the spot on the ticket. Many Southern partisans promoted John Forsyth Sr. for the number two position. However, with Harrison, a military hero, as their opponent, the Democrats needed Johnson, himself a military man, all the more. The elder Forsyth refused to let his name be seriously considered. The final item of business—the adoption of a platform—presented little conflict. The document condemned internal improvements, the assumption of debts, tariffs, banks, and interference in domestic institutions (read slavery).[39]

To the great annoyance of the Democrats, the national Whig Party decided to hold a "ratification" convention in Baltimore to coincide with the Democratic gathering. Forsyth went to great lengths to downplay the significance of the Whig meeting. In the first place, he seriously questioned the attendance figures put out by his rivals. Although the Whigs reported a crowd of over twenty-five thousand, Forsyth reported that "six or seven thousand people never before took so much trouble to make themselves ridiculous since the world began." Second, the Mobile correspondent targeted the behavior of the Whig delegates themselves. While the local Whig newspaper claimed, "the people themselves had met in their legitimate attitude of sovereignty to vindicate the constitution and the laws," Forsyth reported that "the whole Sabbath was desecrated by the shouts and revelry, the guzzling of mint-juleps, hard cider, and the tumult and disorder."[40] An early twentieth-century writer described the 1840 campaign as "undoubtedly the most bitter political battle ever waged in Alabama, with more enthusiasm and acid partisanship displayed than in any other contest." Much to the dismay of Forsyth and his fellow Democrats, the Whigs co-opted the popular appeal aspect from the Jacksonians. As one historian noted, "At a time of severe deflation in the wake of the panic, the issue of an expansive currency and the promotion of enterprise possessed great popular appeal. Van Buren wanted to renew Jackson's fight between democracy and aristocracy, but Whigs began to deploy for battle on new and more democratic grounds." Incredibly (and with a straight face), the Democrats appeared aghast that a political party could base their campaign on little more than symbols and emotional appeals. With righteous indignation, the Democrats complained that by the use of "banners of cider barrels, log cabins, coonskins, gourds, and a hundred other such fooleries," the Whigs were "practicing the most corrupt and unprincipled acts that ever men did, by misleading the ignorant portion of the people." After Harrison's victory, Forsyth sarcastically commented that "Should 'Old Tip' repose his wearied limbs in one of the silk damask chairs of the White House, gourds and cider barrels will haunt him with the ghosts of the hecatombs of murdered coons whose skins have greased his way to such a royal state!" With perhaps greater insight or at least greater honesty, the editor of the *Washington Democratic Review* stated that "we have taught them how to conquer us."[41]

Many contemporary observers as well as some modern chroniclers believed that the Whigs sold their political soul for this one chance at victory. Thomas Ritchie, editor of the *Richmond Enquirer,* complained that the Whigs feared voicing any serious position because "this motley multitude, like the monstrous image of Nebuchadnezzar, is made up of such heterogeneous and ill-sorted materials, that they have no great principles on which they can agree."[42] Arthur M. Schlesinger Jr., in his sympathetic treatment of Jackson, addressed the issue of the Whig's adoption of Jacksonian campaign practices, concluding that "the metamorphosis of conservatism revived it politically but ruined it intellectually." Schlesinger declared that "the Federalists had thought about society in an intelligent and hard-boiled way. Their ideas had considerable relevance to the conflicts and tensions of the life around them. But the Whigs, in scuttling Federalism, replaced it by a social philosophy founded not on ideas, but on subterfuges and sentimentalism." While ridiculing the sentimentalism, Forsyth deeply feared the "subterfuges"—among which he considered the Whig's hidden position on abolition, the tariff, and another attempt at a national bank.[43]

The summer and fall of 1840 found the *Register* filled with campaign news, warnings, and predictions. Every issue contained a copy of the Democratic party platform, a list of endorsements, and perhaps most ominously, a standard charge linking the Whigs with abolitionism. It was the latter item that worried Forsyth and his colleagues the most. The editor presented many cases to try to convince doubters that "abolitionists and whiggery were one." For example, he claimed that twenty-nine delegates to the Harrisburg Whig convention were strong abolitionists. Although Whig newspapers denied this accusation, Forsyth held firm. In another instance, he blatantly played the nineteenth-century version of the race card. While attending the Democratic meeting in Baltimore, he had observed a Whig procession consisting of "all the drays and carts of this city with banners flying, horses and harness decked out with ribbons and finery, and cider barrels to stamp the character of the procession." Forsyth's main complaint was that free blacks drove the drays and carts. Thus, he concluded, "The very 'niggers' have turned Whigs, so great is the enthusiasm for Harrison."[44]

As the November election drew near, Forsyth seemed to become more fatalistic. Although he claimed he was no "panic maker," he believed that a Whig victory would be a major boost for the abolitionist cause. As various states held elections, Forsyth's fears became more pronounced. After the September canvass in Maine, he noted that "the Democratic majority in the state is neutralized if not destroyed by the preponderance given to the Whig side by a full abolition vote." Writing of the "coming danger," Forsyth warned Southerners not to be deceived into thinking that the abolitionist charge was simply a Democratic tactic to get votes. In fact, he noted, a "revelation from beyond the grave" could not be clearer. A Whig victory would mean "abolition with or without the union."[45]

Although Van Buren carried Alabama, Harrison won the presidency. The Whigs again carried Mobile County, this time with a total of 1,480 votes to 1,102. Harrison failed to carry any Alabama county north of the black belt. Not one to be accused of being a good loser, Forsyth lamented that "Humbug has lorded it over principles, and for the first time in the history of a not very old nation, fortune has cast upon the highest round of the political ladder a man who we may at least be permitted to say, is not the best qualified for the dizzy height of all his 'illustrious predecessors.'" Forsyth tried to put on a face of relief—relief that for now, for the first time in his young adult life, he could freely criticize an incumbent administration. A week after the final tabulation of the election returns, Forsyth claimed to be "never more relieved; never more happy than at the prospect of being spared from that torrent of vindictive hatred and foul injustice which have so long been poured out by unprincipled partisans upon an administration whose every act, if not right, we believe sincerely to have been founded in honesty and purity of purpose." Anticipating rough times ahead for the new administration, Forsyth looked forward and noted "what rare times we new opposition editors will have!"[46]

One humorous incident, which nonetheless showed the nature of the hard feelings felt after Harrison's election, was the battle of the balls. On 24 February 1841, a group of gentlemen meeting supposedly "without regard to party" (but attended mostly by Whigs), resolved to throw a Harrison inauguration ball. The event was to take place on March 4 at Mobile's Waverly Hotel. In a move designed to demonstrate a spirit of goodwill, the organizers appointed (without first asking) forty distinguished Mobilians—including John Forsyth—to serve as "managers" of the event. Apparently aghast at seeing their names listed in a rival newspaper as managers of a Harrison celebration, Forsyth and many other Democratic loyalists declined the honor. Moreover, in the true spirit of partisanship and one-upsmanship, the Democrats countered by organizing their own ball. This event, clearly promoted as a Democratic ball (although individual Whigs were invited), was held on March 16 at the Alhambra. Forsyth wrote a glowing report of the gala on the morning after: "We have never seen an assemblage of people more inclined to be gay, amiable, and happy." The editor was particularly impressed with the high quality of wines (a dig at the "hard cider" of the opposition) and noted that many of his friends were "guzzling it freely at 2 a.m." According to the review, "politics were banished as life, light, music, beauty, and motion ruled the night."[47]

Supposedly still relishing his newfound status as an opposition editor, Forsyth, on the day of Harrison's inauguration, wrote that the *Register* was "free from the restraints of defensive warfare" and that "from enduring stripes, we came to put the stripes on." One galling insult was the haste with which the new administration replaced Forsyth and the *Register* as the official local printer of federal laws. Ironically (at least for a Jacksonian such as Forsyth), he complained about the rewarding of spoils to Whig supporters. In a fighting mood, the editor presented a long list of things to which the "opposition" paper was now opposed: "We are anti-administration this day. Anti-Tip—Anti-military chieftain—Anti-bank—Anti-latitudinous construction of a plainly written constitution—anti-shinplasters—anti-all the measures which have brought the Federal party into power, though not anti-all their professions. We are anti-Webster, anti-Badger, anti-Granger, anti-federalism in politics; anti-Whigism in all its notions of banks, credit and currency—in its hatred to the hard and 'almighty dollar'—and its affection for baseless operations in commerce and finance!" According to Forsyth and other Alabama Democrats, the Whig party could no longer have the luxury of relying on symbolism and emotionalism. It was time for Harrison to show substance as well as style—"The old hero who has barked up every tree, rowed one way and looked another, upon every public question, must now indicate by executive acts, what tack he means to give to the government."[48]

President Harrison died one month later. The *Register*'s first report of the death appeared on 12 April 1841 in the form of a published letter from Daniel Webster and others. Forsyth cautioned his readers that the information might be a hoax. However, just in case the information was accurate, the same edition contained speculation as to the nature of the future policies of the new president—John Tyler of Virginia. Apparently not overcome with grief, a correspondent to the *Register* noted that "this melancholy incident to the family and friends of the late President will probably produce a radical change in the administration of the Government. Mr. Tyler belongs to the Southern wing of a victorious party of allies. He has always professed to be anti-tariff—anti-bank—anti-Internal Improvement—anti-abolitionism, and was not a little touched with nullification."[49] The city of Mobile did plan a solemn and dignified service in honor of the deceased president. Forsyth served as the secretary for a committee of prominent Mobilians charged with planning the occasion. A lengthy resolution ended a day of remembrance highlighted by a "eulogy upon the character of the deceased."[50]

Partisan politics continued to survive and flourish in Alabama. Perhaps the most blatant attempt at securing and retaining political power ever attempted by a political party in the state's history occurred in 1841. Even before the election of Harrison, state elections of August 1840 reflected the increasing strength of the Whig Party organization. The Whigs gained several seats in the state legislature primarily because of their strength in south Alabama (particularly Mobile County). Even more disturbing to the Democracy was that the Whigs controlled two of the five congressional seats—the fifth district (Mobile) and the third district (Tuscaloosa). As Whig strength continued to rise after the election of Harrison, the swing district, which included Montgomery, appeared ripe for the Whig picking. Governor Arthur P. Bagby proposed a simple solution to this problem. Alabamians would elect their congressional delegation through the "general ticket" system in which an entire slate of Democratic candidates would run against a slate of Whigs. The strategy was remarkably evident. The Democrats who could not carry the Whig districts in south Alabama would be elected because of large Democratic majorities in the northern part of the state.[51]

Shortly after the election of Harrison, John Forsyth latched on to the general ticket idea—explaining the inherent "fairness" of such a system. Forsyth believed the plan to be "consonant with the true theory of representation of the whole people of a state, and the fair and legitimate mode of obtaining the expression of the people's will" and, moreover, "conformable to the spirit of the Constitution, conductive to the perpetuity of State sovereignty, defensible upon principle and equitable in practice."[52] In Forsyth's mind, the justification for the general ticket scheme rested on the simple concept of majority rule. The editor felt that since the Democrats were clearly the majority party in the whole of Alabama, they should have the total voice in the national Congress. William L. Yancey, in his *Wetumpka Argus,* expressed the same rationale, stating: "In three districts out of five, the Whigs have the power of electing a majority of Congressional representatives, while actually in a minority in the state of 6,000 votes. Thus the state is misrepresented."[53]

Governor Bagby called for the general ticket legislation. Introduced by Nathaniel Terry into the state legislature, the scheme eventually became law in January 1841. Although the Alabama congressional delegation's terms expired in March, there was no election scheduled until the following August. When President Harrison called for a special session of Congress to assemble in May, Governor Bagby convened the state legislature to approve a special election (also to be held in May) to fill the congressional positions—to be conducted under the general ticket system. Reaction from the Whig leadership was predictably and understandably hostile. This was not the first attempt by the Democrats to dilute Whig voting strength. For example, Mobile city elections were purposely held in the summer months when many Whig businessmen returned to their northern homes. As Thornton noted, "The trading community which returned each fall and remained through the season of cotton marketing but fled to New York and the resorts with the approach of the summer tended to be Whigs. The backbone of Democratic strength was among permanent residents. For this reason the date for holding the city elections was a matter of bitter partisan conflict."[54]

The day before the special election, Forsyth waxed philosophical about the general ticket. Every citizen, he claimed, would have the "right of making his suffrage perfect in character by preserving his State as an integer in the union, and not a whole composed of five provinces." Again with logic he obviously believed, Forsyth felt that at last "we shall have no one section of the State dividing the majority of the people, and representing them in parts. We shall therefore have a more perfect embodiment of states-rights—a stronger acknowledgment of state sovereignty than we ever had before at Washington. This we consider argument enough for the propriety and justice of that law."[55]

The results of the special election confirmed that the fears of the Democracy were not imagined. The Whig candidates polled more votes in three of the five legislative districts—Mobile, Montgomery, and Tuscaloosa. However, large Democratic majorities in north Alabama made the general ticket scheme plan work just as envisioned by its proponents. The Democrats secured a majority in the total state vote, thus electing their entire slate. Party leaders, however, did not have long to gloat. A provision in the special election bill provided for a statewide referendum on the general ticket system to be decided at the regular August election. Enough Democrats (Forsyth not being among them) apparently listened to their consciences and voted along with the Whigs to repeal the entire system. Not willing to give up without a fight, however, the Democrats tried another scheme. The party, "thwarted in their first attempt to secure unquestioned political supremacy in Alabama," turned to the "white basis" for apportioning congressional districts. This plan would again have the effect of diluting Whig voting strength.[56]

On the national scene, except for his support of a higher tariff, John Tyler frustrated the Whig leadership. Tyler had left the Democratic Party over what he perceived to be overly aggressive action by Andrew Jackson against the South Carolina nullifiers. Tyler's veto of a bill designed to charter a new national bank earned Forsyth's praise—"Thanks to Mr. Tyler's manly firmness, this act of political infamy has been spared the country." With the emergence of Tyler, Forsyth saw the country now containing three rival political parties: (1) the Democratic Party—"coeval with the Constitution and has neither changed its name or principle in all the vicissitudes of time"; (2) the Clay party—"men who are for Clay against the world, for Clay 'right or wrong'"; and (3) the administration party—"right at heart, but woefully perverted, on the principle that evil communications corrupt good morals."[57]

Although sometimes ignored by historians, the late 1830s were important years for Alabama and the Democratic Party. John Forsyth typified partisan editors in that he saw the political battle as more than just a quest for votes. To Forsyth the struggle was more of what Ronald P. Formisano referred to as "political revivalism." Political parties "became moralized even as issues between the parties became less explicit. Tensions rose and never did more voters come to believe that the political drama presented a clear confirmation of good and evil, right and wrong."[58] Even as the nature of politics evolved, so too did the issues. One historian of the Jacksonian period stated that "traditional lines of division between the Whigs and Democrats were forged in the 1830s at a time when the major questions—the bank, tariff, and internal improvements—were, in the main, economic. By the 1850s, these issues, for the most part, were dead ones. The sectional conflict was in the process of redefining the nature of political divisions and challenging traditional party loyalties."[59] Although Forsyth would soon leave his adopted state, for the next decade this sectional conflict defined his political philosophy.

3

"We Are in a Fit of Disquiet"

In the late spring of 1841, John Forsyth Sr. paid his first visit to Mobile. To honor such a distinguished guest, a committee of prominent Mobilians extended an invitation to the now ex-secretary of state to a public dinner to be held to recognize his many accomplishments. The offer (printed in the *Register*), noted that the occasion would be a "slight manifestation of the estimation in which we hold your eminent services as a republican statesman and the regard we entertain for your character as a citizen and a man." The committee also wanted the elder statesman to bring a partisan address "in regard to the startling measures which the party in power are essaying to fix upon the country." Diplomatically declining the invitation, Mr. Forsyth confessed that he had no ideas as to the action of the new administration. He, however, had no plan to go into retirement or seclusion. As a private citizen, the old Jacksonian would be vigilant to "enlighten the public mind, should unwise, unprincipled, or dangerous propositions be made by those into whose hands the power of the federal government has been recently dropped."[1]

A local Whig editor's reaction to this simple exchange shows, in microcosm, the political relationship between John Forsyth Jr. and his father. The *Mobile Advertiser* contained a column entitled, "The Father Against the Son." In this piece, the writer compared the Forsyths' evaluations of the new administration. While the father spoke of measures not yet taken and "ominous" indications, the son was complaining about promises and pledges already broken.[2] While this certainly was a minor distinction, it serves to illustrate the no-win political situation in which the younger Forsyth found himself. His journalistic rivals and political opponents (often one and the same) attributed any noteworthy achievement to the influence of his famous parent. Likewise, critics magnified any personal or political stumble and contrasted such with the sterling career of the senior.

Neither the father nor son realized this visit would be their last together.

Forsyth Sr. returned to his home in the nation's capital to ponder his own political future. Out of political office for the first time in over three decades, he indeed had important decisions to make. His hometown newspaper noted, "His friends and political admirers anticipated for himself higher honors and a more extended field of usefulness." Many were pushing him to make another bid for the United States Senate. In the fall, he came down with what was identified as "congestive fever." He died at his Washington residence on 21 October. His funeral, which took place two days later, was attended by the diplomatic corps, the heads of the executive departments (minus the president), the General-in-Chief of the army, and many other dignitaries. Partisan newspapers across the nation printed flowery tributes. One Georgia editor best summed his long career with these words: "Few men have lived in our day who united, in a more remarkable degree, the accomplishments both of mind and person."[3]

As the oldest son, John Forsyth Jr. faced the responsibility of settling his father's estate. With little explanation, the *Register,* in December, announced the return of the paper to Thaddeus Sanford and S. F. Wilson. Since Forsyth, in the four years he owned the *Register,* had not paid off his own debt to Sanford and Wilson, the paper was transferred back to settle their accounts. The Georgia native uprooted his family—now having two sons, given the birth of Charles in 1837—and returned to Columbus to manage the family lands.[4] While this period can be viewed as the longest interruption in Forsyth's long career with the *Mobile Register,* the next decade was a crucial stage in his personal and political development.

Columbus, Georgia, in 1841 was only thirteen years old, not far removed from a frontier outpost. In returning to his homeland, the young editor certainly could not escape his father's fame. On the contrary, it became even more evident. In 1825, then-Governor Forsyth had pushed a bill through the legislature establishing the village of Columbus at the site of Coweta Falls on the Chattahoochee River. Edward Lloyd Thomas surveyed and mapped out a new city. When the younger Forsyth arrived back in town, he could travel down two major avenues that bore the Forsyth name.

As the heirs of Thomas Jefferson had discovered fifteen years prior, a lifetime of public service does not necessarily contribute to, and, in fact, is often a hindrance to financial solvency. Forsyth faced the daunting task of administering an estate that was tangled in debt, judgments, liens, and loans. Several years later, a Georgia newspaper noted, "Mr. Forsyth [Sr.] died in the service of his country, and left behind little else besides his fame as an inheritance to his family. The responsibilities devolving upon his son have been many and heavy."[5] Since his father died without a will, Forsyth first had to apply for letters of administration for the estate. In an interesting side note, by the time he made application, the Ordinary Court of Muscogee County had already granted administrative power to Alfred Iverson. Iverson, a judge, member of the Georgia legislature, and future United States Senator, was Forsyth's brother-in-law, having married his older sister Julia. Judge Iverson agreed to waive his power of administration in favor of Forsyth.[6]

The first administrative tasks involved securing an accurate list of debts—owed both by and to the estate and taking an inventory of the deceased's property. To identify all of the debts and debtors, Forsyth placed cards in various newspapers around the state. The *Columbus Enquirer* contained this announcement: "Notice is hereby given to all persons having demands against the Hon. John Forsyth, late of said county, deceased, to present them to me properly made out, within the time prescribed by law, so as to show their character and amount. And all persons indebted to said deceased are hereby required to make immediate payment. John Forsyth, Administrator."[7] Forsyth was to discover that he got a much faster response from the former category than the latter.

The inventory proved to be a more time-consuming process. The senior Forsyth had fairly large holdings in several counties, the largest two being in Muscogee and Twiggs. After several delays, including a court-ordered replacement of a set of unreliable appraisers, the inventory was finished in December of 1842 and approved by the court the following March. Besides the land and dwelling, the Muscogee holdings consisted mainly of domestic household furnishings and utensils. The Twiggs County estate reflected a fairly large plantation operation. Included in this part of the inventory were twenty-two head of cattle, ten hogs, twelve mules, various farm implements, and forty-nine African slaves. A tally of the investment in human property shows a total value of $14,125, an average of around $300 per slave.[8]

The second phase of Forsyth's duty was the liquidation of property and the settlement of accounts. The reluctant planter/businessman again placed ads in statewide newspapers—this time announcing his intention to sell real estate holdings in Muscogee, Hancock, Jefferson, Twiggs, Walton, Wayne, Richmond, Irvin, Ward, and Appling counties. After waiting the required four months, the court granted Forsyth permission to begin the liquidation. The first sale began in August of 1843, nearly two years after his father's death.[9]

The annual return records for the next few years reveal the laborious process through which John Forsyth suffered. From 1843 to 1848, the estate transactions were designed to merely break even. Debt payment or normal estate expenses offset every dollar of income. Some of the sources of revenue, in addition to the sale of lands, included net proceeds from the cotton crop (which peaked in 1843 at $1,231.15 and bottomed out in 1848 at $436.20), the sale of a slave taken as part payment for a tract of land ($555), and the sale of an additional thirty slaves ($10,000). Some of the more interesting payments from the estate included a $10,000 note to a Mr. Rothchild for a land debt, the cost of apprehending a runaway slave ($19), and $2.50 for "a coffin for a Negro child." As late as 1850, Forsyth was still overseeing land transactions.[10]

By 1845, Forsyth had made two major decisions. First, he was going to stay in Columbus longer than originally planned and, second, he was going to re-enter the world of journalism. In January of 1845, the former Mobilian returned to the port city to arrange for the sale of his Summerville home.[11] Apparently, he was ready to sink or swim in his native state. He knew, however, that a successful swim required a source of income more dependable than what he was realizing from his late father's estate. Thus, in August of 1844, Forsyth bought the *Columbus Times*. The *Times* was a struggling weekly journal that had been in existence for only three years. Compared with the *Register,* the Columbus paper was indeed a small-time operation. This Democratic organ, however, gave Forsyth not only a source of income but also a platform for his opinions and political ambitions.[12]

The once-again journalist quickly regained his form as a proprietor/editor, Democratic party operative, and source of controversy. Within a few months, he boasted that "The *Times* has become more valuable in our hands, and we can retire at a moments warning, without pecuniary loss." Although his words sounded confident, Forsyth obviously needed additional sources of income. In December of 1845, he landed another coveted patronage job—postmaster of Columbus. It is not clear from the surviving evidence just how earnestly Forsyth sought this job, but the *Savannah Georgian* noted that he certainly *needed* it. In fact, the editor of that journal claimed that the nomination (offered officially by President James Polk) actually came from the solicitation of General Jackson himself.[13] One can speculate that Forsyth or one of his associates contacted Jackson or Polk, or that the former president got word of the financial plight of the son of one of his most trusted lieutenants. In any event, the nomination passed on 15 January 1846, so John Forsyth now had the title of editor/postmaster.

Securing this relatively lucrative assignment did not come without a bitter struggle. Just before Forsyth received his official commission, several newspapers printed a story claiming that he had been dismissed from his United States

Attorney position while still living in Mobile. According to these reports, he was guilty of a default while serving in his official capacity. Several editors came to his defense. The editor of the *Mobile Register* stated that "his resignation was perfectly voluntary, and during his residence here there was never suspicion or reproach established against him in any personal or social relation whatever." The editor of the *Mobile Herald and Tribune* likewise saw the obvious mischief in the story—"The object of it being very plainly to get the appointment of Postmaster at Columbus for some partisan, who probably thinks abuse the best way of diverting the office to his own hands."[14]

After taking the reins, the new postal employee appeared to approach his duties with the same passion that typified his editorial endeavors. Forsyth defended his new employer with what appeared to be heartfelt conviction. This defense falls somewhere between irony, hypocrisy, and near comedy. Editors were generally the most voracious critics of the antebellum mail service. A good part of their product depended on correspondence and materials copied from other newspapers. The editor of the rival *Columbus Enquirer,* for example, subscribed to fifty different newspapers. Unreliable mail service was not only an inconvenience but also threatened an editor's livelihood. During his first stint at the *Register,* there was no more hostile critic of the mail service than John Forsyth. The new postmaster, however, pontificated, "It is much easier for editors to complain, than it is for the head of a vast and complicated department to carry on its machinery with perfect precision." Any interruption in the service was due to railroad schedules, boats which were unfit for duty, and the fact that "the state laws of Georgia endure mud holes for public roads and highways." Thus, he concluded, "No mortal Postmaster General can ensure regular mails." Forsyth did at least apologize for a case where a postal contractor— seeing a chance to make a few extra dollars—dumped his mail sack in Atlanta and instead took on a load of passengers.[15]

One distressing similarity that Forsyth found in the post office and the newspaper business was the difficulty in persuading people to settle their past-due accounts. In his first month on the job, the editor and postmaster position seemed to merge, as he used the *Times* to lash out at unpaid postal and newspaper accounts. He insisted on enforcing the law that forbade extending credit for postage. Anyone with a regular account would henceforth be required to make a cash deposit in advance. When the sum of the deposit was exhausted, the patron would be notified.[16]

Forsyth found other ways to combine the postmaster/editor roles—several of which today would certainly be considered conflicts of interest. For example, a back room of the post office building served as the office of the *Times*. Forsyth would, at times, be quite liberal in his interpretation of the franking privilege and "post office business" when it came to the use of the mark for newspapers. He urged local postmasters (of which he was one) to frank letters to publishers of newspapers (of which he was also one), notifying them of the refusal of a subscriber to take a paper out of their offices, or of the death, removal, or "G.T.T." (a common abbreviation for "Gone to Texas") of a subscriber. The fact that such an arrangement could be used to partisan advantage did not go unnoticed in Whig journals. On more than one occasion, Forsyth was forced to go on the defensive and state, "The editor and the postmaster are two distinct characters, each ready and able in his vocation to defend his position and conduct."[17]

Even though the post office occupied much of his energy, there was little chance Forsyth could stay out of Democratic Party politics for long. By July of 1845, he was a delegate to a Democratic convention at Milledgeville, where he was appointed to serve on the executive committee for the 2nd Congressional District.[18] Since Columbus, like Mobile, was a Whig stronghold, he often found himself on the losing side of political battles. Just as he was becoming more and more involved in local and statewide partisan affairs, the promise of another battle loomed—the Mexican War.

While previously encouraging Anglo settlement, the leaders of Mexico, in 1830, sealed the borders. Enforcing such an edict, however, proved difficult, if not impossible. By 1835, over one thousand Americans per month crossed the border. Relations between Mexico and the United States deteriorated even further when, in March of 1836, Texas declared independence. In July, citizens of the Republic of Texas elected Sam Houston as their first president. Almost from the moment of independence, moves were underway to annex the "Lone Star Republic" into the Union. Early attempts during the Jackson and Van Buren administrations failed. As has been noted, Secretary of State Forsyth fought annexation during both tenures.[19]

With the election of James Polk in 1844, the pro-annexation forces in the nation had a sympathetic ear in the White House. On 29 December 1845, Texas became the twenty-ninth state. A furious Mexican administration broke diplomatic relations with the United States. President Polk, in what was described as a "desire to establish peace with Mexico on liberal and honorable terms," sent John Slidell to make the necessary moves to reopen formal communications.[20] Slidell was refused an audience as tensions increased. The proverbial straw that broke the camel's back was an incident precipitated by a border dispute. The Americans claimed that the southern border of Texas was the Rio Grande River while the Mexicans held to the more northern Nueces. To dramatize the American claim, Polk ordered General Zachary Taylor to move U.S. troops to the Rio Grande. A clash with Mexican forces resulted in eleven American deaths. Polk, in his war message of 11 May 1846, claimed that Mexico had "passed the boundary of the United States, has invaded our territory, and *shed American blood on American soil.*"[21] Congress, buoyed by (for the most part) favorable public opinion, enthusiastically supported the president. Back in Columbus, Forsyth noted that the Mexicans "must be taught the more common virtues of justice, honesty, and good neighborhood—that our title to Texas is a perfectly, legal, moral, and defensible title." To drive the point home, he raged that the "Mexican invasion is an outrage upon the honor and rights of this country."[22]

In preparation for military action, Secretary of War William L. Marcy sent requisitions for volunteers to the governors of eleven states (including Georgia). Even before the official request, Forsyth was sounding the trumpet call: "We have among us many young and ardent spirits, ready and willing to give their services to the country, whenever they may be needed." The eleven states responded overwhelmingly to the call. In Tennessee, thirty thousand respondents met a request for three thousand volunteers. Since none would go home, a lottery was used to select the "fortunate." The governor of Kentucky stopped his volunteer program after the state met its quota in only ten days. Even Ohio, where many leaders saw the war as merely an excuse to extend slavery, filled the ranks quickly and headed south.[23]

Georgia governor George W. Crawford instructed newspapers to print a call for volunteers. Columbus would be the rendezvous point, with June 10 scheduled as the target meeting date. Since the governor expected a surplus of volunteers, he decided that the first ten volunteer companies meeting war department regulations to show up in Columbus would be allowed to go. Among the ten that actually made it was the Columbus Guards, a local volunteer company of which John Forsyth was a long-time member. Forsyth had actually served in the Guards during his first sojourn in Columbus. The state legislature issued a charter of incorporation for the company in 1835 in response to the deterioration of relations between the state and the Creek nation. Forsyth was a 2nd lieutenant in the original organization but had departed for Mobile before the group was activated in the Creek War.[24]

When he returned to Georgia a decade later, he rejoined his old militia company. The peacetime activities of the Guards were often wonderful adventures

which, as Forsyth noted, "to the young men, who are confined closely to mer-
cantile duties, from year end to year end and, with few opportunities for rec-
reation and exercise, a tramp through the woods and weeks inhaling of pure
air . . . will be particularly grateful." One particular 1845 muster, in which
Forsyth participated, may have been the social event of the year. This excursion, from Columbus to Meriwether, included a military ball (where "the merry
hours flew away in music, light, and dancing"), a public barbecue attended by
"an immense crowd of the citizens and ladies," political rallies on the Fourth of
July, and even a stop at the local spa resort. After the several days of "drill," the
men returned, "everyone pleased with the trip, bronzed in complexion, but
strengthened and invigorated in constitution, improved in disposition, and delighted with the toils and pleasures of a mimic-soldier life."[25]

The 1846 "tramp" would not be nearly as pleasing. After heavy rains de-
layed the initial rendezvous date, the full regiment (910 men) assembled on
June 20. The force was divided into two battalions of five companies each. As
per instructions from Governor Crawford, the men elected their own officers.
Henry R. Jackson was elected colonel, Thomas Y. Reid as lieutenant colonel,
Charles T. Williams as major, and John Forsyth as adjutant. Forsyth had to
secure written permission from the Post Office Department in Washington to
leave his job and go with the regiment. With permission granted, he became a
full-time soldier—however, a full-time soldier who realized he still would have
a newspaper back home with readers craving information about the war. In his
last editorial before he marched away, the soldier/editor promised to take along
his "ink-horn" to furnish his subscribers a "description of the Mexicans, their
country, and their rulers."[26] His frequent reports give a firsthand account of the
soldier's experience throughout the ordeal.

Governor Crawford arrived in Columbus to personally give the regiment a
rousing sendoff. He closed his brief, but stirring, address with a dramatic gesture to the road leading out of town. "Soldiers, there is the road to Mexico,"
he shouted. The plan called for the Georgians to march from Columbus to
Chehaw, Alabama, there to board a train for Montgomery. A steamer would
then transport the regiment down the Alabama River to Mobile. From Mobile,
the group would board ships bound for Brazos Island near the mouth of the
Rio Grande. Finally, the men would follow the river to join up with the main
American army and certain glory. It did not take Forsyth and his fellows long
to realize that the road they were taking now would not be just another "pleasurable" jaunt they had experienced many times before. Many of the volunteers

became ill even before they left Columbus. The first death occurred on the second day of the march, before the troops had reached Opelika, Alabama (about twenty-five miles from Columbus). As promised, Forsyth sent reports back home for the duration of his active duty period. His first such letter described "an extremely hot and fatiguing march." He lamented the fact that the regiment's first victim was "cut off in the career of glory and pleasure," which obviously awaited the troops in Mexico. His early reports were, for the most part, optimistic. He, like most of his comrades, was convinced that the First Georgia Regiment would reach Mexico in time to advance with General Taylor and play a decisive role in the coming victory.[27]

Forsyth and the first battalion reached Montgomery on July 2. There he found a city more concerned with making plans for a ceremony in which distinguished citizens were going to lay the cornerstone for the new capitol building than with the visitors from Georgia. Forsyth appeared offended that the city did not put out a more elaborate welcome for the transient warriors. With a slight amount of sarcasm, he noted that "the citizens did not annoy us with the least civility, or demonstration of welcome." The good people of Selma did, however, rise to the occasion. Passing the tall riverside bluffs on the Fourth of July, the regiment was delighted to see the banks lined with citizens who offered "three thunderous cheers."[28]

Several odd incidents marred the trip down the river. In one case, a sleep-walking soldier fell overboard. He was saved and sincerely apologized to the vessel's captain for causing a delay in the journey. Somewhere along the way, the pilot gave a loud blast of the boat's whistle. Some of the volunteers, having never heard such a horrendous sound, thought the boiler had exploded. In panic, they jumped overboard and several drowned. During the lulls in such excitement, Forsyth complained that no brass band had accompanied the expedition.[29]

The group arrived in Mobile in decent shape on July 9. The most exciting news in the port city was the arrival of the regiment paymaster. Each man received $42 in gold—an amount that was supposed to cover one years' allowance of clothes. The army wisely held back a portion of the soldier's pay. Forsyth agreed with the policy because "money poured out into the men's pockets in this city would prove an element of disorganization far too potent for good discipline to restrain." Even with this policy of fiscal restraint, the pay was soon spent on new jackets, red shirts, and boots. Just outside the camp, a carnival-like atmosphere prevailed. Forsyth reported that "extemporaneous confectionaries" had set up stands that tempted the volunteers with melons, peaches, pies, and ice cream. Such temptation, in so near a proximity, "lightened the boys' pockets of many a sovereign."[30]

The "happiest set of fellows you ever saw" left Mobile on the steamer *Fashion* on the evening of July 14. Four days later, after a stormy voyage, the regiment made land at Brazos Island. Before they could disembark, the men had to wait out a torrential rain that lasted upward of thirty-six hours. When at last they came ashore, they were disappointed to find that about three thousand other volunteers already occupied the only suitable campsites. As the rain continued to fall, the Georgians at last found a place to pitch their tents and "crawled into them like drowned rats." At this early stage, Forsyth still appeared confident that his men would soon see action. Rumors of a massive push by Taylor's army filled the camp and perked the ears of the new arrivals. Adjutant Forsyth hoped his troops would "follow from this detestable island this week." Their (hopefully) temporary home reeked of brackish water pockets and ineffective sanitation. The weather fluctuated between "drought and storm." When it rained, the camp flooded and when it was dry, the "sand drift gives us a sample of the terrible sand storms of [*sic*] Zahara."[31]

Four days later, Forsyth was still convinced the Georgia Regiment would be among the first to see action. Certainly he had visions of marching with his men alongside General Taylor into Monterrey. Forsyth took a trip to Port Isabel, near the site where "American blood had been shed on American soil." Some of the men from both sides that had been wounded in battle were still there in makeshift hospitals. He appeared impressed with two Mexican soldiers who both bore serious injuries. One of the men had lost a leg, the other soldier crushed by artillery shot. Forsyth's observations concerning the men give a good insight toward his attitude regarding the Mexican people in general—an attitude that would resurface a decade later while serving as United States minister to Mexico. Although he was complimentary of the bravery shown by individual soldiers such as these, he did, however, note, "This courage can avail them nothing in the conflict with the white race. They must yield to the prowess of the equal courage, and the superior blood and energy of a superior race." Forsyth concluded that Port Isabel was a "miserable little point of black prairie soil, surrounded by a ditch and a few palisades."[32]

After the first week at Brazos, the men seemed fairly content. Their time was spent in drill and other mundane tasks. In a letter dated July 24, however, one can see a few complaints start to bubble up. Forsyth noticed that, when compared with volunteer regiments of other states, the Georgia band of brothers was indeed a shabby bunch. He criticized Governor Crawford for not "opening his heart and the public purse." Another gripe involved the lack of basic services. The regiment seldom saw a quartermaster or commissary. Also, for the first time, Forsyth began to give unfavorable reports about the health of the troops. On one morning, nearly one hundred men answered the sick call—mostly for dysentery, colds, and fever. Perhaps the biggest complaint was what the men saw as unnecessary delays. They had not come two thousand miles from home to drill. Forsyth made an observation that military men throughout history have known: "Inaction in camp is the worst thing for troops."[33]

As the days at Brazos turned into weeks, the leaders of the Georgia Regiment took matters into their own hands. Colonel Jackson decided to visit General Taylor's headquarters to "get a position" for his men with the advancing columns. Forsyth tagged along to "see the country." The journey to Matamoras was about one hundred miles up the river. Forsyth wrote an interesting travel journal. The two men mingled with the local population as they stopped at several small towns along the way. At one point, the editor got to use the Spanish he had learned as a child living with his father in Spain. He gave stereotypical descriptions of the locals. The women's clothes reflected "exceeding scantiness" and adaptation to a hot climate. The men wore high crowned and broad brimmed hats with bright shirts and pants. The children, up to ten years old, were almost always naked. Invited into a local home, a kind hostess made Forsyth his first tortilla ("did not taste like cornbread"). The traveler concluded the women were "amiable and kind-hearted people," but the men were "treacherous and false."[34]

Colonel Jackson and his young aide arrived in Matamoras on July 30. Pleased to find French, American, and Italian "eating houses," the pair enjoyed their first "Christian meal" since leaving Mobile. Their dining was helped by bottles of good St. Julian, "which was not wanting in the feast." After this respite, they went to the local theater, run, coincidentally, by a Mr. Hart, who had once lived in Columbus. On the walk back to their room, the men took the advice of a citizen and stayed in the middle of the street to avoid an attack—not from Mexicans, but from their own countrymen. Apparently, since the United States army took the ancient city, "gambling, drinking, knocking down, and robbing" were "fashionable amusements." Jackson and Forsyth made it back safely to their cots. Before going to sleep, they both loaded their pistols (also at the advice of a local) and placed them nearby.[35]

The following morning, the well-rested duo put on their best military garb and proceeded to Taylor's camp. When they finally got to meet with the general, they were convinced that the moniker "Old Rough and Ready" was appropriate. Coming upon a collection of ragged tents, they "approached one of the shabbiest we saw, and were told that was General Taylor's." Sitting under a tree on a block bench, the "old gentleman" received them "politely, but without the least ceremony or fuss." Apparently, Taylor told Jackson what he wanted to hear. The regulars would soon be moved to Camargo with the volunteers to follow. Forsyth sent back a mixed impression of Taylor. The general was "as he has been described, a plain—very plain looking man. He looks like an old planter, who had never seen a uniform, much less had one on." He did like the old soldier's "manners and appearance." The Georgian confessed that Taylor's appearance challenged his "anticipation of the halo of chivalric glory to be discovered in the atmosphere surrounding a military hero's head." In other words, Taylor was no Andrew Jackson. It is also apparent that Taylor did not convince Forsyth about the coming movement. He closed his report by noting, "We return to camp tomorrow and I fear shall be detained there a month."[36]

Forsyth was also beginning to realize the degree to which politics affected military campaigns. He noticed the obvious discrepancy in the treatment of regular troops and volunteers. While wagonloads of water and other basic supplies passed the volunteer encampment, not a "wagon or a hoof of transportation" attended to the citizen soldiers. The men were exhausted from the backbreaking task of carrying water from the river to the camp when the chore could have been much more easily accomplished. Said the adjutant: "Two or three wagons would supply all the troops here with water and save an immense waste of strength and breath by the soldiers." He could only surmise that "regular soldiers would not be treated so." Even the long awaited plan to break camp caused controversy. On August 5, Colonel Jackson finally got orders to proceed to Camargo. The Georgia regiment was listed as the eighth of ten regiments scheduled to move out. The standard procedure had been to move in the order in which you arrived at Brazos. However, the Mississippi Regiment, which was a late arrival, had jumped past Tennessee, Alabama, and Georgia. Forsyth claimed that the only possible reason for this injustice was that the Mississippian's colonel—one Jefferson Davis—was General Taylor's son-in-law. Actually, Davis was Taylor's *former* son-in-law. He had married Sarah Taylor on 17 June 1835, but his bride succumbed to malaria less than three months later.[37]

The euphoria of the anticipated move died down as two more weeks went by with no action. The remainder of Forsyth's letters from Mexico took on a more somber tone. Running out of topics on which to opine, he wrote a blistering account of the "myriads of crawling, flying, stinging, and biting things" of the camp. One morning while eating breakfast (standing up, since there was nowhere to sit), Forsyth felt something crawling up his leg. Grabbing the "mystery creature" while disrobing, he "beheld a villainous looking creature of black and yellow with a long, bony tail." He took the creature to the regiment doctor where it was identified as a Mexican scorpion, "as poisonous as a rattle-snake." In addition to scorpions, the area was infested with spiders, centipedes, "hordes of flies," and a "gang of locusts." At night, these plagues were joined by "the music of frogs," the barking of prairie dogs, and at least one panther. These annoyances could certainly bring "death to one's patriotic emotions." In his first reference to going home, Forsyth noted that he longed to "get back from the land of half-bred Indians and full-bred bugs."[38]

Adding to the increasing feelings of melancholy was a greater frequency of death among the volunteers. On August 14, Forsyth reported, "Three of our poor fellows have gone to their long home." Three days later, two more were added to the list of those "who have died in this far off country and whose bones repose upon the banks of the Rio Grande." He also sadly commented that one could never get used to the "almost hourly funeral corteges" from some of the regiments that passed by the camp."[39] The command discharged several sick and/or disabled men, who promptly forsook "glory" and went home. As these men returned to Georgia, Forsyth warned the homefront population to be on guard against the "doleful accounts" of the regiment's condition. Trying to put a bright side to a gloomy situation—a skill that would come in handy during the early 1860s—he (falsely) claimed the health of the men was improving.

Only a day or two after the glowing communication, Forsyth himself fell ill. No report from him reached Georgia for two weeks. On August 24, he let the hometown people know that he was himself again and would soon report back for duty. During the two-week period, several more men had died and Colonel Jackson endured a bout with the measles. Perhaps owing to the lingering effect of his illness, Forsyth appeared particularly grumpy in late August. The precision drill, once a source of great pride, now became drudgery. "We are becoming extremely tired of the monotony and inaction of the camp and anxious to go forward." He even blasted his Columbus newspaper staff for a misspelled word in an issue of the *Times*. The fault was obviously with the typesetter since, he roared, "I never write a word unless I know how to spell it." He was also beginning to realize that the war might end before the Georgia Regiment even got close to any action. He had mixed emotions over such a prospect. "While our boys look with dutiful eyes towards friends and home behind them, and will be rejoiced at the signal to return; I believe there are but a few, who would not be more pleased to return after a good bout with the enemy."[40]

On August 29, more than two months after Governor Crawford pointed out the "road to Mexico," companies of the Georgia regiment began to deploy up the river toward Camargo and Taylor's main force. Forsyth found a double joy in the event in that the hoped-for glory might at last arrive, and he needed new material for his subscribers as he had "exhausted" every possible angle of camp life. Even two thousand miles from Georgia, the editor could not escape controversy. The editor of the *Macon Messenger* attacked Forsyth for his criticisms of Crawford (over the funding issue) and for what appeared to be slanted coverage in favor of the Columbus Guards. Never one to ignore a slight, Forsyth devoted an entire letter to his rebuttal. In both cases, he felt the facts backed up whatever he had written—Crawford *had* been tight with the purse strings and the Columbus militia *did* deserve extra praise.[41]

By September 1, the regiment was finally steaming up the Rio Grande toward Camargo. Forsyth traveled on a boat with 250 of the regiment's men. The party stopped at Matamoras to drop off seventy-two sick men so they could recuperate in "clean, comfortable, and well-ventilated quarters." Twenty-seven of seventy-two died in the next two weeks. Now that the Georgians were in route to a "healthy country," and he thought the worst was over, Forsyth admitted he had been holding back some of the more depressing news from his readers. Now he could "without fear of alarming the friends of our men at home, speak more freely of the sickness through which we have passed."[42] The actual numbers were indeed alarming. The regiment left Columbus with 910 men. On a recent morning, they could only muster 340. The effective force had been about 400 for the past few weeks.

The trip to Camargo took six days. The journey was not uneventful as the men got to tour Reynosa during a stop. Here they saw their first performance of the fandango (although Forsyth slept through it). One member barely escaped drowning when he fell overboard. What was left of the regiment reached Camargo on September 4. According to the weary editor, "Everything looked warlike in the extreme." What he saw upon arrival hit him with a cold dose of reality. There were dozens of other volunteer regiments already stacked alongside the banks of the river. Of over fourteen thousand volunteers, only about two thousand had actually been sent forward. He finally wrote what had probably been on his mind for weeks: The volunteers "are marched out here a thousand to two miles from home—we are stuck down in a hot plain, drinking tepid water, and eating bad bread and pork in a manner that seems to say your services are not wanted—you are only in the way." In one of the biggest under-statements of his career, Forsyth concluded, "We are in a fit of disquiet."[43]

Two weeks later, his personal "disquiet" was coming to an end. Sickness again caused Forsyth to skip a couple of weeks in his reliable correspondence. When he got somewhat better, he was ordered to take a detachment of sick (himself included) back down the river to Matamoras. Realizing that the regiment was probably never going to be involved in any decisive campaign, he agreed to leave without a fuss. He was now convinced that the regiment was "permanently encamped" at Camargo and that "the next movement will be homeward." Forsyth left Camargo for good on September 16. He deposited thirty-two sick men (one man died in route) at Matamoras two days later. In his last report from Mexico, he waxed philosophically about the "sufferings of the poor fellows." He observed that one's blanket became a valuable possession. When a soldier was sick, the cloth became his bed on the ground. When he died, it became his coffin. When the group reached the hospital, they found the facility crowded with over seven hundred sick and dying men.[44]

Nearly three weeks elapsed before the people of Columbus heard any news from their citizen soldiers. Imagine their surprise when a letter dated October 8 arrived from Pensacola, Florida. Forsyth left the Rio Grande on September 20, bound for New Orleans aboard the schooner *Gen. Worth*. The adjutant, who had not yet had a pleasant experience on water during his brief military career, reported, "our passage was most unfortunate." The voyage took eighteen days, during most of which time the ship was "buffeted about the gulf, a prey to headwinds and storm." When they were six days out, the captain "lost his time" and therefore could not determine his exact longitude. The already-weakened passengers were running low on water and food. Four of the men died in route and were buried in the "deep blue water of the boisterous gulf." Not knowing where they were, they made a run to the nearest land they could find. The party ended up at Cape St. Blas, the entrance to Apalachicola Bay (three hundred miles east of New Orleans). The crew and passengers (literally) limped into Pensacola. When they finally landed, they were "without a pint of water or a pound of bread or meat on board." Forsyth reported his weight to be 114 lbs. He went to Mobile to reunite with his family and, from there, thankfully back to Georgia.[45]

Forsyth officially resigned his commission on November 30. Back in the field, the Georgia Regiment eventually left Camargo and went to Monterrey. Their only duty there was guarding money trains and supplies. They did enter Tampico and Vera Cruz but never once came within shooting distance of the

Mexican army. The service time of the men who remained did not expire until June of 1847. The lack of hostile engagements notwithstanding, the regiment paid a tremendous price in human suffering. Only 450 volunteers mustered out in 1847, of which 315 (including Forsyth) had resigned before the one-year enlistment ended. Incredibly, 145 had "gone to their long home."[46] While the regiment unfairly received some criticisms for its "inglorious" record, most (at least in Georgia) understood. The editor of the *Milledgeville Southern Recorder* stated, "Although they have been prevented by circumstances beyond their control from participation in the brilliant battles of the day, they endured so much and have as ardently desired to be in the midst of the conflict as the soldiers of any other state."[47]

After his tour of duty, Forsyth returned to Columbus and his dual role as editor and postmaster. The proposed attempts to settle the disputes that emerged over the new territories acquired at the expense of the United States' southern neighbor prompted a second "fit of disquiet" and led to a realignment of Georgia's political parties. The Mexican War victory and the one-sided provisions of the Treaty of Guadalupe-Hidalgo actually led to John Forsyth's only break with the national Democratic Party.

Georgia's antebellum political structure was similar to what Forsyth experienced in Mobile. The Whigs and Democrats matched up very evenly. It was not uncommon for the state's congressional delegation to be made up of four Whigs and four Democrats. In the 1846 congressional races, Georgia's voters cast 30,300 votes for the Democrats and 29,526 for the Whigs. Both state parties saw themselves as a vital part of national organizations, with each side trying to align itself with a Northern faction. The Democratic leaders believed the interests of the planters could best be served by an alliance with Northern labor. The conservative tendencies of one would serve as a check on the other. The Whigs, on the other hand, wanted an alliance between the planter class and the bourgeois capitalists of the North. Thus, they were champions of Clay's American system. This so-called fusion system had both good and bad points. It was good in that it kept the North divided. It was bad in that it also kept the South divided.[48]

Each side was championed by some of the more notable figures in antebellum Georgia history. The Whig leaders included John M. Berrien, George Crawford, Alexander H. Stephens, and Robert Toombs. For this study, the two latter men are the most important. Born a month before Forsyth, Stephens had a distinguished career in the Georgia legislature and the national Congress. He would later serve as the vice-president of the Confederate States of America.

Toombs, likewise, rose through the Whig Party ranks, serving as a state legislator and in both houses of Congress. He eventually served in the U.S. Senate
as a Democrat and secretary of the treasury for the Confederacy.

The Jacksonian Party was ably led by the likes of Howell Cobb, Henry L.
Benning, Charles J. McDonald, and Herschel V. Johnson. Cobb was elected six
times to Congress, served as speaker of the United States House of Representatives, governor of Georgia, secretary of the treasury (under President Buchanan), and a major general in the Confederacy. Benning, a Columbus resident,
would later serve as the vice president of the 1860 Baltimore Democratic convention and became a brigadier general in the Confederacy. McDonald was the
governor of Georgia when Forsyth returned to the state. Johnson served in
positions ranging from governor to United States Senator and Stephen A.
Douglas's running mate in the election of 1860.

The debate between the Whigs and Democrats found expression in partisan
newspapers across the state. Nearly every important city claimed a journal devoted to one of the parties. In Athens, one could read the (Democratic) *Southern Banner* or the *Southern Whig*. In Milledgeville, the Whig *Southern Recorder*
took aim at the Democratic *Federal Union*. The *Savannah Republican* (Whig)
competed with the *Georgian*. Forsyth's *Columbus Times* exchanged blows with
the Whig *Enquirer.*[49]

Even before the end of the Mexican War, the existing party structures came
under pressure. The very issue of the war itself caused many Southern Whigs
to abandon their national party loyalty in order to support President Polk. The
major point of contention, however, came as a result of the Wilmot Proviso.
On 8 August 1846, David Wilmot of Pennsylvania offered an amendment to
an appropriations bill that stated: "As an express and fundamental condition of
the acquisition of any territory from the Republic of Mexico . . . Neither slavery nor involuntary servitude shall exist in any part of said territory, except for
crime, whereof the party shall first be duly convicted."[50] The full impact of the
proviso did not become evident until after the Treaty of Guadalupe-Hidalgo.
Southerners began to feel that the national congress was out to destroy their
sacred institutions. An often-heard complaint was that the Mexican lands had
been conquered by the "blood and treasure" of the entire nation. Why then,
was the South to be excluded from its benefits?[51] The Wilmot Proviso had two
important effects. First, many Southern Democrats became less hesitant to
speak openly of secession. One Georgia penman advised that the South should
start making plans "in case we should be driven out of the Union."[52] Even
Toombs called the debate a "struggle to secure equality and avoid degradation."

The proviso, although never passed, had a galvanizing effect. One historian noted: "The view that the southern states must secede if the Proviso should be enacted was probably more widespread in the South than the view in 1860 that the election of Lincoln would make secession necessary."[53]

The second major effect of the proposed legislation was the shift in, and ultimate collapse of, the old Jacksonian party system in Georgia. Both sides had to determine which loyalty was more important—to the national party or to the South. Some Whigs (such as Berrien) moved to the Southern position, whereas others (Stephens and Toombs) remained in the Whig mainstream. On the Democratic side, Cobb stands out as an important leader who kept his national allegiance. Forsyth himself was at first reluctant to abandon the national Democratic Party. In July of 1848, he criticized William L. Yancey's advocacy of the so-called "Alabama Platform." Yancey wanted not only a repudiation of measures such as the proviso but also a congressional guarantee of the protection of slavery in the territories. The Alabama fire-eater was on the front line pushing for the formation of a Southern Rights Party. Forsyth accused Yancey of trying to "break up the organization of the great Democratic party throughout the union." Yancey was, according to Forsyth, wasting his time because "Whoever throws his pigmy weight against the rock of the Democracy, courts his own destruction, and will be crushed like an egg-shell in the encounter."[54] The loyal Jacksonian was not yet comfortable with the idea of abandoning the party of his father in favor of a new, Southern organization. Simple political reality kept Forsyth from jumping ship. The proviso was most likely not going to pass in Congress and, even if it did, a Democratic president would veto it.

The presidential election of 1848 sent Forsyth over the side. Even though the Whigs had been against the Mexican War, they knew the value of having a war hero as their candidate. People were unsure about where General Taylor stood on political issues. The fact that Taylor was a Southern slaveholder did not dampen the enthusiasm of even the Northern Whigs, which caused a blurring of traditional party lines. Many Southern Democrats were drawn to the general over the Northerner Lewis Cass. Although some Northern Whigs felt uneasy about voting for the "Hero of Buena Vista," nothing eased their consciences like the prospect of victory. The manner in which the Whigs promoted Taylor helped lead to the sectional nature of the campaign. They presented Taylor as the "Southern Candidate" or a man with "no-party" appeal.

Forsyth and the *Times* came out in favor of Cass. The editor's biggest concern was that Taylor had pledged not to interfere with Congress. He saw this promise as meaning that, if elected, the general would not stand up against the Wilmot Proviso. That the so-far unacceptable piece of legislation still had a pulse sent Forsyth into the waiting arms of the Southern Rights movement. After Taylor's victory, Forsyth complained that "The people have not acted wisely to elect a ruler without accurate principles." He warned his readers of both political parties that "a day of fearful struggle or deep humiliation is at hand." He was particularly upset about the number of Southern Democrats who had voted for Taylor. This act, he felt, would lead to the passage of the proviso, since the bill "heretofore defeated by the aid of Northern Democratic votes will be defeated no longer."[55] Now the Democrats would vote along sectional lines for the proviso. In his first public commitment to the Southern Rights movement, Forsyth wrote words that would show up a decade later during another states' rights debate: "The hour is at hand when Mr. Calhoun's long cherished idea of a Southern Rights party will be realized, or the Southern states are the degraded satellites and vassals of the North." He now felt that the only hope left for the South was an "undivided union, in the merging of all party lines, distinctions and issues in the great cause of Southern rights."[56]

Not only did the lifelong Democrat want to organize a new party, but he also, for the first time, became an open advocate of secession. In a letter written to Howell Cobb just a few days after Taylor's election, Forsyth complained that "We are beaten at all points and have truly lost all but our honor. I foresee that the South has to submit to the degradation by exclusion from a joint domain, or push resistance to the verge, if not over the verge, of revolution of the government."[57] In an editorial appearing at about the same time, he wrote, "Better disunion with our honor bright and our rights secure than union without either." Sounding more and more like Calhoun, the son of the man who staunchly supported Jackson during the nullification crisis noted, "We trust when the hour comes there will be, for once, union in the Southern councils; that the whole energy of its spirit of resistance and defense will be around, that party prejudices will be swallowed up in the paramount duty of self-preservation and the North will be told, the hour that the deed of our degradation is consummated, is the hour that will make us two people."[58] In simple terms, if the proviso became law, the South should take steps to leave the Union.

A month of postelection reflection only served to harden Forsyth's stance. He now tried to use arguments of principle and logic along with the appeals to emotion. The basic issue involved was that of equality. Forsyth compared the current situation to the one faced by the American colonists before the Revolution. Critics of the Southern Rights movement said that slavery probably would not flourish in the territories anyway. While this claim might be true, Forsyth pointed out that the colonists who complained about taxation were not really overburdened by taxes. At stake was the "principle of perfect equality and communion of rights, interests, privileges, and burdens between all the states." Moreover, if the South submitted to the proviso, what future "degradation" could they expect? The abolition of slavery in the District of Columbia, the prohibition of the slave trade between states, and, finally, the abolition of slavery within the states all loomed in the future. Now was the time to take a stand. For the only time in his career, Forsyth called for a new political organization outside of the national Democratic Party. He appealed to "all Southern men *without distinction of Party*" to come together. Sooner or later, the South would have to "meet the alternative of resistance, even to disunion, or a surrender of the institution." It was time to forget past party differences and "unite the South in a vigorous effort to stay Northern madness and injustice, and thus to save the Union."[59]

Once in office, Taylor did nothing to alleviate the fears of the Southern Rights men. Several actions actually hardened the new party alignment. First, Taylor appointed several Free-Soilers (such as William Seward) to key positions in his administration. Second, he promoted immediate statehood for California and New Mexico. The third action affected Forsyth directly—Taylor took advantage of the spoils system. During the campaign, the general claimed that he "loathed proscription for mere opinions sake." In other words, he would not replace men who held patronage jobs simply because they were on the other political side. Postmaster Forsyth was both shocked and furious when, in June of 1849, he was removed from his job and replaced by Columbus Whig Joseph Lee. Georgia's Democratic and Southern Rights newspapers soundly criticized this "act of sheer black-hearted proscription." The postmaster was removed, they noted, "because he took a part in the last canvass and advocated the principles of the Democratic party with his pen."[60]

By the time the Thirty-first Congress convened in December of 1849, Forsyth and many of his fellow Democrats were in an apprehensive mood. Although the Wilmot Proviso had been (twice) defeated, the territorial issue would not go away. The California statehood question now dominated the halls of Congress. In late 1849, the people of California held a state convention during which they adopted an antislavery constitution, elected a governor and a legislature, and formally applied for admission to the Union. Southerners realized that if California entered as a free state, the Missouri Compromise was a dead issue and slavery might be banned from any future states carved from the Southwest. Forsyth saw California's admission as a "preconcerted plan to defraud the South of her property." The scheme was "nothing more or less than the Wilmot Proviso in disguise."[61]

As passions on both sides of the slavery issue grew, threats of secession became more commonplace. On 29 January 1850, Henry Clay presented the Senate with a series of resolutions he hoped would settle this sectional controversy. The package, known in history as the Compromise of 1850, contained five major provisions: (1) California would be admitted as a free state; (2) the Utah and New Mexico territories would decide the slavery question for themselves; (3) the Texas-Mexico boundary dispute was resolved, and Texas would receive $10 million from the U.S. treasury; (4) the slave trade would be banned in the nation's capital; and (5) a more stringent fugitive slave law would be enforced. Since Southerners saw little benefit for themselves in the "compromise," reaction was swift and, predictably, hostile. Politically, the Clay plan exacerbated the already-occurring party realignment. Georgia's political leaders were forced to take a stand on the compromise measures. Toombs and Stephens, believing the compromise was the best hope for a solution, remained in the national Whig camp. John Berrien, on the other hand, broke with Clay and gravitated toward the states rights fold. On the Democratic side, Howell Cobb, who owed his speakership to a national appeal, came out in support of the bills. Forsyth's group, including Benning, Johnson, Iverson, and McDonald, became more staunch in their sectional leanings.

After the introduction of the compromise, Forsyth's feelings became crystal clear. Calling the proposals an example of "Northern aggression," the partisan editor felt that the time had come to sever the Union—"Peaceably if possible, forcibly if necessary." Not impressed with the "theatrical displays" of Clay, he called for "justice and not compromise." Wearied of what he saw as Northern intervention, he wanted to be "let alone or to be alone as an independent Southern Confederacy." The editor of the *Augusta Constitutionalist*, realizing the watershed nature of the Compromise of 1850, noted that "Future struggles in Georgia would be between 'Clay's Compromise party' and the supporters of the Nashville Convention."[62] In the summer of 1849, a gathering of Mississippians called for a general Southern convention to be held in Nashville to discuss Calhoun's plan for Southern unity. As the compromise worked its way through Congress in the winter and spring of 1850, the upcoming convention gained a new importance. Critics of the proposed convention claimed it was designed to promote disunion by unconstitutional means. Southern Rights men were quick to respond. Forsyth reminded his readers that the Congress of 1776 was also "unconstitutional." How could a protest against Clay's violation of the Constitution be unconstitutional? Forsyth's friend Benning wrote Cobb a letter in which he gave his opinion of the slavery question. Forsyth would echo his main points many times in the future. First, the North already had the *will* to abolish slavery; second, the North was rapidly acquiring the *power* to execute this will; and third, these two positions being true, abolition was inevitable unless something "should be done to change the will of the North, or stop the acquisition of power."[63]

Forsyth was strongly in favor of Georgia's participation in the Nashville Convention. While the debate on the omnibus bill continued, he supported the decision of the Georgia legislature to elect two delegates from each of the eight congressional districts to attend the meeting. The *Times* endorsed Benning and Martin J. Crawford to go to Nashville. It appeared that Calhoun's dream of Southern unity would at last be realized. This dream, if it did come to pass, would do so without Calhoun. The weekly issue of the *Times* that carried Forsyth's endorsement of both the convention and the selected delegates also had its columns draped in black as a sign of mourning over the death of the South Carolina statesman. The passing of Calhoun, along with the adjournment of the state legislature, seemed to cool the partisan passions before the elections for the convention delegates. In the April canvass, an embarrassingly low turnout did not bode well for the Southern Rights cause. Only 3,700 votes were cast in the fifty-four counties that bothered to open the polls.[64]

Called to order on June 3, the Nashville Convention itself was somewhat anticlimactic. Since the compromise bill was still languishing in the Senate, the focal point of the gathering was uncertain. Forsyth allies Benning, McDonald, and Crawford, among others, represented the Empire State. While Forsyth praised the actions and resolutions of the gathering, he was not pleased with the lukewarm participation. Six slave states had not even bothered to show up while several came without full representation. Texas and Arkansas had only one delegate each.[65] The effort to unify the South had, at least at this moment, failed once again. An obviously disappointed Forsyth could not help but wonder, "Have the people of the South fallen so low already, that we are driven to the alternative of taking the best terms our masters choose to give us? Are we already defeated?"[66]

In July, despite the best efforts of Clay and Daniel Webster, the Senate rejected the compromise. Two events resuscitated the package. The first was the death of President Taylor. His successor, Millard Fillmore, was an avid proponent of the plan. The final passage of the bill, however, can be credited to a man with whom Forsyth would one day form a strong political alliance— Stephen A. Douglas. Senator Douglas took Clay's omnibus package and introduced each section successively. Through clever legislative maneuvering, he was able to secure passage of each part. The bills were passed and signed into law in September. The Georgia Southern Rights movement was about to make a brief comeback.

Before the final passage of the Compromise of 1850, Forsyth and his fellow Southern Rights men called for a convention to meet in Macon on August 21. It was at this meeting that the Southern Rights Party of Georgia was officially born. The Whig press was quick to label this gathering a collection of "disunionists."[67] The Macon delegates (including Forsyth) loudly condemned the "omnibus surrender." The assembly went on record as favoring an extension of the Missouri Compromise line to California and in strong support of the Nashville Convention resolutions.[68] The gathering heard lighting-rod speeches from Yancey of Alabama as well as Rhett of South Carolina. As was typical, crowd estimates varied, depending on the reporting source. Various printed reports placed the crowd in a wide range anywhere between eight hundred and five thousand.[69]

Within the Southern Rights Party itself, two factions emerged. The "Ultraists" (including Forsyth) openly advocated secession while the moderates—of the Cobb, Stephens, and Toombs mold—favored preservation of the Union. Members of the party had to tone down their appeal from "union or disunion" to "resistance or submission." Forsyth himself had no problem with the disunion aspect of the new party. In route to one of their meetings, he wrote: "To preach 'the Union' when the Union should be tied and brought to a halt in its career of Constitution breaking; to preach party, when party has been the Delilah that has shorn the South of her strengths, and placed her the hapless victim of the North—this may be loyalty to the Union, and fidelity to party, but it is deep and barefaced treachery to the South."[70]

After the final passage of the Compromise, Georgia's Governor Towns called for a convention to decide how the state should respond. The make-up of the elected delegates to this statewide assembly would have a dramatic effect on the future course of the state, if not the Union itself. A headline in the *Times* left little doubt where Forsyth stood: "The Georgia Convention—Secession the Remedy."[71] Although some in the Southern Rights Party tried to downplay the disunion appeal, Forsyth became bolder. Rather than being a struggle between "union and disunion," the upcoming convention would decide between "disunion and abolition." Moderates were naive in clinging to "our glorious Union" when "Congress has entered on the crusade in league with abolition, to crush down the rights and liberties and destroy the property, prosperity, and wages of every man who lives in the excommunicated region of the South."[72]

On October 15, the Muscogee County "Southern Rights Resistance Party" met to select their delegates to run for the state convention. Forsyth was present, representing the Columbus upper town district. After a "free and unreserved interchange of opinions," the meeting nominated Alfred Iverson, John H. Howard, Martin Crawford, and William Yarder to run. Delegates chosen by a "Constitutional Unionist Party" would oppose these men. This party was made up of a mixture of some moderate Democrats (such as Cobb) and the overwhelming majority of the state's Whigs.[73]

The delegate vote took place on November 25. The election turned out to be a disaster for the Southern Rights movement. Forty-two thousand votes were cast for "acceptance" candidates, while only twenty-four thousand went to the Southern Rights men. Less than twenty of ninety-three counties chose the "disunionists." At the December convention, the 264 delegates adopted the "Georgia Platform." This document pledged the state to accept the Compromise and remain loyal to the Union. One of the resolutions adopted at the meeting did state that Georgia would "resist, even to a disruption of the very tie which binds her to the Union," any act which threatened slavery in the District of Columbia or the fugitive slave law.[74]

After this stinging rebuke, the Southern Rights Party leaders looked toward the 1851 governor's race. The convention had signaled the completion of Georgia's political realignment. The Union and Southern Rights Parties took the place of the Jacksonian Democrats and Whigs. The Southern Rights Party contained men, who, like John Forsyth, agreed with the late Calhoun that a geographic party offered the best hope of protecting the Southern institutions. The Union men, on the other hand, still clung to the balance of national power system of politics.[75]

In the weeks leading up to the gubernatorial contest, Forsyth wrote perhaps his best manifestos on his Southern Rights philosophy. These writings go a long way in understanding Forsyth's future role in the presidential election of 1860. Deflecting criticism that his stance was disrupting the national Democratic Party, he replied that "it is not only a high duty but a fixed necessity on the part of the friends of Southern Rights to maintain a separate and distinct Southern organization." Forsyth felt that no other party—including his beloved Democracy—could protect Southern rights without "lowering its standards, abandoning its cause, and sacrificing its principles." In espousing such a philosophy, Forsyth had come full circle since his 1848 criticism of Yancey. In 1851, Forsyth heaped praise on Yancey as a model Southern Rights man. Ironically, the man who would be one of Yancey's most outspoken adversaries in 1860 now noted "His [Yancey's] career has been a success of magnificent triumphs, won by a commanding eloquence and powerful intellect in a just cause."[76]

The Southern Rights Party met in convention in May of 1851. Forsyth was an official delegate from Muscogee County. The delegates ("A finer looking body of men we have never seen assembled on a similar occasion") took a "resolved stand against Northern encroachments and the craven spirit of Southern submission." They nominated former governor Charles J. McDonald to be their standard bearer. The group also adopted a platform consisting of twelve resolutions that spelled out the now-familiar positions of the party.[77] In the meantime, the Constitutional Union Party nominated Howell Cobb as its candidate. As has been noted, the 1850 crisis had separated Cobb and his national brand of Democracy from the Southern Rights branch. Forsyth was openly hostile to his old friend. One of his *Times* editorials stated, "Mr. Cobb's own course separated him from the Democratic party." Cobb's sin was that he "voluntarily abandoned the Democratic party of the South to enter into a broader, and as he hoped, stronger National Union organization." Forsyth tried to convince the voters that a vote for Cobb was another indication that Southerners were afraid to do anything that might offend the North.[78]

The October election brought yet another crushing defeat to the Southern Rights Party. Cobb captured 59.7 percent of the vote, getting a popular majority of more than eighteen thousand. The Union candidate carried all but twenty-one of ninety-five Georgia counties. Cobb's victory came with coattails. Unionist candidates won six of the eight congressional seats and secured large majorities in both houses of the state legislature. This second defeat took the steam out of the Southern Rights engine. Many of the Southern Rights men—including a reluctant John Forsyth—began to trickle back into the national party organization. By March of 1852, a Southern Rights version of a Democratic convention adopted the 1848 National Democratic Convention's platform as its own. At the 1852 Baltimore national convention, the credentials committee admitted States Rights and Union delegates jointly. Cobb and his Union faction also moved back to the mainstream. In 1852, the reunited Democrats won back the Georgia statehouse and control of the legislature.[79]

The Southern Rights Party and Forsyth's stay in Georgia came to an end at about the same time. By the end of 1852, he had "retired" from the *Times*. He planned to return to Mobile, not as an editor, but to start a business that was "more remunerative in its character."[80] A decade later, Forsyth would still be explaining the political stand he had taken in Georgia. In 1850, Forsyth was a states rights secessionist at odds with the national Democratic Party. Ten years later, he was a national Democrat at odds with Alabama's states' rights party. Certainly the twelve years back in his native state were among the most eventful of his life. Although he left Georgia with no intention of returning to journalism and politics, local and national events would force him back into both.

4

"Cannot We Pause a Moment to Think of Our Country?"

John Forsyth returned to Mobile in 1853 with no intention of returning to the *Register*. The once-again Mobilian poured whatever capital he had amassed into a lumber mill project to be constructed on an island across the river from the city. Before the mill turned out its first product, fire completely destroyed the entire venture. Falling back on his most notable skill, Forsyth returned to the *Register* in September of 1854, there to remain (except for his two-year assignment to Mexico) for the next twenty-three years. He joined with John Y. Thompson and Jacob Harris to purchase the *Register*. In November of 1854, Thompson, suffering bad health, sold his interest to Lewis A. Middleton, formerly of the *Mobile Herald*. By August of 1855, only Forsyth and Harris remained. In June of 1859, Forsyth became sole owner and editor.[1]

By the time Forsyth returned to Alabama, a dramatic change was underway in the nature of state politics. As late as 1848, Southern Rights issues were not the dominant part of the political dialogue in the state. With the exception of presidential elections, "Southern" issues did not figure prominently into the state and local political equation. By the early 1850s, however, campaigns turned almost exclusively on Southern Rights issues, with competing parties "hurling the epithet of traitor at each other." According to J. Mills Thornton, perhaps the central event of the 1850s was the exclusive association of the Southern Rights disputes with the presidential canvass and their integration into the general politics of the states. The Kansas-Nebraska Act, the political realignment (featuring the death of the Whig Party, the emergence and collapse of the American/Know-Nothing Party, and the emergence of the Republican Party), and the election of 1856 ensured that this period received great editorial attention.[2]

Forsyth reentered the world of journalism during the first year of the administration of Franklin Pierce. Pierce, who won a truly national (as opposed to sectional) victory, entered office on 4 March 1853, apparently with the support of a unified Democracy.[3] Forsyth praised Pierce as a man who "sacrificed himself politically in his own section of the Union by a bold and consistent maintenance of sound constitutional opinions" and "the loyal and eloquent advocate of the just rights of the slave states to immunity from anti-slavery disturbance and interference."[4] Alabamians were additionally pleased with the choice of their own William Rufus King as Pierce's vice president (King died in April of 1853, having never presided over the Senate). To add to the tranquility, many naively believed the Compromise of 1850 settled the slavery question once and for all. By the time Congress assembled in December of 1853, a growing number in the Democratic Party expressed dissatisfaction with, or hostility toward, the administration. No single issue of the 1850s disrupted the Pierce administration, the Democracy, and the Union more than the controversy over the Nebraska Territory.

The failure of the Compromise of 1850 to bring closure to the slavery question soon became painfully evident. Holman Hamilton, in a book aptly entitled *Prologue to Conflict,* noted that the compromise did nothing that its backers had promised to either side: California's senators in the 1850s were generally Southern sympathizers; slavery existed to some extent in Utah and New Mexico during all or part of the 1850s; slaves were still bought and sold in the nation's capital; and the fugitive slave law caused more problems than it solved.[5] As had been the case in Georgia, the compromise was a major issue in Alabama's state elections of 1851, with radicals pushing secession and moderates favoring the agreement. With the tenuous compromise precariously serving as the official arbitrator of the slavery question, the nation soon erupted over the proposed organization of the Nebraska Territory. A detailed study of the background, evolution, and results of this plan goes a long way toward understanding the connection between Stephen A. Douglas and the State of Alabama, and more important for this book, the bond between Douglas and John Forsyth.

Many national statesmen realized the potential problems associated with the acquisition of the large amount of territory resulting from the Mexican War. The South was in no hurry to organize the Nebraska Territory. Because of the Missouri Compromise of 1820 and the fact that the territory lay above the 36°30′ parallel, the area would be legally unavailable for slavery. After the Gadsden Purchase of 1853, Southern leaders looked forward to exploiting the most easily accessible land route to the West Coast. Although many standard histories of the Nebraska Territory properly emphasize the role of slavery in the debates over the new territory, a much more practical matter deserves attention—the sectional competition over Pacific railroad routes. In his detailed study of the impact of railroads on the Kansas-Nebraska Act, Frank Hodder noted that while the Eastern and Southern newspapers quarreled over slavery, the "practical men" were working for federal land grants and state subsidies. David M. Potter likewise claimed that there was little ideological division over the question of slavery or the black (although, as Potter stated, one side did want to bring their Negro slaves to the territory while the other side did not want them to enter, slave or free).[6] The organization of New Mexico as a part of the Compromise of 1850 gave a Southern route a great advantage. Unless the Northern territories (Nebraska) could also be organized, an equal opportunity would be lost. Here begins the seldom-mentioned connection between Douglas and Mobile.

Douglas's interest in railroad construction began in 1836, when he served in the Illinois state legislature. He helped secure passage of grants for the construction of the first rails in that state. Once in Congress, he tried to secure federal land grants for the Illinois Central and complete a "northern cross" route. Political realities soon set in. Southern opposition to federally financed internal improvements placed Douglas's ambitions in jeopardy. To ensure support for his Illinois Central project, Douglas needed the support of powerful Southern senators, such as William Rufus King and Jefferson Davis. Although King and Davis opposed the improvements, the two senators believed in the principle of legislative instructions.

In November of 1849, Douglas quietly came to Mobile and the headquarters of the Mobile Railroad Company. As early as the 1830s, local promoters envisioned a railroad line that would connect the port city with the upper Mississippi, Missouri, and Ohio River basins. The line would run from Mobile to a point just south of Cairo, Illinois, near the conflux of the major river systems. The idea was to take a (large, it was hoped) part of the trade that was controlled exclusively by New Orleans. By 1847, public interest in the venture was such that public shares were being sold. Eventually, the city of Mobile fathers voted a special property tax to bring additional capital to the project. Despite these efforts, the company was nearly bankrupt when Douglas hatched his scheme. The senator proposed to attach his Illinois Central project to those of the Mobile and Ohio companies. The line would link the Gulf of Mexico with the Great Lakes. Local officials jumped at the chance and began to secure support in the state legislature. When Douglas returned to the Thirty-first Congress he attached the Mobile to Ohio grant to his Illinois Central Act. In so doing he not only secured the passage of his own bill but also secured railroad construction between Chicago (where his own landholdings increased in value) and the

Gulf of Mexico, in the process diverting the Mobile and Ohio route from St. Louis, its original destination. By the time Forsyth (always a supporter of any venture that would improve the port city's commercial prospects) returned to Mobile, he already admired Douglas, the "gallant statesman and orator."[7]

Douglas now turned his attention to a transcontinental route to the Pacific with its terminus in Chicago. Since Forsyth's support for Douglas in the election of 1860 stemmed largely from his agreement with the "Little Giant" on the Nebraska question, a careful analysis of the Kansas-Nebraska Act is warranted. To facilitate Douglas's plan to span the continent, the region west of Iowa would have to be organized and settled. One exasperated Missouri congressman exclaimed, "In the name of God, how is the railroad to be made if you will never let people live on the lands through which the road passes?"[8]

The controversial life of the Kansas-Nebraska Act began in February of 1853 when the House passed a territorial bill.[9] Since the land was clearly above the Missouri Compromise line, slavery was banned. In the Senate, Southern opposition killed the bill. Senators such as David Atchison worried that if the new territory indeed came into the Union as free, then slave-state Missouri would be besieged on three sides by abolitionist forces. Many miles from the land in question, Forsyth wrote that "if Kansas is a Free State, Missouri is then girt on three sides by abolition neighbors. The consequence must be to drive slavery from the borders to the heart, and finally southward into Arkansas. If the South loses Kansas, it loses Missouri."[10] On 4 January 1854, Douglas, by now chairman of the Committee on Territories, reported a new bill to organize the territory. Basically copying the language of the Compromise, Douglas suggested that "popular sovereignty" (a term which Forsyth would defend countless times in 1860) be used to determine the status of the territory when it became a state. This reasoning was not good enough for Southerners, who felt that since slavery would be barred during the territorial phase, it was highly unlikely that enough proslavery voters would be present for the eventual state elections. A revised version of the bill specified that popular sovereignty would also apply during the territorial phase—a clear repudiation of the Missouri Compromise. A final version officially called for the repeal of the 1820 agreement and split the territory into two separate pieces—Kansas and Nebraska. This bill passed the Senate on 3 March 1854, while the House gave its approval on May 22. President Pierce signed the bill into law on May 30.

When Douglas had reported his bill to the Senate in March of 1854, he noted that it might cause a "little controversy." The truth of this classic understatement became evident immediately. Douglas explained the rationale for proposing the measure by stating in his own Senate report that the new law advanced "certain great principles, which would not only furnish adequate remedies for existing evils, but, in all time to come, avoid the perils of similar agitation, by withdrawing the question of slavery from the halls of Congress and the political arena, committing it to the arbitration of those who were immediately interested in, and alone responsible for, its consequences."[11] In a letter to Howell Cobb, Douglas explained that "the great principle of self-government is at stake, and surely the people of this country are never going to decide that the principle upon which the whole republican system rests is vicious and wrong."[12] Supporters such as Forsyth saw a simple logic in Douglas's plan. In their minds the concept of popular sovereignty represented the truest of democratic principles. The Kansas-Nebraska Act simply replicated the logic behind the Compromise of 1850. In Forsyth's opinion, the "honest intention of the law was to leave the question of the institutions of the embryo state to be determined by the bonafide emigrants to the territory who were to be its future and permanent citizens." Anyone who could not understand this concept was guilty of "ignoring the Democratic principle of the capacity of men and communities of States to govern themselves."[13]

Obviously, many were indeed "guilty." The most scathing attack came from Senators Salmon P. Chase of Ohio, Charles Sumner of Massachusetts, and others in the form of a document entitled an "Appeal of Independent Democrats." These senators saw the bill as a "gross violation of a sacred pledge, as a criminal betrayal of precious rights, as part and parcel of an atrocious plot." Taking their hostilities to new levels, the Northern partisans attacked the defenders of slavery "not on the merits or demerits of their position, but on the grounds that they were vicious, dishonest, and evil." The appeal closed with the promise that the authors would "go home to our constituents, erect anew the standard of freedom, and call upon the people to come to the rescue of the country from the domination of slavery. We will not despair; for the cause of human freedom is the cause of God."[14] Ironically, whereas in 1854 through 1856 the debate over the Kansas-Nebraska Act was mainly a North versus South contest, when Forsyth defended the Act and its author in 1860, he defended it from attacks by fellow Southerners.

In the two years between the passage of the Kansas-Nebraska Act and the election campaign of 1856, national politics clearly attracted the attention of Forsyth and his readers. In Alabama, as in most of the South, there had been no demand for the extension of popular sovereignty into the territories acquired from the Louisiana Purchase. Until the Kansas-Nebraska Act, the western region received very little attention. In the contested region itself, the issue appeared to be almost a fabrication. As Potter noted, the majority of the inhabitants apparently did not care very much one way or the other about the slave issue. By 1855, however, Forsyth pointed out to Mobilians that "the abstractions of the slavery debate have become momentously practical." In the North, many people came to believe what the abolitionists and Free-Soilers had been warning all along—a slave-section conspiracy existed to dominate the nation. In the South, editors such as Forsyth protested the blatant abuse of "natural" government by such forces as the Northern emigrant societies.[15]

A trip to New York City in the late summer of 1855 seemed to harden Forsyth's perception of the sectional rift. The northern excursion served several purposes. The first and most practical reason was to escape the brutal seasonal heat of Mobile. Second, Forsyth appeared to be toying with the idea of leaving the *Register* for a more lucrative market. While in New York he toured the offices of the *Herald,* the *Times,* and the *Tribune.* Observing the lack of a true southern Democratic paper, and perhaps with himself in mind, Forsyth reported: "To a man of proper character and parts, and backed by the necessary capital to make a successful start, a true States Rights and Southern newspaper in this city opens the most splendid of modern enterprises." Finally, the month-long visit allowed the perceptive editor a chance to gauge for himself the prevailing sentiments of his Northern brethren regarding the territorial issues. The sentiments he observed were indeed disturbing. He felt the Northern press was guilty of promoting a "spirit of unrestrained violence." By the time he was ready to return to Alabama, he concluded: "If the Democratic principle of faith does not save the Union, it will not be saved."[16]

The ideological debate (or what Forsyth had previously referred to as the "abstraction") over the Kansas-Nebraska Act soon gave way to a physical struggle to control the anticipated vote on slavery. Having lost the battle in Congress, the antislavery forces determined not to lose the literal war. In May of 1854, Senator William H. Seward threw down the gauntlet: "Come on then gentlemen of the slave states—since there is no escaping your challenge, I accept it on behalf of the cause of freedom. We will engage in a competition for the virgin soil of Kansas, and God give the victory to the side which is stronger in numbers as it is in might."[17] Placing the blame squarely on Northerners determined to "precipitate an abolition population from New England upon the territory with a view to shape future destinies," Forsyth and his fellow editors answered the challenge. Claiming that they were occupying the high ground, the *Register* announced that "while the South is not disposed to push its institutions on a people that do not want it, it will not be satisfied to be cheated out of a virgin country, admirably adapted to slave labor, by the affective officiousness of intermeddling abolitionists. It has therefore to choose between losing its vast stake in this new region of settlement, or meet the movements of its enemies by counteracting action."[18]

As the competing factions poured in and proslavery and antislavery groups formed rival governments, the South, becoming increasingly paranoid regarding its position in the Union, decided to fight fire with fire. Although Forsyth piously complained of the "daring outlaws of Kansas who have brought their treason" and the "fanatics and traitors who have been hoping to convulse the society and obtain a triumph for the villainous cause," he realized that only Southern intervention would balance the scales. Forsyth concluded that the only way to accomplish a just solution was to "raise money and send Southern men who desire to emigrate in whose strong arms and firm hearts, our rights, interests, and power will find protection."[19]

To answer what the South perceived as clearly a one-sided Northern provocation, appeals soon appeared for aid to the rightful inhabitants of Kansas. An 1855 correspondent wrote the *Register,* saying: "Men of the South! Would you preserve your equality in the Union! Would you protect your property from the reckless rapacity of agrarian legislation? Would you defend your families from outrage—Your firesides from pollution—your beautiful country from the bloodshed and horrors of servile war? To Arms!" This writer concluded that "if [Kansas] is surrendered to our enemies, the Nebraska bill is worthless; our equality in the U.S. Senate gone; and the doom of the South unalterably fixed."[20]

One of the more daring efforts to transport Alabama men and money into the troubled area came under the leadership of one Colonel Jefferson Buford. Buford came through Mobile seeking support in March of 1856. Forsyth heartily endorsed this "patriotic undertaking" to lead a band of Southern emigrants to Kansas. Colonel Buford pitched his plan to a group of leading Mobile citizens (including Forsyth) at the Battle House Hotel. Convinced that the effort needed cash more than ready men, Forsyth issued an appeal to civic pride: "We hope the contributions of Mobile will be generous and large in proportion to the interest which the community has in this great question." Noting the sizable donations already committed by Georgia and South Carolina, Forsyth admonished Mobilians to "imitate the example and back up the firm determination of Missouri, that the nefarious plottings of the Northern abolitionist societies, Sharps rifles to the contrary, notwithstanding, shall be defeated at all hazards in Kansas."[21]

The passage of the Kansas-Nebraska Act was very significant for the nation as well as Alabama specifically. Neither Douglas's objective of railway extension nor the South's objective of slavery extension came to fruition. However, at least four major results had long-term implications for the nation, state, and Forsyth's future. First, because of the passage of the act, positions both for and against slavery became more firmly entrenched. Although the South won the legislative victory, the act, combined with the Fugitive Slave Law, the Ostend Manifesto (which advocated the purchase or seizure of Cuba by the United States), and the proslavery territorial government of Kansas, was a major defeat in the propaganda war. Forsyth employed deadly serious (and prophetic) prose when he noted that "if it be distinctly ascertained that the people of the North deliberately resolved not to respond to the guarantee of slavery, then should the South organize an independent government, and protect its rights by force."[22]

Second, the debate over the act forever corrupted the concept of popular sovereignty. Partisans both North and South would come to criticize Douglas (and, in Alabama, Forsyth) for his doctrine of "squatter sovereignty." The third and perhaps most significant result of the act was the effect it had on the Democratic Party. The act seriously damaged the power of the Democracy in the free states and also upset the bisectional balance of power within the party. After the act, the Northern wing of the party experienced fantastic losses. The results of the 1854 congressional elections document the carnage. Sixty-six of the ninety-one free-state Democrat incumbents went down to defeat. Only seven of the forty-five Northern representatives who voted for the act returned to Congress. Whereas in 1852 the Democrats controlled all but two Northern states, in 1854, the party *lost* all but two.[23] Finally, Douglas's legislative "triumph" caused Democrats such as Forsyth to call for strict unity among what was left of the national organization against the rise of new political factions. In October of 1855, Forsyth warned that "the South has but to stand firm and be united to triumph over the most persevering and impassioned enemy that a peaceful country was ever subjected to." He also hoped that "the crisis coming upon the country would lift true men of all parties above the miasmic vapor of prejudice and partyism into the clear and upper atmosphere of principle."[24] In retrospect, Forsyth was overly optimistic, as the most drastic legacy of the Kansas-Nebraska Act was the coming political realignment.

In December of 1855, Forsyth identified four parties among the "masses of the people"—the Democrats, the "Seward or Black Republicans," the Free-Soil Know-Nothings and the Southern Know-Nothings. For better or worse, each of these parties faced significant change in 1855 and 1856. Forsyth did not even include the Whig Party in his roster, stating that the Whigs were "so poorly represented as hardly to be worth considering as an element of any power."[25] After the demise of the Whigs, the Democrats looked forward to a virtual free reign in the South. Competition between the Whigs and Democrats had basically been between Southern partisans trying to outdo each other as protectors of slavery and champions of the South. Democrats believed that the victory in the Kansas-Nebraska ordeal proved the soundness of the national Democracy regarding slavery and should eliminate all Southern opposition to the Democratic Party. Although historians have produced many volumes concerning the 1854–60 rise of the Republican Party, the fastest growing political force in many parts of the nation (and particularly in Alabama) was actually not the antislavery Republicans but the antiforeign American or Know-Nothing Party.[26]

Although antislavery rhetoric and actions reached fever pitch after the Kansas-Nebraska Act, many in the nation saw a bigger threat in the form of increasing (particularly Roman Catholic) immigration. Even though Americans liked to imagine themselves as a "sanctuary for the world's victims of poverty and oppression," anti-immigrant movements enjoyed great success throughout early American history. Several secret fraternal organizations of nativists emerged in the 1840s. One of these was the Order of the Star Spangled Banner, a New York group, founded in 1849. When questioned about their order, members replied, "I know nothing." By 1854–55, the Know-Nothings achieved national prominence, electing eight governors, more than one hundred congressmen, the mayors of Boston, Philadelphia, and Chicago, as well as thousands of local officials.[27]

Since Mobile was one of the few Alabama Know-Nothing strongholds in the 1850s, a few details about the organization are in order. Economic dislocation as well as religious prejudice brought many members streaming into the party. Nationwide, immigration reached new heights in the 1840s and 1850s. Between 1846 and 1855 more than three million immigrants arrived in the United States. This figure represented 15 percent of the 1845 population—the highest percentage increase in U.S. history. To put these numbers in perspective, consider that although immigration had never reached an annual rate of one hundred thousand before 1842 nor two hundred thousand before 1847, it exceeded four hundred thousand three times between 1851 and 1855. In 1850, the city of Mobile contained 4,086 foreign-born citizens. By 1860, the foreign-born total reached 7,061—an increase of 72.81 percent.[28] Each immigrant represented a potential competitor in the workplace and, as such, stirred much resentment.

Economic dislocation was certainly a major fear that led people into the nativist fold. However, since 87 percent of all immigrants went to free states, numbers alone cannot explain the party's Southern drawing power. In the South, with few crowded cities, Forsyth could rhapsodically condemn nativism, stating: "nothing more selfish, contracted or bigoted, can be conceived in morals or politics, and nothing more shortsighted and unpatriotic when viewed in relation to the best interest of the country, with its boundless territorial waste and wilderness awaiting development, and eager to wave with yellow grain and blossom like the rose under the toiling hands of labor."[29] Religious prejudice also played a role in the party's brief Southern success. Southerners, like their Northern Protestant counterparts, harbored much animosity toward Roman Catholics. Since, after the 1840s, more than half of the immigrants were Roman Catholic, the Know-Nothing Party appealed to many Southerners, especially in Mobile. Mobile had a larger than usual Roman Catholic population, going back to its founding as a French settlement. By the end of the 1850s, membership in the Roman Catholic Church ran a close second to the Methodist, and the value of Roman Catholic Church property more than doubled its closest rival denomination.[30]

At least three factors led to the Know-Nothing hatred of Roman Catholics. First, the perception existed that the Catholics, blindly loyal to the Pope, forced their religion on others. Catholic Archbishop John Hughes of New York once wrote: "The object we hope to accomplish is to convert all pagan nations, and all Protestant nations. Protestantism is effete, powerless, dying out . . . and conscious that its last moment is come when it is finally set, face to face, with Catholic truth."[31] A second perception was the notion of the Catholic as drunkard. As one contemporary noted, "It is liquor which fills so many Catholic homes with discord and violence, darkens newspaper columns with so many accounts of Irish rows, brawls, and faction-fights, fills our prisons with Irish culprits, and makes the gallows hideous with so many Catholic murderers."[32] Finally, the Catholics, attacking the godlessness of public schools, sought tax support for Catholic schools or tax relief for parents who sent their children to such schools.

Although sheer immigration numbers did not excessively affect Alabama, and, outside of Mobile, there was no large Roman Catholic concentration in the state, the Know-Nothing party did briefly become a powerful force in Alabama politics and a major concern for Forsyth. In Alabama, the rise of the Know-Nothing Party had far greater political than ideological implications.[33] Although the decline of the Whig Party in Alabama and the rise of the Know-Nothing Party were obviously related, the question is, which caused the other? Already weakened by the Compromise of 1850 and its subsequent secession movement, the Whigs did not survive the Kansas-Nebraska fight. In Alabama, redrawn legislative districts, the national Democratic nomination of Alabamian William Rufus King for vice president in 1852, the appointment of Mobile Democrat John Archibald Campbell to the United States Supreme Court, and most important, the abolitionist sentiment of many Northern Whigs, finished off the statewide organization.[34] Traditional scholarship held that the Know-Nothing movement emerged in the vacuum created by the disappearance of the Whig Party. The party gained as much strength from its availability to political refugees as from its anti-Catholicism. Newer research seems to indicate that intensified prejudice against Catholics, hostility to politicians, and impatience with the established parties caused the formation of the Know-Nothing Party, which, in turn, led to, rather than benefited from, the collapse of the Whigs.[35]

Regardless of how they came into existence, the Know-Nothings presented a very real threat. In 1854, the party experienced great success at the national, state, and local levels. In Massachusetts, the entire state senate and 376 out of 378 state representatives came from the American Party. In the 1854 Alabama elections, the party furnished the mayors of both Montgomery and Mobile. The American Party held a state convention in 1855 and also set up the *Montgomery Mail* as its statewide organ. Nativism temporarily became an issue almost as important as slavery. By the spring of 1855, Democrats across Alabama began to plan for the upcoming state elections and for the 1856 presidential race.[36]

Forsyth and the state Democratic organization began a calculated assault on the Know-Nothing Party. The goal of Forsyth and his colleagues was to paint the American Party as a danger equal with Republicanism. This attack centered on three issues. First, Forsyth claimed that, American Party propaganda notwithstanding, the Know-Nothings were not a "Southern" party. After the 1855 state elections, Forsyth failed to comprehend "how a secret order, imported from the North with all its paraphernalia, signs, oaths, grips, etc., could reasonably be an invention got up especially for the benefit of the South." Perhaps overly paranoid, Forsyth saw the "obtrusion of the Know-Nothing question into Southern politics as an event calculated and certain to divide and weaken the South in its vital struggle with the powers of Abolitionism."[37]

Second, Forsyth blamed the Know-Nothing Party for Republican victories in the North and feared that the party's continued existence could jeopardize the Democratic chances in the 1856 presidential race. In Forsyth's mind, the nation only needed two political parties. The Democratic Party—"defending the Constitution and the rights of the states, standing unflinchingly on the Nebraska legislation and maintaining the right and the justice of the repeal of the Missouri Compromise"—countered the Republican Party—"warring upon the Constitution, the Bible, the Union and the Nebraska legislation, as all so many monuments of the Southern institution of Slavery, upon which they have declared a deadly and Carthaginian warfare." If the Know-Nothings were indeed sympathetic to the Southern cause as they claimed, then Forsyth wondered: "Where is the necessity of this separate and distinctive organization in this State or in any State in the South? Where the need of *two* parties aiming at one end and animated by the same purpose?" Having seen the Republicans elect a Speaker of the United States House of Representatives owing to bickering between rival Democratic factions, Forsyth feared similar results in the coming presidential race, stating, "The American Party cannot by any possibility elect its candidate before the people. The best and worst it can do is to defeat the Democratic nominee and elect the abolition candidate."[38]

Finally, Forsyth saw Know-Nothingism as dangerous because it distracted the attention of the electorate from the more important issue of slavery and abolitionism. As 1855 came to a close and the national election year approached, Forsyth wrote: "As the slavery question is to be the great issue that will loom up and absorb all others, in the presidential election, it is perfectly obvious that all minor and collateral issues will be ignored and forgotten as the combat on the main point thickens." According to Forsyth, the Know-Nothings represented just such a "minor and collateral issue." The American Party organization was "beating its party drums, blowing its party whistles and looking after its party interests, while the Republic is in danger and serious men are pondering the means of defense." Likewise, "The foreign and religious features of Know Nothingism, taken in their largest significance, were of small moment to this section of the Union when compared with the overshadowing issue which every man saw had to be settled with the enemies of our domestic peace and safety."[39]

William J. Cooper Jr. compared the Know-Nothing Party to a meteor. Like the celestial object, the party appeared initially as a bright flame, then, just as rapidly, burned out. The party could not survive a plunge into the politics of slavery. Much like the Whigs, the Know-Nothing Party had to take a stand on the Kansas-Nebraska Act. At their national convention of 1856, Know-Nothing delegates split over the slavery issue. The defeat of a platform plank calling for the restoration of the Missouri Compromise and the adoption of a vague, proslavery platform drove many delegates out of the meeting. After the defeat in 1856, the party died. The "Northern Americans" gave up their dream of a separate party and fused into the Republican Party.[40] John Forsyth pronounced both a eulogy for the Northern wing of the party as well as an invitation for the Southern: "They will find that 'Americanism' is dead at the North and has become swallowed up, with rare individual exceptions, in the voracious jaws of Black Republicanism. It is to the *Democratic Party alone* that the South and the country can look for salvation and championship in the struggle with Seward fanaticism."[41]

The rise of "Seward fanaticism" posed a definite threat to Forsyth's Democratic Party. Described by its enemies as a "rag-tag group of Free-Soilers, abolitionists, disgruntled Whigs, unhappy Democrats, Know-Nothings, and opponents of the Kansas-Nebraska Act," the Republicans had a vision of attaining majority party status among antislavery groups. The demise of the Whig Party, coupled with the emergence of the Know-Nothings, led to a competition in the North for the right to be the main opponent of the Democrats. The Republican Party traced its origin back to 1854 when these various groups organized protest meetings against the "Nebraska outrage." Calling their organization (successively) Anti-Nebraska, Fusion, People's, and Independent party, the name Republican caught on.[42]

With the national Whigs no longer a factor, the Republicans had to compete with the Know-Nothings for the loyalty of a block of voters both anti-Catholic and antislavery. The problem the Republicans faced was convincing the voters that slavery was more of a threat to American values, rights, and liberties than was Roman Catholicism. Although on the surface it appeared that the Republicans and Know-Nothings could simply blend into one party, two problems prevented this merger. The first centered on basic ideological differences. While the antislavery movement did grow out of the same evangelical Protestant milieu as nativism, the abolitionists, Free-Soilers, antislavery Whigs, and later the Republicans denounced the antiforeigner movement as a form of bigotry, not so unlike slavery.[43] Second, the Republicans, much like Forsyth (but from a different angle) felt the nativist cause distracted from the real issues. Charles A.

Dana of the New York *Tribune* stated that "neither the Pope nor the foreigner can ever govern the country or endanger its liberties, but the slave breeders and slave traders *do* govern it."[44]

Escalating their antislavery rhetoric, the Republican Party condemned not just the sin but the sinner. The 1850s marked a definite change in the philosophies of political parties. Majority rule came to be seen as the elimination of the minority. A political opponent was not just one who held a differing opinion but one who sought to destroy a way of life. Thus, Forsyth stated that the contest between the Republicans and the Democrats was a "war of extermination" waged against social institutions. The election became the "holy work of putting down the treasonable, insane conspiracy against the peace of the Southern States and the Constitution of the Union."[45]

This abstract battle between the opposing forces took concrete form in May of 1856. South Carolina Representative Preston Brooks physically assaulted (with a cane) Massachusetts Senator Charles Sumner in retaliation for Sumner's "Crime Against Kansas" speech. In the speech, Sumner pushed for the admission of Kansas as a free state, exposed the "inherent evil nature" of Southerners, and insulted Brook's relative, Andrew P. Butler. Brooks's violent response did wonders for the Republican Party. Sumner broke new ideological ground by attacking the morality of slaveholders themselves. The caning of Sumner served to focus attention on the divisive nature of slavery to the exclusion of other issues. Although Forsyth questioned the wisdom of the choice of location for the assault, he did feel that "Sumner has been well whipped" and "got no more than he deserved." As Sumner's biographer noted, when violence of this nature took place in the halls of Congress, could the Union long endure? Ralph Waldo Emerson (a friend of Sumner) lamented: "I do not see how a barbarous community and a civilized community can constitute one state. I think we must get rid of slavery, or we must get rid of freedom."[46]

For Forsyth and the *Register*, the first half of 1856 was consumed with comments on the coming presidential election. As the Alabama State Democratic Convention prepared to convene in January, Forsyth warned that "a new period in our history is at hand, when the power of the Democratic people is again to be severely tested." When the year started, each daily edition of the *Register* carried a banner endorsing President Pierce for reelection. Forsyth believed Pierce had fulfilled all expectations of Southerners. The president had tried to obtain Cuba, he opened the remainder of the Louisiana Purchase to the possibility of slavery, and he had vigorously attempted to enforce the Fugitive Slave Law. Forsyth approvingly exclaimed that Pierce's record was "as pure and spotless as any man who was born and lives South of the Potomac," and he was the "loyal and eloquent advocate of the just rights of the slave States to immunity from anti-slavery disturbance and interference." Forsyth also worried that if the South rejected Pierce, it would be difficult to ever get another Northern man to stand up for Southern Rights. Most importantly, Forsyth believed that any attempt to replace Pierce as the party's nominee could lead to a disruption that might, in turn, hand the election to the Republicans. This campaign was not the time to allow internal party politics to explode. Forsyth, trying to be a moderate voice, wrote, "in our party bickerings and controversies, cannot we of the South disagree and dispute without doing injustice to the true friends of our common cause, and without putting the union in jeopardy by an act which tends immediately to sectionalize and abolitionize the entire North. In other words, in our hot pursuit of party triumphs, cannot we pause a moment to think of our country?"[47] Taking a stand opposite of that which he had taken in 1850–52 (but one to which he would return in 1860), Forsyth pushed for a national ticket/platform as opposed to a more Southern position.

Pierce was, however, not without his critics. Many Northern Democrats complained that the Pierce administration's acquiescence to the slavery faction had upset domestic tranquility, hurt the Democratic Party, and subsequently weakened the Union. On the other hand, his appointment of some antislavery men to patronage positions and his alleged sponsorship of antislavery resolutions while in the New Hampshire legislature pushed some Southern Democrats forever away from the Pierce wing of the party. By the mid-1850s, the president found himself assaulted from both sides. It was impossible to convince Northern Democratic voters to accept a program of slave extension, and it was equally difficult to persuade the South to relinquish the disproportionate power that resulted from slavery.[48]

Forsyth saw the upcoming campaign as a "war to the knife" and a "life and death struggle." Even before the nominee was known, he was (at least outwardly) confident of a Democratic Party victory. His optimism was based on several factors. First, he felt the Democracy was fighting for a "sacred cause." The struggle was one of self-defense and clearly backed by the Constitution. Second, the issues were crystal clear and could not be hidden or evaded. According to Forsyth, there was "no alternative but resistance." Finally, victory was certain because the Democrats were still the only national party. It was crucial that the Democratic partisans not let distractions take their focus off of the ultimate goal. He suggested a new motto for the party: "Everything for the cause and nothing for men."[49]

By late spring of 1856, Forsyth began hedging his bets. Under the bold printed endorsement of Pierce, he began to add the words "subject to the decision of the National Convention." Selected from the state of Alabama at large as a delegate to the convention, Forsyth realized that the nomination could go to Pierce, Douglas, or Pennsylvania's James Buchanan. Unlike five years earlier, Forsyth was now acting like an unwavering party man. He wrote that "it is fortunate that in such a choice the Republic can suffer no detriment, and that upon whichsoever of them it falls, the Democratic Party will be satisfied, and support him with a cordial enthusiasm, and the whole people will find a sure presage of a wise and patriotic administration, in the integrity, honor, and statesmanship of the candidate."[50]

The 1856 Democratic National Convention opened in Cincinnati on the first Monday of June. Forsyth and the Alabama delegation cast their votes for President Pierce on each of the first fifteen ballots. No candidate could get the needed vote total. After much discussion and back-room negotiations, on the seventeenth ballot Buchanan received the (unanimous) nomination. James Buchanan had a long and distinguished record of public service. Ten years of service in the House, ten more in the Senate, and five years in the diplomatic corps as minister to Russia and Britain, all gave credence to his candidacy. However, perhaps Buchanan's most desirable quality was the fact that, unlike both Pierce and Douglas, he had been out of the country during the Kansas-Nebraska controversy and thus had no "taint of responsibility."[51] Forsyth was a part of the official delegation that conveyed the wishes of the convention to Buchanan on his farm in Lancaster.[52] Soon after the nomination, the *Register* (quickly changing its headline endorsement) referred to "old Buck" as "the man whom we would point at among all others, as the one best calculated to confirm the wavering, and unite those already strong, in the Democratic faith." Forsyth was likewise pleased with the party platform. In a letter written from Cincinnati, he stated it was "sound as a nut." He had nothing but praise for the Northern delegates for their willingness to stand up for Southern principles. In fact, he reported, they "would have made it stronger if language could have done it, and the South had desired it."[53]

When John Forsyth returned home from the Democratic Convention, he still realized an important struggle lay ahead. In his (somewhat partisan) opinion, the convention was "the most important political assemblage in the annals of American History since the convention that debated and framed the Constitution of the United States." The *Register* chief saw the "Black Republicans" as preparing to fight a war to the death against the social institutions of the

South. The coming political season had "consequences so momentous as to defy description." The editor warned his readers that the presidential canvass would determine "whether the power of the federal government shall pass into the hands of the abolitionists and be wielded for Southern destruction or whether the Constitution which guarantees Southern safety shall be maintained as the permanent law of the Union." According to Forsyth, a simple comprehension of political mathematics should be enough to alarm any Southerner. If no more slave states entered the Union, the South would soon lose its power in the U.S. Senate. He envisioned a scenario whereby the Congress would in rapid succession repeal the Fugitive Slave Law, amend the Three-Fifths Compromise, and with the resulting legislative majorities, pass an amendment to abolish slavery in the entire nation.[54]

Forsyth's involvement in the campaign of 1856 was just beginning when the *Register*, on July 24, abruptly issued this notice: "John Forsyth, Esq., the Editor of this paper left this city, yesterday, for Washington City, whither he has been called by his recent appointment as Minister to Mexico."[55] President Pierce, now in a virtual "lame-duck" status, apparently rewarded Forsyth's support with the appointment to replace the recently resigned James Gadsden. The official notification came from Secretary of State William L. Marcy in a communication dated 4 August 1856. When news of the appointment became public, a distinguished group of Mobile citizens, "without reference to party," sent Forsyth a letter requesting the privilege of hosting a dinner in his honor. The *Register* printed Forsyth's reply—one of his most heartfelt and perceptive writings ever. After the obligatory thanks (yet declining the offer), Forsyth became reflective, "as a Southern Man speaking to Southern Men." Expressing long-held fears, the editor, now in his mid-forties, wrote of the Union "in imminent danger from a wild spirit of revolution which has demented the Northern Mind." If that "revolutionary party" won the election, Forsyth concluded, "questions of the utmost gravity that can be presented to a people, will immediately demand solution." While not exactly sure what the solutions were, Forsyth knew that, first, "we cannot with safety and honor submit to a government based upon Black Republican principles," and, second, "the crisis demands a thorough union of hearts, hands, and votes at the South."[56]

A second such "valedictory" provoked a hostile rejoinder on the pages of the *New York Times*. On 6 October 1856, the *Times* reprinted a lengthy writing in which Forsyth bid farewell to his *Register* readers. In the address, Forsyth noted: "The integrity of the Federal Union depends on the election, by the popular vote, of James Buchanan." A "Black Republican" victory would be tantamount to a "revolution" that would be just cause for leaving the Union. The new minister concluded that while he would not take action against the Union, disunion held no fear, "as a Southern man," if forced upon him. The *Times* blasted Forsyth as the "newly appointed Minister to Mexico, who with his commission and outfit in his pocket, and a sworn servant of the Union, preaches up treason to his employer." The Northern journal also suspected sinister motives behind Forsyth's proclamations. His fear over the coming election could stem from the fact that he needed a Democratic victory to keep his newly acquired position.[57]

By 1856, Northern and Southern editors were hurling blame and the labels of revolutionaries and traitors at each other. The sectional issues—once naively thought solved by the Compromise of 1850—became more pronounced in the first years of the "critical decade." Thus was the state of the Union as John Forsyth sailed for Mexico.

5

"Sacrificed on the Altar of Duty"

At the 1856 Democratic National Convention, John Forsyth had led an unsuccessful effort to renominate President Franklin Pierce. Forsyth, the head of the Alabama delegation, remained stubbornly loyal to Pierce long after most of the party regulars had abandoned the cause. Apparently appreciative of such allegiance, Pierce, two months later, appointed the Mobile editor to replace General James Gadsden as United States Minister to Mexico. Gadsden, best remembered for the successful negotiations that resulted in the last cession of territory needed to complete the current boundaries of the continental United States, had faced recall after repeated complaints by the Mexican government. This was not the first time Forsyth's name had come up for a diplomatic post. In 1854 he was touted as a possible appointment to the consulate at Havana, Cuba. One letter, endorsed by twenty-five members of Congress, noted his "high order of talents, undoubted patriotism, and a devotion to the best interest of the country." Another, sent by Alabama Senators Clement C. Clay and Benjamin Fitzpatrick, praised his "attainments as a scholar and a lawyer." Forsyth's Mexican tenure as "Envoy Extraordinary and Minister Plenipotentiary" was, without doubt, the most frustrating period of his life. Having to deal with what he believed to be an inferior society, coupled with what he felt was a treacherous betrayal by the Buchanan administration, Forsyth ended his two-year diplomatic stint with the bitter conviction that he had been "sacrificed on the altar of duty."[1] Between 1856 and 1858, Forsyth experienced a humiliating rejection of personally conceived and negotiated treaties, received pressure from his own administration to pursue schemes he believed to be ill-advised and possibly illegal, prematurely recognized a revolutionary government on his own authority, broke off relations with his host country over a questionable cause, and left the foreign post under duress from both the Mexican and American administrations.

William L. Marcy, United States secretary of state under Pierce, wrote to

Forsyth that, "owing to the past disturbed state of Mexico and to other causes, our relations with that republic require particular attention at this time." Forsyth arrived in Mexico during the period of Mexican history known as the Reforma. The process that led to the disenchantment of the Liberal Mexican Reforma leaders can be traced back at least to Mexico's independence from Spain (1821). President Buchanan did not exaggerate when, in his Second Annual Message to Congress, he stated that, "Mexico has been in a state of constant revolution almost since it achieved its independence. One military leader after another has usurped the government in rapid succession; and the various constitutions from time to time adopted have been set at naught almost as soon as they were proclaimed." The facts certainly bear him out. From independence to the Ayutla Revolt (the initial event of the Reforma), Mexico experienced forty-five government changes. The average life span of a government during this period was nine months. Five successive constitutions served as the law of the land during the three decades of tumult. Accompanying the political chaos was a marked physical decimation of the proud nation. Before the Treaty of Guadalupe-Hidalgo, Mexico claimed 1,725,000 square miles of land. After the treaty and the subsequent Gadsden Purchase, the total area dropped to 767,000 square miles.[2]

Mexico in the first half of the nineteenth century faced many important and divisive issues. Most prominent were the ideas of political legitimacy, constitutional government, relations between the center (Mexico City) and regions, the impact of Liberalism, types of social arrangements and land ownership, problems of the political economy, and above all, the relationship between church and state. Complicating these issues was the competition between various groups within the nation that claimed exclusive responsibility for their solution. Prior to the Reforma, several groups "shared" power. The Roman Catholic Church, army, private militias, landed gentry, guilds, commercial corporations, and even Indian communal villages, all vied for regional or national authority. While most likely oversimplifying the situation, the Liberals and Conservatives formed the two basic political divisions in Mexico, and as such, competed for Forsyth's attention and support. To the Liberals, the process between independence and Ayutla was "a continuing liberal and democratic struggle against the forces of political and clerical oppression, social injustice, and economic exploitation." The Liberals gained their support from a wide cross-section of society. The progressive element of the metropolitan Creole elite and urban intelligentsia as well as provincial lawyers, landowners, professionals, and some army officers could be numbered in the Liberal camp. A surprising number of peasants and industrial workers were also of the Liberal persuasion. Many in the former group saw the Liberal program as a way to end social and ethnic injustices while members of the latter—growing in number owing to the rise of the urban factory workers—found little comfort in the status quo. Both groups saw the Liberal movement as an outlet for basic discontent.[3]

Regardless of their background, Liberals held certain principles dear. They were in favor of individualism, were antimonarchy, felt the Indian communal properties (*ejido*) system hindered loyalty to the state, and, most important, felt the Roman Catholic Church was too powerful. Richard Sinkin stated that the "tap-root of radicalism in Mexico was then detestation of the Catholic Church."[4] The church was an all-encompassing power that affected almost every aspect of Mexican life, literally from birth to death. Roman Catholicism had dominated the Mexican power structure since colonial days because of its great economic wealth and legal privilege. The tremendous wealth came from both real estate and invested capital—both of which Liberals believed ensured the status of the church and obstructed the country's development. The privileges (*fueros*) of the church ranged from tax exemptions to jurisdiction in criminal cases.[5]

The Conservatives, on the other hand, viewed the process of the same period as "a succession of senseless efforts to destroy Hispanic traditions, to substantiate alien ideals and values, and by so doing, to condemn the country to perpetual anarchy, dictatorship, and moral corruption." Conservative support came from absentee communal landowners, large merchants, army officers, promonarchists, and high clergy, as well as a great number of the impoverished laity. The church's view of government was indeed simple. The best that one could expect from any civil government was for that institution to support and defend the Roman Catholic Church. Centralism was therefore the most effective way to run the nation. Man, because of his sinful nature, could not be expected to govern himself wisely. God instituted the church to basically protect himself from man. Long before the days of *Iturbide,* Roman Catholicism was the official, protected religion of the nation. Religious toleration was a doctrine of the devil himself. Any Liberal attempt at reform faced clerical opposition.[6]

The initial event of the Reforma came during the final act of General Antonio López de Santa Anna's many performances as Mexico's ruler. When Santa Anna took office in April of 1853, the rules of his regime included religious intolerance, strong central government, the abolition of the federal system and popular voting, a strong army, and no congresses. These affronts to Liberalism, coupled with what its leaders viewed as the disgraceful loss of land to the United States by the Gadsden Purchase, solidified the opposition of both the Liberals and some moderate conservatives. Mexico appeared ripe for a Liberal uprising comparable to those underway in the United States and Europe in the mid-nineteenth century.[7]

Opposition to Santa Anna was most pronounced in the southern state of Guerrero. General Juan Álvarez ruled this isolated area as his feudal domain. Seeing his local autonomy threatened, Álvarez protested Santa Anna's demand for central authority. Objection turned to mutiny, and mutiny evolved into insurrection. Led by Álvarez, along with General Thomas Moreno, Colonel Florencio Villareal, and Colonel Ignacio Comonfort, the rebels withdrew recognition of the Santa Anna regime. The 1854 "Plan of Ayutla" (named for the town from which it was proclaimed) called for the removal of Santa Anna, the election of a provisional president by representatives appointed by the commander-in-chief of the revolutionary army, and an "extraordinary" congress to produce a new constitution.[8]

Important Liberal leaders such as Benito Juárez, Melchor Ocampo, Ponciano Arriaga, and Ignacio Ramiréz saw the overthrow of the old regime as the "renewal of the liberal struggle to complete the work of independence by removing the last vestiges of Mexico's colonial heritage." However, as Forsyth soon discovered, the word "complete" was obviously inaccurate. The Liberals entered a grave period. James C. Scott described this revolutionary moment as an "interregnum." As is true in most revolutions, the critical moment occurred between the moment when a previous regime disintegrated and the moment when the new regime was finally in place. As events unfolded, it became painfully clear that the Ayutla revolt failed to secure internal tranquility. The Conservative forces had not been decisively defeated. Although the abdication of Santa Anna deprived the Conservatives of a charismatic leader, they still held a formidable social and economic stranglehold on the populace. This Conservative remnant played a crucial role in the other two major events of the Reforma period—the civil war and the (post-Forsyth tenure) French intervention.[9]

After Ayutla, the Liberals formed a new government with Alvarez as president. Comonfort served as minister of war, Ocampo was the minister of foreign affairs, while Juárez headed the ministry of justice. The leadership represented a new generation of reformers untainted by failures of previous Liberal governments. The progressive leadership did not have the luxury of a honeymoon period. Swift and extreme opposition awaited their earliest attempts at reform. Initial efforts to eliminate military and ecclesiastical privilege created such an uproar, that, in December of 1855, Álvarez willingly resigned the presidency in favor of Comonfort. Comonfort's relatively moderate stance was perhaps the only way to preserve what little gains the Liberals realized.[10]

It was into this chaotic environment that Forsyth, who confessed to Marcy that diplomacy was a field "entirely new to me and in which I have no other guide than the instructions of the Department and my own inexperienced judgments," cautiously entered. After a "pleasant run" of five and a half days on the cutter *McLeland*, Forsyth arrived in the Mexican capital on 15 October 1856. A few days later, he sent word to his diplomatic counterpart, Juan Antonio de la Fuente of a desire to arrange a formal meeting with the president of the Mexican Republic.[11] Forsyth presented his credentials to President Comonfort on October 23. In an address prepared for the occasion, he pledged that his mission would "bind our two countries together in the enduring bonds of a cordial good-will, amity and peace." In his response, Comonfort likewise vowed "every day more and more to cement the mutual friendly relations which happily bind the two nations, which from the historical antecedents of the two countries, the similarity in their forms of governments, their well-comprehended interests and their destinies, should be cultivated with diligent anxiety."[12] Unfortunately, this warm (albeit hypocritical) personal exchange represented the high-water mark for both Forsyth and Comonfort in regards to United States–Mexico relations.

President Pierce specifically defined Forsyth's Mexican mission as having five goals. The lame-duck president instructed Forsyth to negotiate a reduction in certain Mexican trade tariffs, promote improved commercial relations between the two nations, settle outstanding American claims against the new republic, establish a postal treaty, and secure transit rights across the Tehuantepec isthmus. Forsyth's first major diplomatic snafu came as a result of his attempt to go beyond this charge. Less than three weeks after lamenting his lack of diplomatic experience, Forsyth went to great lengths to explain to Secretary Marcy the inadequacy of United States' policy toward its southern neighbor. Forsyth felt that a conventional diplomatic approach would not secure lasting advantage for the United States. Writing to Marcy in November of 1856, he noted the "prevalent and growing sentiment among intelligent Mexicans, is that without the intervention, aid, or guarantee of the United States in some form or other, a stable Government can never be secured to this people." Unlike many Southerners in the United States who favored a policy of land acquisition, Forsyth promoted a plan whereby the United States could "enjoy all the fruits of annexation without its responsibilities and evils." Lest one think that Forsyth harbored an enlightened view of diplomacy, consider that one of the main benefits he saw in his protectorate scheme was that it would "secure for our countrymen the enjoyment of the rich resources of the Mexican country, without the danger of introducing, into our social and political system, the ignorant masses of the Mexican people."[13]

In fairness to Forsyth, one must note that the protectorate idea also had support among some of the Liberal leaders in Mexico. Mexican Minister of Foreign Affairs Miguel Lerdo de Tejada (who had replaced Antonio) broached the subject with Forsyth in a meeting held on 16 December 1856. Still smarting from the Treaty of Guadalupe-Hidalgo and the Gadsden Purchase, many Liberal leaders saw the investment of U.S. dollars as a defensive maneuver—the only way to avoid future annexations.[14] Lerdo boasted to Forsyth that the current Mexican government was the best and most liberal in the nation's history. However, the Mexican diplomat was also convinced that the regime "could not sustain itself against the disorganizing element now unhappily rife throughout the country, without the pecuniary aid of some friendly power." Lerdo felt out Forsyth as to the possibilities of large loans from the United States in exchange for commercial and/or transit privileges. Along with a transcript of this meeting, forwarded by Forsyth to the State Department, the American minister stated his opinion that the time was right to take advantage of Mexico's dire financial straits. Forsyth admitted the plan would be expensive but, in his judgment, "it is not easy to perceive how a few millions can be disbursed from our plethoric Treasury with superior results and profit and advantage."[15]

Lerdo's resignation a few days after his interview with Forsyth did not deter the novice diplomat's optimism regarding the protectorate idea. Confident that President Comonfort was willing to make a deal, Forsyth believed the new Mexican Minister of Foreign Relations, Ezequiel Montes, shared views similar to Lerdo. Correct in his assumption, Forsyth, on 2 February 1856, submitted drafts of the Montes-Forsyth treaties—three treaties and one convention. The first treaty was a trade reciprocity arrangement, which provided for free trade on mutual land and river frontiers. The second was a postal treaty while the third dealt with specific commercial provisions. The convention provided for a joint commission to adjust private claims. The most significant part of the treaty, however, was a loan provision—surpassing any authority given to Forsyth from Washington. Forsyth's proposed treaty called for a loan to Mexico in the amount of fifteen million dollars. Seven million dollars of the loan was to remain in the treasury of the United States. Three million dollars of this total would be used to settle American claims against Mexico while four million dollars would retire the English Convention Debt. The remaining eight million dollars was to be paid to the Republic of Mexico upon ratification of the treaty. The intertwined duty and trade provisions in the Montes-Forsyth agreements meant that ratification guaranteed protectorate status.[16] The language of the treaty made clear that, without the loan, the entire deal was off. Inexcusably, Forsyth held the expressed goals of the administration hostage to his own unauthorized policy.

The Mexican Liberals considered the Montes-Forsyth treaties to be a great diplomatic victory and lobbied for U.S. ratification. The agreements would minimize British influence by ending Mexican indebtedness and diverting most Mexican foreign trade into U.S. sources. These provisions essentially represented what Lerdo had requested back in the previous December. Increased trade with the United States resulting from frontier reciprocity, rebates on duties, and regular steamer service promised to bind the economies of the nations and attract a flood of Yankee capital and technology.[17] Certainly Forsyth could not also have helped but understand the importance of this deal for the economy of Mobile, which, as a major Gulf of Mexico port, stood to profit tremendously from expanded Mexican trade.

Unfortunately for Forsyth, the President of the United States did not support his diplomatic effort. Before receiving any official notice, Forsyth attained copies of the *New York Herald,* which contained news of Pierce's rejection. Official news finally arrived. In the last correspondence sent from the Pierce administration to Forsyth, Secretary Marcy conveyed the president's displeasure. Marcy noted that Forsyth clearly overstepped his authority, stating, "As your instructions had no reference to the subject of . . . a large loan by this Government to Mexico—it required most deliberate consideration on his [Pierce's] part before taking any definitive action upon it."[18] Even though Pierce did not approve of the treaties and refused to submit them to the Senate for its advice, being in the last days of his term, he did not specifically reject the proposals—leaving the fate of Forsyth's handiwork to the new president, James Buchanan.

If Forsyth was discouraged by Pierce's rebuke, he surely could not have been optimistic over the chances of his treaties under Buchanan. The glowing, albeit late endorsement of the new president notwithstanding, the late Democratic convention was not the first time a Forsyth had clashed with Buchanan. Some twenty years earlier, Buchanan unsuccessfully tried to convince President Martin Van Buren to dump Forsyth's father as his secretary of state. The senior Forsyth repaid Buchanan's hostility by rejecting the Pennsylvanian's first report as the chairman of the Foreign Relations Committee (ironically dealing with

Mexico). In a stinging memorandum, Forsyth Sr. had sarcastically remarked that "the Committee seems to have had an imperfect knowledge of the facts in relation to our affairs with Mexico." The two men never again missed an opportunity to try to derail the career of the other. As late as 1840, Buchanan worked feverishly behind the scenes to ensure that Forsyth Sr. did not become the Democratic Party's vice-presidential nominee.[19] Forsyth Jr. was seen as a leftover appointee who would have to be retained in order not to ruffle the feathers of the already-fragile Democratic Party family.

The younger Forsyth's fears were realized when he received his first communication from the new administration. Lewis Cass, Marcy's replacement as secretary of state, informed Forsyth that Buchanan agreed with Pierce's evaluation of the treaties and, like his predecessor, refused to submit them to the Senate for consideration. Cass conveyed instructions for Forsyth to communicate this decision to the Mexican government as conclusive.[20] Forsyth, perceiving the rejection of his work as a personal affront, refused to give up without a fight.

After receiving the bad news from both Marcy and Cass (in the same mail), Forsyth composed a lengthy defense. His arguments centered on at least three main points. First, he claimed that, while true enough his instructions did not mention anything about loans, a door had opened, which he felt could not be ignored. Comparing his unforeseen opportunity to that which befell negotiators of the Louisiana Purchase, Forsyth justified his actions. Second, a policy of direct land acquisition (especially popular with Buchanan) was not practical. Forsyth noted that "in the Plan of Ayutla which brought the Comonfort government into power, the alienation of the national territory is deprecated as an act little short of treasonable, and the President himself is pledged on the record in the strongest terms, against ever consenting to it." Finally, perhaps realizing that his second argument would not dampen the administration's appetite for Mexican land, Forsyth demonstrated how his plan would eventually result in land acquisition anyway. Forsyth stated that he "regarded a loan to Mexico as a species of floating mortgage upon the territory of a poor neighbor, useless to her, of great value to us, which in the end would be paid, could be paid with honor, and could only be paid by a peaceable foreclosure with her consent." The minister believed that since it was impossible to acquire territory immediately, he "did the next best thing, which was to pave the way for the acquisition hereafter."[21]

Even after official communications from successive administrations, Forsyth stubbornly pressed ahead. His diplomatic mistakes began to evolve from merely "inexperienced judgments" to possible deception and insubordination. During a routine interview with Montes, the subject of the treaties came up. Forsyth told Montes that the American government was on the verge of ratifying the treaties. Encouraged by this report, Montes conveyed the information to Comonfort. Forsyth even had the audacity to ask the American administration to speed up its approval of his treaties, as Comonfort would leave power in a few months. Apparently trying to explain to Forsyth the meaning of "no," the administration reiterated its rejection of Forsyth's work. Buchanan informed Forsyth that the minister was mistaken in harboring any hope that the Montes-Forsyth Treaty would ever see the light of the U.S. Senate. In words strangely similar to the aforementioned used by John Forsyth Sr., President Buchanan criticized the younger Forsyth's "misapprehension which you obviously entertain respecting [Buchanan's] views on the subject of further negotiations."[22]

In what was thought to be his final word on the Montes-Forsyth Treaty, President Buchanan served notice that he would send his own drafts of treaties for Forsyth to negotiate. The promised manuscripts arrived in July of 1857. Apparently not wanting to leave anything to chance, the Buchanan administration clearly spelled out exactly what it desired—sending drafts (reported to be in Buchanan's own handwriting) of two treaties for Forsyth to present. One of the treaties involved an attempt to adjust the Mexican-United States border to acquire more Mexican territory. Buchanan had long dreamed of expanding the borders of the United States at the expense of its weaker neighbor. The administration instructed Forsyth to attempt to purchase the province of Lower California, nearly all of Sonora, and the part of Chihuahua north of the thirty-eighth parallel. The total sum to be offered was twelve million dollars with an option to go as high as fifteen million. Recent historical events such as the Gadsden Purchase convinced Buchanan that the Mexican leadership—public professions to the contrary notwithstanding—would eventually be forced to dispose of these remote holdings. Buchanan tried to convince Forsyth of the potential impact of these negotiations, claiming that, if he succeeded, "This will be productive of great and enduring benefits to your country and entitle your name to be enrolled in the list of her most distinguished Diplomatists."[23]

It was at this point that Forsyth made a mistake all too common among diplomats—he forgot that he was merely a *conveyor* of American policy, not a *formulator*. Responding to Buchanan's instructions in September 1857, Forsyth claimed the proposals placed him in an "untenable" position. In a lengthy letter, Forsyth elaborated on the inadequacies of Buchanan's policy. He offered his personal misgivings regarding both treaties. The purchase of Mexican territory was, according to Forsyth, "hopeless from the beginning." The minister to Mexico accepted Comonfort's sincerity in his pledge that he would "sooner throw himself from the Palace window" than surrender any more Mexican soil. Comonfort confided personally to Forsyth that "each President has his system. The system of Don Antonio [Santa Anna] was to sell his country; mine is to preserve it."[24]

While lecturing the president of the United States on the shortcomings of his orders obviously entails a lack of judgment, Forsyth's next move bordered on insubordination. Convinced that the boundary treaty was ill-advised, he refused to submit it (much as Buchanan had refused to submit the Montes-Forsyth Treaty to the U.S. Senate) to the Mexican minister of relations. Forsyth, who wrote that he was "thoroughly persuaded of the facts and unwilling to jeopardize the influence I have been able, with great care and attention to acquire with the government; unwilling to subject my own government to the certainty of an official rebuff of its overtures," requested an interview with Comonfort to try to work out some other sort of agreement.[25]

The second document concerned access rights across the Isthmus of Tehuantepec. As Cass noted, "the value and importance to Mexico of a Rail Road across the Isthmus of Tehuantepec can scarcely be overestimated. In this the United States are, also, deeply interested. The proximity of the Isthmus to our shores, the salubrity of the climate, the adaptedness of the ground for the construction of the Rail Road, and the great diminution of the distance in comparison with other more southern routes between our Atlantic and Pacific possessions—all conspire to point it out as preferable to any other route of our own territory."[26]

Although Buchanan believed that an 1853 treaty (part of the Gadsden Purchase agreement) guaranteed the United States the right of transit, he felt the agreement should be "confirmed, extended and rendered more specific." In the confused state of Mexican politics, several competing factions claimed to possess a legitimate grant allowing them to develop the transit route. In 1857 Colonel A. G. Sloo of New York organized the Tehuantepec Company for the purpose of fulfilling a contract to construct a rail passage across the isthmus. Unable to raise enough money to pay the Mexican government for the construction rights, he had borrowed a large sum from Francis P. Falconet, a British citizen living in Mexico. After Sloo failed to pay his debt, Falconet took possession of the contract. Sloo's group, however, still felt they had the legal right to pursue the project. To complicate matters even more, the Mexican government had already sold the grant to a Mexican, Jose de Goray, in 1842.

Also in 1857, the Louisiana Tehuantepec Company was formed with Emile la Sére as president. Among the prominent backers of this venture were Louisiana Senators Judah P. Benjamin and John Slidell. The new company's charter authorized Benjamin and la Sére to travel to Mexico to try to negotiate new concessions from the Mexican government. Several weeks before this trip, Slidell had visited President Buchanan to seek the administration's support for the Louisiana Company's aspirations. The president was more than happy to oblige. As la Sére and Benjamin prepared to depart for Mexico, Buchanan ordered Forsyth to "make known to the Mexican Government the object of their missions and to give them such aid in its accomplishment as you may deem advisable and effectual."[27]

In the same correspondence in which Forsyth expressed disapproval of the expansionist land purchase scheme, he likewise voiced reservations about the proposed deal concerning the Tehuantepec transit rights. Forsyth's objections centered on two concerns. In the first place, the United States offered no monetary compensation in exchange for the grant of such a right. Forsyth reminded Buchanan that, ten years prior (when the Pennsylvanian was the secretary of state), the United States offered Mexico fifteen million dollars for basically the same right-of-way deal. This was most likely a not-so-subtle reminder of Forsyth's earlier failed diplomatic effort because, under his rejected treaties, U.S. loans would have secured trade and transit preferences.

The second objection was much more personal in nature. Forsyth clearly resented Buchanan's sending of Benjamin and la Sére to conduct negotiations. Forsyth reported that "my assistance has not been requested, nor have I been consulted in any steps of the negotiations. Indeed from the attitude in which the public credence and the public press have placed these gentlemen, my aid was not at all needed. They have figured in the papers of the capital as the 'American negotiators.'" He went on to note that "report has taken the form of open remark that Mr. Benjamin was possessed of secret and ample powers from the Government and that, for the time being, the functions of the U.S. legation in Mexico were in abeyance." Even more wounding to Forsyth's already injured pride were the reports that he no longer had the confidence of the administration and that "a treaty would only be made after his recall."[28]

Hurt feelings aside, the intrigue behind the Tehuantepec affair went much deeper. Significantly, the major players in the drama all had connections to major factions in the Democratic Party. Benjamin (whom Robert Toombs promoted to replace Forsyth as minister to Mexico) and la Sére were both strong Buchanan supporters. La Sére, reported in one contemporary source to have survived eighteen duels in his lifetime, co-owned a Louisiana newspaper with Slidell, another strong Buchanan stalwart. Pierre Soulé, former U.S. minister to Spain and, like Forsyth, a supporter of Stephen A. Douglas (Buchanan's main party rival), represented Sloo's interest. Soulé, also a personal friend of Forsyth, ironically was on the same steamer that transported Benjamin and la Sére to Mexico. Soulé came to Mexico to try to regain the transit grant for the Sloo faction. With Forsyth backing the Soulé mission, the Tehuantepec affair became a microcosm of the United States' Democratic Party squabbles.[29]

Two weeks after Forsyth submitted his objections to Washington, he proceeded to make a bad situation even worse by offering unsolicited views of what he felt to be a more suitable course of action. Once again, he directed the administration's attention back to his rejected treaties of the previous February. He still believed he could secure a deal based on what he had already negotiated, with only minor adjustments. The impertinent minister even sent detailed maps and diagrams to get his points across. Forsyth still insisted that any successful transit negotiation (both through the isthmus and a northern province route) could only become reality as a result of pecuniary considerations. He even had a price in mind: "I am of the opinion that twelve millions of dollars will be required for the whole, and this may be divided at pleasure between the equivalents. That is to say, six millions for commerce, and three millions for each of the transits; or eight millions for the former and four millions for the two latters." This "project" (as Forsyth termed it) perhaps sounded reasonable until one remembers that Forsyth's specific instructions ordered him to negotiate the same deal with no monetary considerations whatsoever. The Minister Extraordinary concluded his plan by stating, "I have thus, in the discharge of what I consider my duty, indicated to the Department, the policy which in my opinion can be embodied in the form of a treaty with Mexico."[30]

A fascinating scenario began to unfold even before Forsyth received an official reply to this communication. Benjamin and la Sére concluded a private deal with the Mexican government—however at far less advantage than they had expected. They placed the blame for these shortcomings squarely on Forsyth. On 3 October 1857, Buchanan received a lengthy letter from the two gentlemen in which they strongly condemned the "treacherous conduct" of Forsyth. Cass forwarded a copy of the letter back to Forsyth, commenting that the charges were "of so grave a character that it seems due to you that you should have an opportunity to reply to them." Benjamin and la Sére brought at least three major charges against Forsyth. Benjamin apparently kept a detailed diary of what he termed the "disgusting details." The first charge concerned the way in which Forsyth represented the Benjamin and la Sére mission to President Comonfort. As of Saturday, August 29, the two gentlemen felt certain they had secured a very fair and lucrative deal with the Mexican leader. However, on the following Monday, they were perplexed to learn that the terms to which both parties had agreed had been significantly altered—to their disadvantage. They claimed that Forsyth, sometime during the weekend, met with Comonfort and convinced the ruler that the United States government had removed its "protection" from the Tehuantepec Company. The Louisianans complained that, "after stating in our presence to the President of Mexico that our mission met the cordial approbation of Mr. Buchanan and that he was instructed to aid us, Mr. Forsyth went secretly to the Mexican President at the most critical point of our negotiations to contradict what he had said in our presence."[31]

The second complaint had to do with Forsyth's relationship with Soulé and the rival Sloo grant. Although ordered to give any needed assistance to Benjamin and la Sére, Forsyth appeared to promote the rival company. Benjamin and la Sére bitterly complained: "Mr. Forsyth, with a full knowledge that Mr. Soulé had come to Mexico for the purpose of defeating us in a measure which our Government desired to aid, introduced Mr. Soulé to the President of Mexico with a high eulogium on his character, position and influence in the U.S. and listened to a long discourse made by Mr. Soulé to the President in opposition to the measures which Mr. Buchanan wished to accomplish . . . lending by his expressive silence the weight of his official influences to a gentleman whose avowed purpose was to thwart measures which Mr. Forsyth was instructed to favor."[32] Soulé's own correspondence seems to sustain this charge. In a series of letters to Needler R. Jennings, a New Orleans businessman with ties to the Sloo claim, Soulé revealed some of the behind the scenes maneuvering involving himself and Minister Forsyth. On at least one evening during his stay, Soulé dined with Forsyth and discussed his mission in great detail. With Forsyth's help, Soulé arranged to make sure his meeting with President Comonfort took place only after la Sére and Benjamin's. The implication of such action was clear—Forsyth, who sat in on the first meeting, could supply information that might be beneficial to Soulé before the second meeting. Indeed, after Soulé's audience with the president, Forsyth carefully compared and critiqued Comonfort's reaction to the rival arguments.[33]

Finally, Benjamin and la Sére alleged that Forsyth made "slanderous" remarks regarding their operation. Referring to the pair as mere "speculators," Forsyth warned the Mexican government of potential legal complications if the

Tehuantepec Company received official grants. Forsyth also allegedly accused the two of paying bribes of up to one million dollars in exchange for their concessions. Benjamin and la Sére felt that, because of Forsyth's actions, the deal was far less lucrative than it should have been—and most certainly would have been with the cooperation of the legation. Not only did the Tehuantepec Company have to assume claims (totaling over one million dollars) against the Mexican government brought by rival companies, but also, the length of the grant was reduced from seventy-five years to sixty.[34]

Within a week of receiving a copy of this "extraordinary indictment," Forsyth angrily penned an elaborate defense. The minister felt the charges were not just against his official performance but also an attack on his integrity and honor as a gentleman. Attributing most of the report to misrepresentation, gossip, innuendoes, and "unmitigated falsehood," Forsyth concluded that Benjamin and la Sére were simply trying to find a scapegoat for their own ineptness. According to Forsyth, the charges rested "upon no firmer foundation than those apprehensions, suspicions, and prejudices, which are easily traceable as the parents of their difficulties, losses and blunders throughout this business." In his own mind, Forsyth's only crime was that he had not permitted himself to become the "pliant tool of a clique of Tehuantepec speculators which for ten years past have constantly kept this legation in hot water."[35]

Becoming increasingly defensive, Forsyth commented that he was "fully aware that some persons with ulterior objects [an obvious reference to Benjamin and la Sére] have been active in their efforts to obtain my recall, and that the telegraph and the press have been but in requisition by kindred agencies to misrepresent my conduct and to affect that end." Appearing to come very close to offering his resignation, Forsyth requested a vote of confidence: "There is a question that admits the toleration of no ambiguities or doubt. In the judgment of the Government, I have done wrong or right—Which? I ask. In the confidence of the Government I am or I am not—Which? I ask. Honored with the mission without solicitation by myself or my friends, I came here no office-beggar, and I certainly shall not stoop to ask to return here upon any other terms than those of confidence in my integrity and patriotism, which prompted the voluntary tender of this mission to me."[36]

Although Forsyth feigned indifference regarding the status of his foreign mission, he was working behind the scenes to save his reputation, if not his job. He dispatched a letter to Stephen A. Douglas explaining the entire situation and asking for the senator's support. Forsyth explained to Douglas that the entire controversy stemmed from the fact that Benjamin himself wanted the

Mexican post and that Slidell was determined to force a recall. He hoped the Illinois statesman would speak up for him against certain criticism from the administration. It is interesting to note that Forsyth also sent Douglas copies of his rejected treaties. He hoped Douglas would examine them and lend his "valuable encouragement." He confided to his friend that if he could successfully complete the treaty negotiations, he would "go home and leave this mission for somebody else—even Benjamin, an eleventh hour Democrat." However, he continued, "to be recalled to make way for such a Democratic novice, after my life of devotion to the cause, would be a pill that I could hardly digest."[37]

Before he had time to further ponder his future plans, a salvo came in the form of yet another communication from Cass. By November 1857 (after he had already reviewed the complaints of Benjamin and la Sére), Cass had read Forsyth's correspondence concerning the Tehuantepec and boundary treaties. Secretary Cass (and by implication, President Buchanan) could not conceal his frustration with the headstrong minister. Cass, himself a former diplomat, proceeded to give Forsyth a primer on the proper conduct of a United States minister: "Your position is that of an agent . . . it was your duty to carry into effect the instructions of your principal, both in the letter and the spirit whether you fully approve them or not." The seventy-year-old Cass had obviously forgotten that he himself once resigned from a diplomatic post rather than carry out orders sent from then Secretary of State Daniel Webster. Cass continued this "lesson" by noting that Forsyth's impertinent style of diplomacy "would make the foreign policy of the Government dependent on the individual opinions of the respective ministers, and would compel the President, instead of controlling the action of our public agents, himself to receive their instructions, and regulate his conduct by their views." Cass hoped that Forsyth would eventually agree with Buchanan's Mexican policies, but the old general explained, "it will none the less be your duty, I need hardly say, to make your official action conform to it, and to endeavor to secure its success with the Government of Mexico."[38]

Events in Mexico soon forced all parties to turn their attention away from this diplomatic stalemate. On 17 December 1857, Forsyth reported that "a complete revolution has just occurred in this city, the result of which is the overthrow of the constitution . . . the dispersion of Congress, and the investment of Gen. Comonfort, as the sole organ of the Government, with dictatorial powers."[39] Conservative forces under the leadership of General Félix Zuloaga began to purge the capital of Liberal influences. Zuloaga temporary propped up the moderate Comonfort perhaps to retain some semblance of legitimacy. The "Plan of Tacubaya" was the first stage of what became the War of the Reform, a civil war pitting the Conservatives against the Liberals.[40]

Presiding over a nearly bankrupt nation, the weakened Comonfort began to soften his opposition to the disposition of Mexican territory. As early as the prior November, the general had sounded out Forsyth on the possibility of such a deal. Forsyth, stung by the harsh criticism received directly from the administration, as well as indirectly from the Mexican and American newspapers, began to sound more and more like Buchanan. During the first week of 1858, Comonfort sent word that he desperately needed $600,000 in order to raise six thousand troops to "pacificate" the country. Forsyth replied to the besieged general that he could "promise pecuniary succor in but one way, and that was in consideration of a cession of territory." Forsyth was now convinced that the desperate times would force Comonfort to follow the earlier course of Santa Anna. In typical condescending tones, the minister noted that "in money matters, these people exhibit a puerility and lack of common sense and prudence, which is incredible to all but eye-witnesses."[41]

On 9 January 1858, Zuloaga abandoned Comonfort, and the civil war resumed in earnest. Soon three contending armies marched in the streets of Mexico City—Liberals, Conservatives, and a small force that remained loyal to Comonfort. On January 21, Comonfort fled the capital and escaped to Vera Cruz. Here began the events that led to Forsyth's most controversial act of his two-year diplomatic tenure. Benito Juárez formed a Liberal government at Guanajuato on January 19. Four days later, in the capital the Conservative faction, boosted particularly by the army, declared Zuloaga president. Forsyth had to decide which government to recognize. Surprisingly, on his own authority, he decided to recognize the Zuloaga regime only four days after its formation.[42]

On January 25, Forsyth received a communication from Luis Cuevas, the new minister of foreign relations under the Zuloaga administration. His official response (thus extending United States de facto recognition) came only two days later. Forsyth sent word to Cass of his action. In this important correspondence, he spelled out several reasons for his "hasty" action. First, the Zuloaga government held the capital, and thus, had to be considered the "de facto" government. Forsyth noted that it had always been the custom of the diplomatic body to recognize the government in a capital. Second, reports of a constitutional government in exile were, at the time, based only on "hearsay and newspaper reports." Third, he argued that since Comonfort (the then-constitutional president) had agreed to the Plan of Tacubaya (which overturned the Constitution of 1857), no constitutional government could legally exist. Fourth, no Liberal forces under Juárez had contested the recent proceedings in the capital. Fifth, there was little chance a Liberal government would win, even if one did exist. Finally, no official communication had come from a Liberal government.[43] In a bizarre twist of fate, just as Forsyth finished the above correspondence, a communication did arrive from the Juárez government. In a brief note, Melchor Ocampo, minister of relations under the Liberal regime, requested that Forsyth deal only with representatives of the Juárez faction. Although Forsyth outwardly expressed sympathy for the Liberal cause, he replied to Ocampo that "had your communication been received two days earlier, it would have been in my power to have replied to it in a manner and form from which I am now disbarred."[44] Forsyth proceeded to recite the same reasons to Ocampo that he had just penned for Cass. Ironically (considering his recent indiscretions regarding the boundary and Tehuantepec negotiations), he stated that no matter his personal feelings of sympathy, he must follow official diplomatic procedures.

Forsyth's decision to recognize the Zuloaga government haunted him for many years. One does not have to be cynical to seriously question each of Forsyth's stated reasons for the action. For example, his claim that control of the capital required the recognition of the government ignored historical precedent. After the Ayutla revolt, General Gadsden extended recognition to the Alvarez government at Cuernavaca. Likewise, the 1848 Treaty of Guadalupe-Hidalgo was signed with a government located in Querétaro. Forsyth's claim that he did not have information about a rival, Liberal government except through "hearsay and newspaper reports" also appears weak. Surely a man of Forsyth's background and local contacts could discern which newspapers published reliable information. Mexico City's *El Heraldo* carried complete coverage of Juárez's establishment of the Liberal government, including a list of cabinet members.[45] The constitutional argument is equally puzzling since Comonfort, before his departure, recognized Juárez (who as minister of justice was next in line for the presidency) as the constitutional president. The complaint that no Liberal force came forward to combat Zuloaga in the capital failed to disclose that Juárez was arrested in the first hours of the coup. Only the last argument—that no official communication arrived from the Liberals—appears valid, if true.

In later years, President Buchanan criticized the "indecent haste" shown by Forsyth in his recognition. Mexican historian José Fuentes Mares went even farther, charging that Forsyth lied about the dates on which he received the successive communications from Ocampo and Cuevas. According to this scholar, the purpose of the alleged deception was the belief that the Zuloaga government would be more receptive to a land cession. Indeed, in the same letter in which he explained his decision to recognize the Conservative regime, Forsyth reported that he was "feeling the pulse" of the Zuloaga government on the subject of territory.[46]

Forsyth began to exert increasing pressure on Cuevas to get the Mexican minister to relinquish the desired territory. In March 1858, the American envoy presented another proposed treaty (again forwarded by the U.S. administration). Knowing that the United States Senate would soon adjourn, and that he was planning on taking a leave of absence from his post, Forsyth urged deliberate haste in acceptance. The treaty basically contained the same provisions that Forsyth found "untenable" a year prior. This time Forsyth, perhaps wiser if not humbler, accepted the administration's logic that the northern land served no purpose to Mexico and could only be developed by the United States, whose population would eventually "expel these savages and replace them by a thrifty and intelligent population, which would not only render the Mexican frontier entirely secure, but would enrich it by the productive industry and lucrative trade which everywhere follow the footsteps of American emigration and settlement." American expansion into the coveted territory was inevitable since the "great author" of the laws ordained it. Expressing Darwinian logic concerning the encroachment of the "thrifty and intelligent" United States' population, the American envoy noted that it was an act of "provident statesmanship" to conduct foreign policy according to natural laws. Forsyth also suggested to his Mexican counterpart that the United States was being generous since "if it were actuated by a policy purely selfish, might fold its arms and quietly await the operation of their cause with absolute confidence that this would give the regions as harvest fields and homes to those who speak the tongue of its rapidly augmenting population."[47] In simpler terms, if Mexico did not accept the offer of payment, it should be prepared for another Texas scenario.

Apparently not convinced that the "great author of the laws" wanted Mexico to liquidate its national possessions, Cuevas replied that the boundary change was "neither conductive to its true interests, nor its good name, whatever advantage it might realize as just compensation." Cuevas understood, much as did Comonfort (at least in the earliest months of his administration) that "a new loss of territory would entail grave internal disorders and postpone more and more the restoration of peace."[48]

At this critical impasse, one can see the beginnings of a plan to either force the Mexican government to accept the deal or precipitate a change in that government in favor of one that would. Forsyth's diplomatic correspondence became increasingly inflammatory in tone. Upon receiving Cuevas's official rejection of his offer, Forsyth, in a thinly veiled threat, replied that "when in the fullness of time, the consequences obeying unchangeable and universal laws shall have ripened into realities, the forecast and the generosity of the U.S. will have been vindicated in the proposals which Mexico has just rejected." Cuevas took the last remark as a personal threat from Forsyth and not as an official statement of United States policy.[49]

Forced for the second time to report to the American administration the failure of a treaty negotiation, Forsyth, this time, appeared genuinely remorseful. Remembering his past rebukes, Forsyth assured his superiors that he had "left no stone unturned" to insure the success of the negotiations with the Zuloaga government. Even though Zuloaga remained inflexible, he harbored cautious optimism, noting that "Mexican administrations are short-lived, and the present one already exhibits unmistakable signs of decay." In a subsequent communication, Forsyth smugly noted: "I can see no ray of hope for this country. It appears to me to be irretrievably lost, as every nation must be that possesses neither honesty nor common sense in its rulers."[50]

The treaty that Forsyth had presented to Cuevas contained stipulations that Mexico and the United States would themselves settle claims by their respective citizens against the other nation. Since the Mexican government rejected the treaty, all claims were back on the table. Thwarted by the current Mexican regime in his boundary objectives, Forsyth decided to use Mexican "outrages" as the pretext for future concessions. Just such an "outrage" presented itself when, on 15 May 1858, the Zuloaga government, strapped for finances, issued a new tax policy. The decree levied a 1 percent tax on all real or personal property valued in excess of five thousand dollars. Forsyth believed the "tax" to be a forced loan—from which United States citizens should be exempt. Forsyth complained that the measure did not "come at all within the purview of the theory or laws of taxation, as they are understood and exist among civilized nations, but that, on the contrary, stripped of its flimsy veil, it is a simple and naked forced loan." Any U.S. citizen who paid the tax, according to Forsyth, would be "exposed to subsequent extractions without excuse and without limit." His objections to the so-called tax centered on three concerns. First, it was "irregular and unusual in its inception." The measure did not come from any customary legislative process but rather from a "sudden and unexpected decree." Second, the "tax" had a very strange exemption policy. A fairly large group was either above or below the range of people who would be subject to the tax. Those who were affected, however, faced excessive collection policies. Finally, Forsyth complained about the means of appropriations of the collected funds. Most of the money was earmarked for troops engaged in the ongoing civil war. Cuevas, once again refusing to be intimidated, denied these accusations and countered that "the decree shall be punctually and exactly executed."[51] For once Forsyth received the full, if only temporary, backing of the Buchanan administration. Relations between the two nations approached low ebb.

The incident that precipitated a break in relations involved one Salomen Migel—a United States citizen living in Mexico. Having resisted the tax decree of May 15, Migel was ordered banished form the republic. Apparently trying to turn this incident into an issue between the two governments instead of one between the Mexican government and a private citizen, Forsyth informed Cuevas that Migel simply did what "was counseled and advised by him [Forsyth] as the representative of the United States." Escalating the rhetoric to new levels, Forsyth claimed it was his solemn duty to "warn the Mexican Government that if any American citizen is subject to an arbitrary expulsion from the Republic for this cause, that that Government will take the step upon the peril of its responsibility to the sovereignty of the United States." Although Cuevas felt Forsyth's note was so "vehement and offensive" as to not deserve a reply, he nonetheless informed Forsyth that the banishment of Migel would be enforced. Employing a comment that probably cut Forsyth like a dagger, Cuevas noted that since the Buchanan administration had not supported Forsyth's mission in the past, the present case would probably be no exception. As it turned out, Cuevas was correct. President Buchanan, in a later message to Congress, concurred that this tax was not a "forced loan." Three days later, Forsyth informed Cuevas that he was suspending relations between the two nations pending further instructions from his government.[52]

Forsyth hoped his decision to break off relations would be endorsed in Washington, and he would soon be authorized to recognize the Liberal government of Juárez. Incredibly, he still steadfastly held on to the belief that Buchanan would realize the folly of territorial expansion. Forsyth reported that there was little hope of concessions even if the Liberals did come into power.[53] The only feasible alternative would then be his never-abandoned idea of a United States economic protectorate over its southern neighbor. Forsyth badly overestimated Buchanan on both counts. The president saw, in the break in relations, an excuse to remove a minister who had been a political opponent and who had consistently argued over policy matters. Buchanan sanctioned the action taken by Forsyth and ordered him to withdraw the legation. The minister was to request his passport and immediately proceed to Vera Cruz for a return to the United States. Cass wrote to Forsyth: "Your action upon the occasion and the circumstances attending it, have led the President to consider the condition of Mexico and the state of our own relations with that country. Both are equally unsatisfactory."[54]

Even the timing of Forsyth's withdrawal prompted a controversy. Forsyth knew that the Mexican government had officially requested his recall. He was, however, not sure if Buchanan had agreed. His first knowledge that his government was sending a ship to transport him home was read in a Mexican newspaper. Another paper in the Mexican capital wrote that "the order to withdraw the legation of the U.S. from the Republic is simply an order of recall . . . and is an act of complaisance to the Mexican Government, done in obedience to Zuloaga's request." To prove to the Mexicans that he was not being forced out and, quite possibly, to antagonize Buchanan, Forsyth sent word to Cass that he would not be ready to leave for another two months.[55]

Conditions in the capital continued to deteriorate as Forsyth prepared to withdraw. One of his last dispatches noted that "even in the unhappy history of Mexico, the past has been a month of dark and disgraceful record. Evil and only evil fills the land."[56] On August 26 the beleaguered minister officially requested passports for himself and the rest of the legation. He also made an official request to José de Castillo Lanzas (the fifth Mexican minister of foreign relations with which Forsyth dealt during his two-year tenure) for a military escort to accompany his group from the capital to the coast. It was not until October 14 that Forsyth informed his host country that he would be leaving six days later. On October 18 he complained that the escort offered by the Mexican government was insufficient for the "present condition of the roads disturbed by civil revolution and infected . . . with robbers." When the Mexican government still would not increase their offered escort, Forsyth threatened to take matters into his own hand. He implied that he would call for United States' troops to provide the protection "befitting the dignity of the occasion."

Lanzas continued to insist that the escort he had offered—consisting of little more than a couple of soldiers riding on top of the official carriage—was sufficient.[57]

It was not until October 19, the day before the scheduled departure, that the Mexican minister confessed as to the real problem. In a letter that could not have made Forsyth feel very confident, Lanzas admitted that he did not want to send a large contingent of soldiers with the American legation because they "would be destroyed by the constitutionalist bands or the robbers that infest the roads." In his last official communication with the Mexican government, Forsyth dropped all pretensions of diplomatic courtesy and unloaded much of his pent-up frustration. He noted that he could just wait in the capital city until an adequate escort was provided but he was anxious to leave, "preferring to brave the chances of robbers and assassination on the road to remaining in Mexico, subject to the insults and slanders of the servile newspaper organs of the Government; to expose my friends to the vengeance and prisons of the Government because they are my friends; to have my house surrounded by Government spies as if I were a malefactor; and my own servants converted into spies within my dwelling."[58]

In one last parting shot, Forsyth penned a comment that he probably felt could apply not only to his Mexican hosts, but also equally to President Buchanan, Secretaries Marcy and Cass, as well as Benjamin and la Sere. Forsyth stated that he preferred to deal with the robbers on the highway because "These at least will assail me openly and with arms in their hands and I can, in the same manner, resist them."[59] Finally, on October 21 the American Legation made its way to Vera Cruz. In route, the party encountered and actually defeated a band of armed robbers. The entourage recovered thirteen stolen mules from the thieves. This was John Forsyth's only triumph in Mexico.

6

The "Disturber" of the Democracy

John Forsyth returned to Alabama in November 1858 with every intention of returning to his diplomatic post. After the Juárez forces gained the upper hand in the Mexican War of the Reform, the beleaguered minister hoped to be able to extend recognition to the Liberal regime and continue his policy of economic and territorial expansion. President Buchanan, however, had other ideas. Buchanan realized that Forsyth's return to the United States presented a chance to be rid of the impertinent diplomat once and for all. In December, Forsyth traveled from Mobile to Washington at the request of the president. He soon learned that the administration had no intention of sending him back to Mexico. In his Second Annual Message to Congress, Buchanan referred to Forsyth as the "late minister to Mexico."[1] Taking this affront as a personal insult to his honor as a gentleman, he asked Buchanan to allow him to briefly return to Mexico where he would then resign. The president refused to consider Forsyth's request so the fuming minister submitted his resignation on 7 February 1859—to be effective on March 2.

During the first few months of 1859, a bitter war of words between the supporters and critics of Forsyth took place in several of the nation's most prominent (and partisan) newspapers. On 10 May 1859 the *New York Times* published a "Letter from the Hon. John Forsyth, late Minister to Mexico concerning the Administration." In this lengthy discourse, Forsyth told his side of the Mexican controversy. The editor included personal letters written to President Buchanan along with responses. Buchanan returned one particularly hostile letter with only the words, "Disrespectful, ungrateful, and absurdly unfounded." Just after his resignation, Forsyth wrote to Stephen A. Douglas, stating that "Mr. Buchanan has put a gulf betwixt himself and me by the most shameful treatment, forfeiting all my respect for him as a gentleman as well as confidence in him as a just and upright magistrate."[2]

As Forsyth accepted that his diplomatic career was over, he once again turned his attention to state and national issues. In June, the *Register* noted Forsyth's return to full-time management of the paper as sole owner and editor. Forsyth wrote: "I come back to take the undivided responsibility of the conduct of this journal with political principles not only unchanged, but indurated by the reflections which two and a half years of separation from the press have afforded me to make upon my past political career." As for the administration, Forsyth claimed his falling out with Buchanan would in no way affect his loyalty to the Democratic Party. As a crucial presidential election approached, it was time to "let bye gones be bye gones."[3]

The months leading up to the election of 1860 were among the most eventful and controversial of Forsyth's entire career. During the nomination and platform adoption processes of the national Democratic Party, several important themes either came to light or resurfaced. First, the territorial problem, far from being solved, became more explosive than ever. Second, Forsyth left the majority of his own state party to support the presidential aspirations of Stephen A. Douglas. Third, the campaign gave perhaps the best example of the influence of national arguments on local concerns. Finally, Forsyth played an important role in the Charleston and Baltimore national Democratic conventions and the resulting disruption of the national party.

Understanding the continuing uproar over the territories requires a brief review of the situation. The nation's leaders had debated the dilemma over slavery in the territories, and the question of congressional authority over it, since the Ordinance of 1787. As we have seen, the acquisition of the New Mexico Territory and California after the Mexican War, the Wilmot Proviso, the Compromise of 1850, and the Kansas-Nebraska Act each, in turn, brought the question to the national forefront. The furor that developed over the ill-fated Wilmot Proviso led Southerners to close ranks on the issue of states' rights. William L. Yancey's Alabama Platform went in the opposite direction. Yancey believed the federal government had a duty to protect slavery in the territories and that slaveowners had the right to take their slave property into the territories without interference. The debate of 1850–51, in which Forsyth (then editor of the *Columbus* [Georgia] *Times*) sounded like an avid secessionist, resulted in a patchwork compromise. Stephen A. Douglas, while serving as the chairman of the Congressional Committee on Territories, emerged as a key national figure in 1854 as the author of the Kansas-Nebraska Act. This bill brought the phrase "popular" or "squatter" sovereignty to the forefront of political debate.[4]

The territorial question remained unanswered as the presidential election of 1856 drew near. Cincinnati was the site of the Democratic National Convention. Prior to this gathering, the Alabama Democracy met in Montgomery. Two future foes—Forsyth, elected chairman of the instructed delegation, and Yancey, in charge of the Committee on Resolutions—worked in relative harmony. Yancey pushed for the Alabama Platform provisions with Forsyth's acquiescence.[5] At Cincinnati, the debate concerning the nominee and the adoption of a platform took on a sectional tone. The quest for the nomination was between Douglas and the Pennsylvanian, James Buchanan. Buchanan was openly friendly to the South and sympathetic to her institutions while Douglas was already notorious among many Southerners for his popular ("squatter") sovereignty position. With his eyes on 1860, the ambitious Douglas reluctantly conceded the nomination to Buchanan, who pledged to serve only one term.

The adoption of a platform was somewhat more complicated. Facing increased pressure at home while at the same time trying to win a national election, delegates from both the North and South, including Forsyth, sought words that would please their constituents. As a result, the final platform was intentionally vague. While the document forcefully stated the principle of "non-interference by Congress with slavery in state or territory or in the District of Columbia," it did not clearly spell out if a *territorial* government could or could not exclude the institution. Thus, in 1856 the Democratic Party had sustained the principles of nonintervention and popular sovereignty. The ambiguity satisfied political leaders in both the North and South since they could interpret the document as they pleased.[6]

With the election of Buchanan, Southerners had a president who was sympathetic to their cause. A favorable ruling in the 1857 *Dred Scott* case (which rendered the Missouri Compromise as well as the Kansas-Nebraska Act invalid) also solidified the Southern position regarding the territories. Why then was the South in such a political uproar before the election of 1860? One must first determine how Stephen A. Douglas, a man jeered in Northern cities for his *pro*-Southern views, became the epitome of abolitionist-like evil in the Southern mind. This vilification of Douglas mystified Forsyth. In a series of letters between Forsyth and William F. Samford, a candidate for governor of Alabama in 1859, the Mobilian stated: "When in the autumn of 1856, I sailed from this port, I left Judge Douglas the most popular northern statesman in the South. When I returned, in the fall of 1858, he was the best abused man in it."[7]

At least three actions by the Illinois senator in the late 1850s contributed to his fall from grace. His rejection of the proslavery Kansas Lecompton constitution, his Freeport Doctrine (in which he stated that the people of a territory could effectively exclude slavery from a territory by refraining from the adoption of positive legislation) and a lengthy article he wrote for *Harpers Weekly*, in which he attempted to show that the relation of the territories to the union paralleled that of the American colonies to Britain, all helped fuel Southern animosity. The two latter issues rankled many Southern tempers. For example, at the Charleston Convention of 1860, the Mississippi delegates carried copies of the Freeport speech to use as ammunition. However, the Lecompton situation convinced Yancey and the other firebrand Southern partisans that the South could no longer rely on the national Democratic Party for the protection of slavery rights and that the safety of the South demanded the formation of a Southern party.[8] Douglas was in the delicate position of having to hang on to his Illinois Senate seat while at the same time not damaging his national ambitions, which depended on Southern support. He soon fell out of favor with both the administration and a majority of the Southern leaders. By casting his vote against the Buchanan-supported, proslavery Lecompton constitution, whether on principle—as Forsyth claimed—or because of political reasons, Douglas never gained the support of a solid South.

The second issue—Forsyth's support of Douglas—requires an investigation into why Forsyth chose to buck the Southern mainstream, prompting the *Montgomery Advertiser* to characterize him as "the solitary Douglas traitor in the legislature." John Forsyth, a man whose editorial writings in the early 1850s reflected the Southern Ultra (a term used here to designate a firebrand secessionist) position, supported a man routinely referred to in the South as "Traitor Douglas." Forsyth's contemporaries, puzzled by his "rebellion," offered many cynical explanations. Among the speculations were Forsyth's hopes for another ministerial appointment, a contract for the United States printing operations, or payback for Douglas's role in securing the Illinois Central Railroad for Mobile.[9]

Forsyth himself claimed, "It is so much more simple and convenient to sum up one's political position by 'D———n Douglas,' than enter into a knotty explanation."[10] For much of 1859 and 1860, the *Register* was Forsyth's means of offering his explanation. The editor's reasons for supporting Douglas fell into three main categories—ideological, political, and personal. Forsyth often expressed an ideological divergence from many of his Southern brethren regarding the territorial issue. The most divisive issue regarding the territories was the controversial policy of "popular sovereignty" as espoused by Douglas. Critics of this concept felt that Douglas had corrupted what many saw as popular sovereignty in its truest form—congressional control. When Congress exerted authority over a territory, the "voice of the Nation at large was heard on the subject, and every interest was consulted and debated." Conversely, if a relatively small group of settlers ("squatters") in a territory had control over issues such as slavery, than the will of the entire people—the Nation, to whom the territory belonged, would be muted. One outspoken opponent believed that the idea of popular sovereignty was in direct opposition to the principles established by the founding fathers in the Constitution. This particular writer ended a lengthy pamphlet against popular sovereignty by noting that he "would rather seem wrong with Mr. Jefferson than be right with Mr. Douglas."[11]

Forsyth took the position that there was no such thing as "squatter" sovereignty. This term could only apply to an unorganized public territory. The "squatter" in this sense was merely an occupant with no power of self-government. However, once a territory became more formally organized, the term "popular" sovereignty was accurate since the settler was now a citizen of the United States. Forsyth agreed with Douglas that the Lecompton constitution was a good example of unabashed squatter fraud and, as such, deserved rejection. Forsyth wrote to Samford: "The Constitution by that [Lecompton] name came to Congress, the most atrocious and bare-faced emanation of 'Squatter Sovereignty' that has ever been presented to the public eye." He placed the blame for the Lecompton disaster squarely on the administration. The proslavery document was one which, according to the editor, "Mr. Buchanan in an evil hour, thrust upon Congress, and to which he recklessly committed the Democratic Party."[12]

Just as the transformation of Douglas in the Southern mind amazed Forsyth, so too was he baffled by the metamorphosis that prompted avowed advocates of states' rights to push for congressional supervision of the territories. How could men, many of whom were willing to dissolve the Union over any perceived threat to their rights, not concede to the citizens of an organized territory the sovereignty over their own affairs? In a lengthy speech before the Alabama House of Representatives, Forsyth explored the irony of the notion that an "extreme southern rights friend claims *jurisdiction for Congress over the question of slavery in the Territories.*"[13] Benjamin Fitzpatrick was one of those men to whom Forsyth referred. In an 1859 letter, the Alabama senator explained his views on the subject of "squatter sovereignty." In his opinion, since Congress did not have the power to *exclude* slavery from the territories, then there was no way that body could delegate such a power to a territorial legislative body. However, since Congress *did* have the obligation to protect property, it had the right to intervene if a territorial body tried to exclude slavery. Therefore, the majority of the residents of a particular territory really had little say as to what laws governed the institution of slavery.[14]

While an ideological kinship no doubt existed between Forsyth and Douglas, certainly political considerations also played a role. In March of 1859, Forsyth, who had officially resigned his diplomatic post a month earlier, wrote to Douglas to explore his position on popular sovereignty and slavery in the territories. Even before being assured of an ideological compatibility, Forsyth in essence promised his unconditional support. Apparently, political and practical concerns also weighed heavily on the editor's mind. On the practical side, Forsyth felt protective legislation had little chance of passage and, even if passed, would serve little purpose in a territory where the people were against slavery or where climate or other geographical factors made the institution unfeasible. He knew a split in the Democratic Party would most likely turn the federal government over to the "Black Republicans." In pledging his support, Forsyth confided to Douglas his opinion that no Southerner could get more than the slave-state vote and possibly could not even unite the entire South. According to the editor, the South "must have a sound Free State man to keep the issue from being purely sectional." A full year before the presidential election, Douglas told a friend that Forsyth and the *Register* were "making a glorious fight on the right line." At about the same time, the (Washington, D.C.) *National Era* noted that "There is one gentleman in Alabama, so far as we can learn, who openly and boldly avows himself to Douglas, and it is John Forsyth of Mobile."[15]

The *Register* staff hammered out editorials warning against letting "abstract" issues such as states' rights lead to a victory for the abolitionists. When the *Montgomery Advertiser* accused Forsyth and the *Register* of putting Douglas's interests ahead of the South, the terse reply was, "Which of the two is the better friend, he who helps another to commit a gross injustice, or he who warns against, and seeks to prevent it?" As editorial tempers flared, Forsyth wrote to the *Advertiser* and argued prophetically: "You have sworn for the South that it will not tolerate a Black Republican government. Then set your house for it, because if you do not throw down your firebrand tests and close up the Democratic ranks, as sure as the hand on the dial will travel on to the appointed time, so sure will you have that Black Republican Administration. And then, gentlemen, what becomes of your claim for protection in the Territories?"[16]

A third, and perhaps most important factor behind Forsyth's loyalty to the Little Giant, was a common personal animosity both felt toward President Buchanan and his administration. If Forsyth was in the mainstream of Southern thought during the early 1850s, as well as immediately after the election of Lincoln, something made him turn against the current in the interim. One common denominator between the journalist-politician and Douglas was a falling out with Buchanan. The Buchanan-Douglas relationship never mended after the Lecompton folly, while what Forsyth saw as the deliberate sabotage of his Mexican mission led him to remark that "of all men living he [Forsyth] liked Mr. Buchanan the least."[17] The respective breaks with the Buchanan administration occurred at about the same time, driving the two casual acquaintances into a solid alliance. Douglas would be the sword through which Forsyth could attack Buchanan and his allies. Many anti-Douglas Southern papers noted Forsyth's bitterness. Opposition editorials blasted Forsyth and his newspaper as traitors to the Southern cause. They felt he supported Douglas only to grind a personal ax against Buchanan, who "turned him out of office." In one letter, Forsyth summarized his two main political positions as "defense of Douglas and opposition to Buchanan."[18]

The third concern centers on the relationship between national and state issues. Three separate 1859 state or local races demonstrated the interest of the Alabama electorate with the territorial issue and Douglas. In the Alabama gubernatorial election, William F. Samford ran against Andrew B. Moore. Samford was a devoted states' rights Ultra who routinely referred to Douglas, Forsyth, and others of like persuasion as "semi-abolitionists." The east Alabama penman was also an unflinching supporter of Yancey's ambitions, as well as a proponent of the Alabama Platform. Samford attacked Moore, another conservative states' rights Democrat, for refusing to call a state secession convention after Congress had passed the Kansas-Conference Bill. A second race—the contest for the Mobile District seat in the United States Congress—was no less divisive. This race pitted James A. Stallworth, a friend of Forsyth, against F. B. Shepard. Stallworth, the incumbent, faced criticism for his vote on the "Kansas matter." In June of 1859, Stallworth and Shepard met in a debate at Bladen Springs. The questions centered on the Douglas dilemma. Shepard spent much of his debate time in a verbal assault on John Forsyth. Forsyth reported to Douglas that he and Shepard narrowly escaped a duel. Stallworth used equal efforts to defend his editor-friend. The third canvas, which directly involved Forsyth, was the selection of four representatives from Mobile County to serve in the Alabama house. On July 9 the Mobile Democracy met in the city amphitheater to nominate their ticket. The assembly selected Forsyth (who reportedly declined a nomination to run for the United States House of Representatives), Percy Walker, Alexander B. Meek, and G. Y. Overall to run for the four spots. A rival Democratic group in Mobile, billing themselves as the "Democratic States' Rights Party," also met to select an opposing slate.[19]

With the voters of Mobile scheduled to go to the polls on the first Monday of August, the contest was limited to only four weeks. The campaign's intensity more than compensated for its brevity. Nightly speeches, culminating with boisterous demonstrations and fireworks, pierced the usually placid port city evenings. As the rival tickets polarized opinions, the attacks became more vicious and sometimes even physical. The *Register* contained reports of threatened duels between Forsyth and several of his critics. Forsyth and his staff used the same logic in the campaign that had originally helped convince the editor to support Douglas. To his legion of antagonists, Forsyth reasoned: "You charge me with Douglasism, we charge you with Sewardism" (a commonly used synonym for Republicanism). In one speech before a crowd reported (by Forsyth) to contain "at least one thousand upturned faces," the partisan editor defended Douglas's views of the territorial issues at great length.[20]

The election results seemed to bode well for both Forsyth and Douglas. An overwhelming statewide majority reelected Governor Moore. In Mobile County, the total was 2,047 to 1,290 in favor of Moore. Likewise, Stallworth turned in a strong performance, outpolling his Ultra opponent 1,925 to 1,578. The legislative races also produced impressive tallies. With Forsyth receiving the highest individual vote total, the four men of his ticket swept the at-large race. With 2,075 votes, Forsyth outpolled the best of the opposition ticket by 394 votes.[21] Although too much inference from this data may be a bit presumptuous, one can generalize that, at least before the Democratic state convention, the majority of the people of Mobile County and the state at large appeared to be content with the traditional Democratic Party. In particular, the dismal showing of Samford gave Forsyth much ammunition for future editorials. The newly elected legislator credited his "anti-Buchanan" and "nonintervention" messages as being important factors in his victory.[22]

In his first elected office, John Forsyth took his seat in Montgomery. Several statewide political groups were trying to consolidate their power as the legislative term began. The old Whig remnant now called themselves Constitutional Unionists. Coming primarily from west and central Alabama, they wanted a break with Forsyth's wing of the traditional party. Next were the moderate Southern Rights men. They supported John Breckinridge for president but wanted to remain in the union. Forsyth led the statewide Douglas organization. A small, but distinguished, group of Douglas leaders was centered in Huntsville and Montgomery as well. Yancey led the final faction—the extreme Southern Rights group. The traditional Democrats feared this group wanted a break with the national Democratic Party coupled with the formation of a Southern counterpart. In the eyes of the Yanceyites, Douglas was an evil to be avoided on a level only slightly below the abolitionist and the plague.[23]

Two issues dwarfed all others in the 1859 biennial legislative session. The first was the election of a United States senator. The term of the incumbent, Benjamin Fitzpatrick, was to expire in March of 1861. Yancey hoped to replace Fitzpatrick in Washington. Although the selection was still over a year away, the political maneuvering began early. The *Montgomery Advertiser*, in an editorial entitled "The Treachery of Douglas," fired the first volley. The secessionist paper lambasted Fitzpatrick for his support of the Illinois statesman on the Kansas and Minnesota territorial questions.[24] Yancey, who realized his chance to grasp the reins of the Alabama Democratic Party could be slipping away, pulled out all stops to drive a wedge between the conservative Democracy of Forsyth and the upstart Southern Rights group.

As the senatorial vote drew near, the *Montgomery Mail* wrote a blistering editorial condemning John Forsyth specifically. The journal questioned the loyalties of anyone who would dare support Fitzpatrick. Calling Forsyth the "leading Douglas man in the state," the paper referred to the upcoming senatorial vote as a roll call of the *true* states' rights men, asking, "Who will choose to record himself once and forever opposed to the States Rights party of the South?" The implication that only supporters of Yancey could wear the robes of loyal Southerners clearly offended Forsyth. He challenged the *Mail*'s editor (Johnson Jones Hooper, a Yancey loyalist) to compare credentials. "He [Hooper] must compare records with me, and show that while the richest years of my manhood have been devoted to the cause of States Rights Democracy, while for twenty years I have sacrificed fortune, lived precariously, and more than once risked my life for it, he was *not* during that whole period, a steady soldier in the ranks of its enemies."[25] The ultimate rejection of Yancey in the contest seemed to again indicate that the Forsyth/Douglas cause was gaining momentum. This victory, however, would prove to be the last one Forsyth would enjoy in a united Democratic Party.

The second key legislative issue involved contingency plans in the event of a Republican victory in the presidential election. In October of 1859 the influential *Charleston Mercury* published several "principles" for Southern Democrats. The main thrust of the article was that state legislatures should make provisional plans in the event of a victory by a Republican or (in an unmistakable reference to Douglas) an *unacceptable Northern candidate.*[26] The Alabama Legislature considered a resolution authorizing the governor to call a state convention to determine the course of action in the event of an unfavorable election result. While practically all the legislature, Forsyth included, agreed on the unacceptability of a "Black Republican" administration, opinions differed concerning what to do if Douglas was the Democratic nominee. Forsyth delivered a speech from the floor of the house in which he staunchly defended his friend from Illinois. Satisfied with his effort, he wrote Douglas that only one of the legislators would admit that he would not vote for Douglas if nominated.[27]

State business soon took a backseat to preparations for the Alabama State Democratic Convention scheduled to meet in the capital city in January of 1860. Before this assembly, the various counties selected delegates. The heated discussions that took place in many of these usually routine meetings suggest the gravity of the national conflict. Perry County, for example, passed resolutions stating that their delegates should not support Douglas or any other man who did not advocate congressional protection for slavery. The people of Mobile County selected two competing delegations. While some men, including Forsyth, were named to both delegations, each overall group was markedly different in its respective resolutions.[28]

Forsyth, along with John J. Seibels of the *Montgomery Confederation* and former governor John A. Winston, led the Douglas forces in the state convention. While never more than a small minority in Montgomery, the Forsyth group drew much attention and fire. The *Advertiser* criticized the preconvention stance of the Mobile editor by asking, "Will he [Forsyth] not rise above the level of partyism, and look to his country? Will he not cease to disorganize the people of Alabama in his wild crusade in favor of Douglas, and unite with us in the endeavor to prepare the State for the crisis that seems inevitable?"[29]

With the echo of the opening gavel barely subsiding, the first controversy erupted. After the convention selected Francis S. Lyon as chairman, the rival Mobile delegations faced a credentials challenge. In question was the nature of the call that had advertised the delegate selection. After a spirited debate, the body voted to admit Forsyth and the pro-Douglas delegation. While Forsyth's group most likely gained admission because the overall body knew they were a "harmless minority" and as such could do no damage, Forsyth claimed a great victory.[30] The selection of the members for the committee on resolutions was the next point of disagreement the state convention faced. The composition of this group, in retrospect, sealed Alabama's fate and ensured the split of the Democratic Party. The fourteen-member committee contained at least seven devoted Yanceyites. The great orator could easily influence the other men. Forsyth bitterly complained about being left off of this important group. He felt his years of loyal party service in the trenches certainly more than justified his selection. With Yancey and his gang now controlling these proceedings, the report of the resolutions committee affirmed the 1856 Cincinnati Platform— with the important addition of the main components of the 1848 Alabama Platform. The most significant resolution instructed the Alabama delegation to immediately withdraw if the Charleston National Democratic Convention refused to uphold the stated principles of the Alabama Platform. This time no ambiguity existed.[31]

Forsyth led the feeble opposition to the committee's action. He offered his own set of conciliatory resolutions as an alternative. The Mobilian felt the state delegation should go to Charleston with a spirit of cooperation in order to defeat the "Vandal hordes of Black Republicans." Like the committee, he favored the readoption of the Cincinnati Platform, but with the insertion of the principles of the *Dred Scott* ruling (as opposed to the Alabama Platform) as a guide for the territorial question. In the final vote, Forsyth was one of only three members who voted against the majority resolutions dealing specifically with the issue of slavery in the territories and the threatened withdrawal from Charleston. He then stubbornly insisted that the official proceedings record his name as a negative vote. The convention adjourned with Alabama committed to a platform that, according to Forsyth, would hasten the disruption of the Democratic Party and, ultimately, the Union.[32]

I now turn to the primary concern here—Forsyth's role in the national election process. Forsyth spent much of the next three months relentlessly criticizing the actions of the state convention. He also devoted many hours to pondering an alternative strategy he hoped might secure the nomination of Stephen A. Douglas. The hostile reaction he faced led Forsyth to compare himself to a captain who, on pointing out dangers ahead, faces a mutiny from the crew. In this case, however, feelings were so strong the "captain" appeared to be serving in a foreign navy. Day after day, the *Register* commented on the folly of the late state meeting. Forsyth continued to insist that winning the election should be the ultimate goal of the party. This objective, he felt, should supersede all desires to make a statement on "abstract" issues such as protectionism and states' rights. At one point, he warned that if the Alabama delegates insisted on going to Charleston with their strict anti-Douglas resolutions, the state might as well go ahead and leave the Union beforehand. In the longest and most emotional speech of his brief legislative career, Forsyth warned his house colleagues that if they divided the Democracy on "barren and abstract issues," they would make the "million of abolitionists two millions, and enable them to ravish the Federal government from our hands."[33]

As the ominous gathering in South Carolina drew near, the attacks became more personal. Forsyth printed a letter written by Yancey to James Slaughter, in which the Ultra leader stated: "But if we could do as our fathers did, organize 'committees of safety' all over the cotton states (as it is only in them that we can hope for any effective movement), we shall fire the Southern heart, instruct the Southern mind, give courage to each other, and at the moment, by one organized, concerted action, *we can precipitate the cotton states into a revolution.*"[34] The *Register* seized on this admission as a springboard for several articles that pointed out what its editor saw as a not so hidden agenda of Yancey and his cohorts. Forsyth and many of his fellow writers believed the Yancey-led state convention deliberately adopted an unacceptable platform with the obvious intention of disrupting the party and, ultimately, forming a separate Southern nation.

Never content with the prospect of seeing himself relegated to the sidelines, Forsyth contemplated an alternative strategy. Although not selected as a delegate, he worked behind the scenes in order to have a say in the outcome of the Charleston convention. In late January, he wrote Douglas: "We mean therefore to call meetings in various parts of the state—not to take ground against or denounce the action of a Democratic Convention (for that would be to contradict our own advice and policy to abide by the action of the national Democracy) but to unite all Democrats and *others* who are willing to unite with us in a last effort to save the country from a Black Republican administration."[35] Some saw in Forsyth's call a desire to unite with the fledging Constitutional Union movement in an effort to thwart the radical Democratic wing.

Forsyth tried to convey a favorable impression about the situation. He confided his belief to Douglas that Yancey and his delegation would remain in the Charleston convention and conform to its actions. He envisioned a situation in which the instructed delegation would split into internal factions. He calculated that the group contained eighteen Ultras and eighteen moderates. In a best-case scenario, Yancey's group would walk out of the convention, at which time the moderates would resign and ask for readmission as uncommitted (hence potential Douglas) delegates from their respective districts. He also said that the Alabama state convention had not been a true sampling of the people of the state. The disruptive spirit, just witnessed in Montgomery, was the exception rather than the rule. Either Forsyth was extremely (and naively) optimistic or, more likely, he offered Douglas false hopes. Surely Forsyth realized the three members who had voted against the withdrawal resolutions at the convention were not the only men who represented the true sentiments of the people.[36]

Even nonparticipating observers recognized the impossibility of a unified national convention as long as Douglas was a factor. Murat Halstead, a newspaper correspondent from Cincinnati, observed "the only possible way to keep the Convention together from the start was for the Douglas men to withdraw his name; and then the South, with another man, would have been willing to mitigate the asperities of the slave code platform."[37] Forsyth continued to pump Douglas with glowing reports. In January he wrote: "If you are nominated at Charleston, I believe Alabama will give you [a] 20,000 majority." The next month, responding to continued reports that the senator was receiving advice to withdraw, Forsyth insisted that Douglas stay the course and, "tell your friends that you must be nominated—It will be the very best thing for the Democracy of the South." Through March and into April of 1860, Forsyth regularly corresponded with Douglas, consistently imploring the champion of popular sovereignty to "stand firm," even if advised otherwise by his associates. The optimistic editor claimed Douglas was "stronger, a thousand times, with the Southern people, than the superficial currents set in motion by the Politicians, would indicate."[38] Certainly a man involved in Democratic Party politics his entire life knew the implausibility of such statements. Even as Forsyth outwardly exhibited a wall of confidence, he, for the first time, pondered what to do if Douglas did not receive the nomination. He assumed Douglas could still influence the platform and nomination even if he himself was not the nominee.

Gaveled to order on 23 April 1860, the National Democratic Convention met at Institute Hall of Charleston College. The building, designed to hold eighteen hundred delegates, uncomfortably accommodated upward of three thousand. An early spring heat wave (that pushed the South Carolina temperatures near the 100-degree mark) made matters more uncomfortable for the delegates, floor leaders, and gallery spectators. The official delegates belonged to one of three groups, each on its own mission. Douglas supporters composed a slight majority but knew they could not produce a two-thirds majority necessary for nomination. Their only hope of success depended on a Southern walkout and a favorable two-thirds vote of those who remained. They did, however, have a strong enough voice to control the crucial platform vote. William A. Richardson, a United States representative from Illinois, was their floor leader.[39]

Yancey reigned supreme over the second group—a sizeable faction of the Southerners, particularly the "fire-eaters." Determined to secure the main provisions of the Alabama Platform, they were willing to withdraw to prove their resolve. Numerically, they were a minority of the total body with only about forty votes. Yancey hoped his actions could "nudge the party a bit further along the road to an open acceptance of southern equality." After the walkout occurred, one Southern leader noted that the Yanceyites believed that "reflection would induce the majority to retrace their steps and to present to the retiring states a platform which they could accept with honor."[40]

A third group, sometimes ignored by historians, was the forces loyal to President Buchanan. Known by some as "Old Buck's Boys," they operated behind the scenes to ensure a Douglas defeat. Their leader was Senator John Slidell (the man who had been indirectly responsible for one of Forsyth's Mexican problems with Buchanan) and Jesse Bright. One local Charleston paper reported a rumor that Slidell, Bright, and a banker named W. W. Corcoran had planned to "invest" a large sum of money between them to defeat Douglas. Buchanan's forces hoped the election would end up in the United States House of Representatives, where they could control its outcome. Some still believed a nomination as a "dark horse" candidate would cause Buchanan to back away from his one-term pledge.[41]

Regardless of the personal loyalties or agendas, Stephen A. Douglas was the concern of every delegate. Halstead reported that the senator was "the pivot individual of the Charleston Convention. Every delegate was for or against him; every motion meant to nominate or not to nominate him."[42] After the election of Caleb Cushing of Massachusetts as chairman of the proceedings and a few minor credentials squabbles, the Charleston convention settled down to business. On the second day, the convention made a fateful decision to adopt the platform before agreeing on a candidate. This action made a harmonious convention impossible. As long as the nominee was unknown, neither side was willing to give ground on what Forsyth had consistently dismissed as the "abstract" issue of slavery in the territories.

The platform committee presented the convention one majority and two minority reports. The full body rejected the majority report, which offered the Cincinnati Platform along with the rejection of popular sovereignty and an endorsement of a federal slave code. The convention delegates also rejected the second minority report, which endorsed the Cincinnati Platform as written. The committee then substituted the primary minority report, pushed by Forsyth and the Douglas delegates. It also reaffirmed the Cincinnati document but, in addition, pledged that "the Democratic Party will abide by the decisions of the Supreme Court of the United States (i.e., *Dred Scott*) on the questions of constitutional law."[43]

The body voted separately on each section of the primary minority report. The first section (Cincinnati Platform) carried overwhelmingly. On April 30, after the adoption of the popular sovereignty plank, the walkout occurred. The Alabama delegation, followed by those from Mississippi, Louisiana, South Carolina, Florida, Texas, and Arkansas retired from the convention. The "Bolters" reassembled in another hall in Charleston and adopted their own platform. They then adjourned with instructions to reconvene in Richmond on June 11. Meanwhile, the nomination scenario Forsyth had envisioned failed to materialize (because of an interpretation of the convention rules that required a two-thirds vote of the *total* number of delegates—not just the *remaining* number). After the remaining delegates conducted fifty-seven ballots, Douglas still could not muster a two-thirds majority. Without a nominee, the regular Charleston convention likewise adjourned, to meet again in Baltimore on June 18.[44]

Although the final disruption of the party was still a few weeks away, in Alabama the rush was on to claim the vacated seats for the upcoming Baltimore convention. In Mobile County, the Yancey wing of the party met and selected delegates to a new state convention scheduled to meet on June 4, in Montgomery. Forsyth, through the *Register,* advertised a competing convention that would meet in Selma (later moved to Montgomery) on the same day, for the same purpose. Forsyth wrote to Douglas—clearly defining his inflexible plans. Sending the senator a copy of his printed convention "call," the editor stated: "We have just begun the fight [and] mean yet to drive the Yanceyites to the wall—They are very uneasy [and] we shall not spare them. We treat them as aliens, Bolters separated from the Democracy and refuse to join them in the same convention."[45]

No action in Forsyth's life ever drew so much political and personal hostility. The *Advertiser* referred to Forsyth and his associates as "reckless and ambitious third rate politicians" and "puny braggarts." The editor was singled out as a "vainglorious boaster." Many old party regulars viewed Forsyth as a "disturber" of the Alabama Democracy. The Yanceyites could not fathom why the idea of congressional protection of slavery in the territories, once generally accepted, was now deemed revolutionary. The leading Yancey journal mocked Forsyth when it noted that all *true* Democrats in Alabama held to protection of slavery except the editor of the *Mobile Register:* "He—'wrapt in the solitude of his own originality'—he *alone* had 'Squatter' imprinted on his brow, as, 'gloomy and peculiar,' if not 'grand,' he mournfully gazed across the peaceful waters of Mobile Bay towards Mexico, and querulously wrote of 'Old Buck.'" Yancey's nineteenth-century biographer claimed that Forsyth's "self-conceit led him to attempt to overthrow the Democratic Party."[46]

The competing state conventions met and selected their delegates. The "Bolters" convention sent their members to Richmond, where they planned to regroup and then present themselves for admission at Baltimore. The "squatter" convention sent Forsyth, Seibels, and others directly to Baltimore as replacements for the delegates, who they felt, had resigned at Charleston. Regardless of their open disgust with Forsyth and the other Douglas men, the Yanceyites understood the odds that awaited them at the upcoming convention. The *Advertiser* (correctly) predicted that "Forsyth will carry his delegation from Selma to Baltimore, and mark the prediction that if the Montgomery Convention sends a delegation to Baltimore, it will be ruled out by the Baltimore Douglas Convention (for it is nothing more, nor nothing less) and the Forsyth bogus Douglas delegates under the false name of Democrats will be accepted."[47]

An air of tension settled over Baltimore as the meeting opened on 18 June 1860 at the Front Street Theatre. One delegate brought a prizefighter along to serve as a personal bodyguard while he was on the convention floor. Reports of numerous duels and several fistfights made the newspapers even before the opening session. Murat Halstead noted that the Douglas forces, which now smelled victory, assumed a tone of arrogance. He reported that they were "encouraged by the presence and support of Pierre Soule of Louisiana, John Forsyth of Alabama, and other strong Southern men." After taking care of minor business, the convention selected the crucial Committee on Credentials. Of the delegations that retired from the Charleston meeting, only Alabama and Louisiana now returned with competing delegations. The pro-Douglas delegations from the two states argued that they had fulfilled the request of the Charleston Convention by selecting a new delegation for Baltimore. They also claimed that since the Yancey group was selected for a convention in Richmond, they had no legitimacy in Baltimore.[48]

As the committee deliberated, the convention and the city filled with wild speculations and quarrels. By now, word had leaked out that Douglas was seriously considering dropping out of the contest. Before the final report of the committee became known, Douglas sent a letter to Richardson authorizing him to withdraw his name if the situation warranted. The senator knew the stakes involved in this political drama. He realized that a split Democratic Party "would inevitably expose the country to the perils of sectional strife between the Northern and Southern party." Such a division would cripple his long-held view of "nonintervention" by Congress in the territories. Douglas was willing to "cheerfully and joyfully" sacrifice his goal of the presidency to protect that principle. Rumors were also rampant that the New York delegation, with their thirty-five votes, was about to sell out the Illinois senator. Forsyth worked furiously behind the scenes to make sure Douglas held his ground and cast aside any thought of withdrawal. The credentials committee presented its report on June 21. With symbolism perhaps divinely inspired, the floor of the convention hall literally fell out shortly after the morning call to order. After hasty repairs, John Krum of Missouri presented the majority credentials report. The committee voted sixteen to nine to admit the Soulé (pro-Douglas) delegation from Louisiana, and by a fourteen to eleven tally, accepted the Forsyth group from Alabama.[49]

Isaac Stevens of Oregon presented the committee's minority report. He vehemently denounced the majority decision and insisted on the legitimacy of the Yancey delegation from Alabama. The minority protested that the delegates who left Charleston merely withdrew; therefore, they did not resign. The minority's second complaint took aim directly at Forsyth. Stevens pointed out that, unlike the regular Democratic meeting that was well advertised and attended, Forsyth's call only appeared in three newspapers and was answered by representatives from only twenty-eight of fifty-two counties. Even the nature of the call came under fire. Instead of being a specific address to "the Democracy," the *Register* advertisement issued a general plea to the *people* of Alabama to hold county meetings, and then send delegates to a state convention. Stevens and the minority read this statement as an appeal to people outside the traditional Democratic Party to form a new political organization. When the full assembly took the final credentials vote, the majority concurred with the majority report. By a vote of 148 to 101, the convention accepted John Forsyth and his pro-Douglas delegation. This repudiation of Yancey led to the resignation of Caleb Cushing as chairman and the second "bolt" of the Southern states. With the convention now packed in his favor, Douglas finally received the nomination on the second ballot. In retrospect, John Forsyth and the other Douglas managers achieved a pyrrhic victory.[50]

The remaining choice of a vice-presidential candidate was also somewhat complicated. Forsyth and Seibels promoted Benjamin Fitzpatrick as a man who could take away votes from the Yanceyites in Alabama. Forsyth ignored the fact that Senator Fitzpatrick was not totally committed to the Douglas platform and had actually voted for the Davis slave-code resolution in the Senate.[51] After the nomination was made, Fitzpatrick was torn over whether to accept. He received a flood of advice from Douglas supporters and opponents alike. Seibels informed the senator that "To refuse [the nomination] now would be to cower before your enemies, disgrace your best friends, and place yourself in a most unenviable position." A fellow Alabamian telegraphed Fitzgerald with an injunction to "accept no nomination from the Douglas Convention. Success would not compensate the loss of friends." In his official reply to the nomination, Senator Fitzpatrick declined, noting: "The distracting differences at present existing in the ranks of the Democratic Party were strikingly exemplified both at Charleston and at Baltimore, and, in my humble opinion, distinctly admonish me that I should in no way contribute to these unfortunate divisions."[52] With Fitzpatrick out of the picture, the nomination fell to one of Forsyth's old Georgia associates, Hershel V. Johnson. The "Bolters," with Cushing again serving as their chairman, reassembled and nominated John C. Breckinridge for president and Joseph Lane for vice-president. They also adopted the same platform previously rejected by the majority at Charleston. While the Democrats were between conventions, the Republicans met in Chicago and made somewhat of a surprise nomination of Abraham Lincoln of Illinois for president. Likewise, the Constitutional Union Party chose John Bell of Tennessee to be its standard bearer. Thus, the campaign commenced.

After the grueling nomination and platform-adoption process, the subsequent summer and fall campaign had the potential to be somewhat anticlimatic for Forsyth. A fierce war of words carried on between the *Montgomery Advertiser* and the *Register* quickly dispelled any quietude. As the Democratic Party went in separate directions, the Yancey journal fired away, claiming that "we have no hesitancy in saying that the Mobile *Register* had been more unscrupulous in its abuses and misrepresentations of those who would not bow to the wishes of its demagogical chief than any journal that has ever been published in the State of Alabama." These critics dismissed Forsyth's support for Douglas as blatant opportunism since he, they claimed, hoped for a future appointment in the new administration. Another chance at a ministry, perhaps to Britain, was the carrot, they felt, that Douglas dangled in front of Forsyth's eyes. Yancey, in a Memphis campaign speech for the Breckinridge ticket, asked the assembled crowd: "Will you put those broken down politicians, Soule, Forsyth, [Jere] Clemens, and your [Henry] Footes against this mighty array of genius?" The Douglas men were almost universally labeled traitors to the Southern cause and to the principle of states' rights.[53]

By October, Douglas, aware of Republican victories in several state elections (most notably Pennsylvania), knew he could not win the presidency. He now devoted his energies to the preservation of the Union. Forsyth, however, was not yet ready to give up. The editor implored Douglas to make a campaign swing through Alabama. He promised a warm welcome in Mobile and two thousand Douglas votes on Election Day. Douglas agreed and made plans to arrive in Mobile on 5 November 1860. Even the choice of which steamer Douglas would take from Montgomery to the port city involved political calculations. Forsyth advised the senator to take the *Duke* since its captain was a known Douglas supporter. A delegation, led by the editor himself, met Douglas upriver and accompanied him on a triumphant entry into the city.[54]

On the evening of November 5, Forsyth introduced Senator Douglas from the courthouse steps. The Little Giant, exhausted and only a few months away from death, delivered a two-hour speech to an enthusiastic crowd of around (as so reported) five thousand people. A fireworks display officially ended the 1860 campaign for Douglas and Forsyth as they retired to the Battle House Hotel (Forsyth was living here as his residence was undergoing a renovation). The two men spent Election Day receiving supporters and discussing the national situation.[55] That evening, the pair huddled in the offices of the *Register* to await any election news that might come by wire. Knowing the battle was lost, the two warriors turned their thoughts to the future—how would the South react to the election of Lincoln? Forsyth showed Douglas an editorial he had already written and planned to run in the event of Lincoln's victory. The article urged the immediate calling of a state secession convention to discuss the grave situation. Over Douglas's strong objections, the editor made preparations to insert the message into a coming issue of the *Register.* Douglas left Mobile the following day, bound for New Orleans.[56] He and Forsyth met only once more physically (while Forsyth was in Washington, serving as a Confederate peace commissioner), and never again philosophically.

Over the next several days, the election results confirmed Forsyth's fears. The split Democratic Party handed Lincoln and the Republicans a solid electoral majority. In Alabama, Douglas finished a distant third, behind Breckinridge and Bell. Mobile was one of only five Alabama counties (and the only one not in the Unionist Tennessee Valley) that produced at least a plurality for the Illinois senator. The final tally in the county was 1,823 for Douglas, 1,629 for Bell, and 1,541 for Breckinridge.[57] Although Forsyth boasted of the local triumph, the poll in Mobile County could be attributed to the large number of temporary Northern residents. Almost immediately, plans began to take shape for the calling for a state secession convention. Forsyth closed ranks with the Southern secessionists and served the Confederate cause with distinction.

What then, in conclusion, was the significance of John Forsyth and the other Douglas managers in the disruption of the Democratic Party, the election of 1860, and the ultimate secession of the Southern states? To fully answer this important question, one must investigate the motivations of both the Yancey and Douglas forces in the nomination and platform adoption processes as well as the legality of the Forsyth "replacement" delegation at Baltimore. We turn first to Yancey. It is certainly no secret that the great orator longed (prayed?) for a separate Southern nation. Historians must note, however, that a *desire* for something that eventually happens does not necessarily constitute a *cause* of the happening. Although Yancey was obviously ready for secession, and wanted Alabama to likewise be ready, he did not expect the event to happen in 1860, nor can it be proven that he even desired such an event at that moment. Yancey's stand on the withdrawal resolution at the Alabama State Democratic Convention was not an effort at disunion, but an attempt to prepare the state should such an event become likely in the future. Likewise, Yancey did not go to the Charleston Convention to "precipitate" a revolution but, rather, to persuade the national party leadership to openly accept the concept of Southern equality. There is no reason to believe that Yancey might not have eventually compromised as he had done in 1856.[58]

The role of the Douglas men also requires a brief review. At the first sign of controversy at Charleston—the adoption of the platform—the Yanceyites were perhaps ready to compromise. The majority report, which clarified the Cincinnati platform, might have been acceptable to Yancey, but the Douglas supporters refused to seek common ground. Several weeks before the convention, Forsyth sent a private letter to Douglas in which he told the senator that their side should "refuse to accept any material interpolations" in the platform as it stood in 1856. In fact, many Douglas supporters wanted to force Yancey to make good on his threatened walkout. Such a withdrawal would achieve two of the national party's objectives—brand Yancey as the disrupter of the party and secure the nomination for Douglas. If Douglas was sincere in his offer to withdraw his name at Baltimore, the protest of his managers (including Forsyth) ended such a possibility and guaranteed there would be no compromise for Yancey.[59]

Finally, one must examine the nature of the Forsyth "replacement" delegation that appeared at Baltimore. There can be little doubt that the Yancey group had the legitimate claim for the seats vacated at Charleston. This delegation followed the specific instructions given to them by the official state Democratic convention in January. The Forsyth group, on the other hand, was acting on its own authority without the official sanction of any statewide organization.

The Baltimore credentials committee accepted the Forsyth group because they knew the Mobile editor and his colleagues would make no trouble regarding the platform and also such an action served to punish Yancey for what the committee saw as a plan to destroy the national party and promote secession.[60] Many contemporary newspapers assigned blame for the party split to the Douglas forces and the "bogus" Forsyth delegation. One noted that, rather than a useful Baltimore convention, "The Douglas Managers determined to carry things with a heavy hand, and they did so. Their tone had become reckless, defiant, domineering. They were evidently determined to exclude the regularly appointed delegates from the Southern states and fill these places with creations of their own."[61]

Speculation can be a dangerous practice for the historian—however, one can only surmise the outcome had the Yancey delegation been seated at Baltimore. Certainly, the overall body could have still failed to present an acceptable platform in which case the second walkout would have occurred anyway. However, it would have most likely been to Yancey's advantage to work out some type of compromise—thus being able to claim that he had molded the national party to his own image.[62] The seating of the Forsyth delegation ended any chance for a solution to the Democratic nomination and platform dilemma. Had Forsyth not led a move after the Charleston breakup to select a pro-Douglas replacement delegation, the Baltimore seats would not have been in question. Without the second "bolt," Douglas still would not have had the numbers necessary for a two-thirds majority. The senator may have then withdrawn his name, which would have pressured Yancey to compromise on the platform. A united Democratic Party—while certainly not assured of a victory—would have offered Lincoln a more formidable challenge.

In his masterful study of antebellum Alabama politics, J. Mills Thornton concluded that while Yancey and the fire-eaters usually receive the scorn for the breakup of the Democratic Party and, ultimately, the Union, Senator Douglas and his managers must assume their share of the blame. Likewise, Roy Franklin Nichols noted that when the Southern Democrats encouraged Douglas to step aside, he was willing, but his followers were not. Such managers, he concluded, "forced Douglas to permit the destruction of the Democratic Party."[63] Certainly few managers were more instrumental in that "disturbance" than John Forsyth of Mobile.

John Forsyth Jr. as a young Mobile editor, ca 1837. (Museum of Mobile)

John Forsyth Sr. One of the most notable figures in the early history of Georgia, Forsyth Sr. served as governor, U.S. senator, and secretary of state under Presidents Jackson and Van Buren. (Library of Congress)

John Forsyth served as an adjutant for the Columbus (Georgia) Guards during the Mexican War. (Historic Mobile Preservation Society)

James Buchanan. Forsyth once stated that "Of all the men living, he liked Mr. Buchanan the least." (Library of Congress)

Stephen A. Douglas. Forsyth's unwavering support of the Little Giant in the presidential election of 1860 was the most controversial position of his career. (Library of Congress)

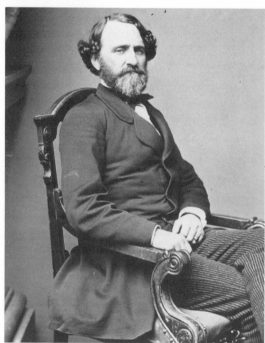

John Forsyth in 1861. (Library of Congress)

General Braxton Bragg. Forsyth
served on Bragg's staff during the
1862 Kentucky Campaign.
(Library of Congress)

John Forsyth in his *Mobile Register* office during
Reconstruction. (University of South Alabama
Archives)

John Forsyth's Grave. Magnolia Cemetery, Mobile, Alabama. (Photo by Lynne Burnett)

7

"The Cause of the Union Was Lost"

Several weeks after Abraham Lincoln's election, John Forsyth wrote a somewhat somber letter to Stephen A. Douglas. He correctly surmised that with Douglas's defeat, "the cause of the Union was lost." More prophetically, he noted that he never for a moment believed that "a giant nation could die without a giant struggle."[1] Many political observers, particularly his former Northern allies, believed Forsyth would "remain" a strong unionist. They soon began to quiz their Southern friend about what they perceived as a change in his attitude regarding secession. In December of 1860, the *New York Times* printed a letter from August Belmont (chairman of the Democratic National Committee) to Forsyth in which he pleaded with the editor to use his influence to resist an emotional response to the recent national election. Wrote Belmont: "Upon the leading national men of the South devolves now the sacred duty to stem the torrent of terrorism, conjured up by rash politicians." Belmont went on to pose two troubling questions. First, he wondered, "Is Mr. Yancey's pro- gramme to precipitate the South into a revolution to be carried out by those patriots who, with you, have thus far nobly fought against him and his nefari- ous doctrine?" Second, "How can our friends in the cotton states reconcile their actions of today with their professions only a few months back?"[2]

In a subsequent letter, Belmont accused Forsyth of being a traitor to the Douglas cause. The New Yorker wrote, "When we Douglas men of the North stood by our colors against the combined onslaught of Black Republicans and the administration, we were upheld in our struggle by the consciousness that we were fighting the battle of the Union and the Constitution against fanati- cism, North and South." After Douglas's death, John Forney, in the official eulogy, mentioned Forsyth, as one of several Southern political managers, who at one time were "*professing* to be his warmest friends." Some prominent South- erners were disturbed by Forsyth's apparent shift. No less than Herschel V. Johnson expressed his disappointment with the Mobile editor. Johnson, who did not want to see his Georgia cohorts rush to secession, complained openly about the stance that Forsyth and other former moderates took on the issue.[3]

In raising such questions, Belmont, Forney, Johnson, and many others exhibited the same misunderstanding of Forsyth's views as had been repeatedly expressed by leading secessionist newspapers during the late campaign. Many equated Forsyth's support of Douglas with a disavowal of states' rights and an unconditional pledge of loyalty to the Union—even under a Republican administration.[4] Neither idea could be further from the truth. As we have seen, throughout the 1850s, Forsyth presented a consistent stance on the issue of disunion. In 1850, commenting on the resistance movement in South Carolina, Forsyth (while serving as editor of the *Columbus Times*) wrote: "Carolina must draw the line boldly and distinctly between the enemies and friends of States' Rights sovereignty and equality. It were better to be conquered in a manly struggle for freedom, and die free, than live the victims of power and the slaves of despotism consolidated of fanaticism and cupidity." Before the presidential canvas of 1856, he had stated that "if Frémont's election should occur, the South ought not to submit, and will not submit." More specifically, the editor had declared, "If it be distinctly ascertained that the people of the North are deliberately resolved not to respect the guarantee of slavery, then should the South organize an independent government, and protect its right by force." Even after the Alabama State Democratic Convention of 1860, Forsyth, while championing Douglas and the Union, still wrote that if a "Black Republican" was elected, he would be of the same opinion as the Ultras. To his old nemesis William F. Samford, he wrote: "If a Black Republican president should be elected by a purely sectional vote, the South resisting and the Northerners uniting against us, this is no Union for the slaveholders to live in. I should go with Mr. Yancey, halter or no halter." Forsyth's expressed goal—one from which he never departed—was to prevent such a victory. His differences with the Yancey faction of the Democratic Party had been over how to accomplish that goal—not what to do if the goal was not achieved. Thus, when Forsyth wrote Douglas that "it seems to me we must part," he typified many Southern Douglas supporters in that he supported the Little Giant in earnest but, when the "cause of the Union was lost," closed ranks with the Southern secessionists.[5]

As the fallout of Lincoln's election settled, Alabama's political attention turned to Montgomery and secession. Forsyth noted the seriousness of the times in an editorial which stated, "No man who has intelligently reflected on the political condition of the country, especially as developed in the presidential canvass just closed, can resist the conclusion that the incompatibility of interests and views between the slaveholding and the non-slaveholding states, or to adapt the phrase of the master spirit of abolitionism, the 'irrepressible conflict,' has at last come to a crisis which leaves but little, if any, hope of those who look upon the Federal Union as the master piece of human wisdom in the science of government."[6]

As discussed in the previous chapter, the Alabama state legislature, in February of 1860, passed a resolution stating that, in the event of a Republican presidential victory, "It shall be the duty of the governor, and he is hereby required, forthwith to issue his proclamation, calling upon the qualified voters of the state to assemble on Monday, not more than forty days after the date of said proclamation . . . to consider, determine, and do whatever in the opinion of said Convention, the right, interest, and honor of the State of Alabama required to be done for their protection." One week after Lincoln's election, Governor Moore fulfilled his obligation. He announced that December 24 would be the election day for delegates to a January 7 convention. Two schools of thought regarding the secession issue quickly materialized prior to the Christmas Eve election. One group—the immediate secessionists (sometimes referred to as "straight-outs")—favored unilateral action by Alabama in withdrawing from the Union. The second group—the cooperationists—ranged from conditional unionists to those who favored secession in concert with the other Southern states. Forsyth now favored the secession convention, but, he wrote, "If the convention should determine to withdraw separately and without cooperation with the other Southern states, then such action shall be referred to a vote of the people at the ballot box."[7]

Since most people believed the final decision of the secession convention would not go before the voters of Alabama, many viewed the election of delegates as a referendum on secession. Conservative cooperationists had trouble mounting a campaign. The *Mobile Advertiser* announced a slate of four conservative candidates (none of which had been publicly nominated). Of these four, two—including a surprised Forsyth—declined to run. The election results ensured Alabama's secession from the Union. The secessionists won twenty-nine counties (fifty-four delegates) while the cooperationists won twenty-three counties (forty-six delegates). Statewide, the popular vote was 35,693 to 28,181 in favor of the secessionist candidates. The breakdown of the vote demonstrated the typical geographical split of Alabama politics. Generally speaking, north Alabama elected cooperationist candidates while south Alabama chose secessionists. Even Mobile County, certainly not a center of secessionist fervor, supported the secessionist ticket. Although the city of Mobile gave Breckinridge only 29 percent of its vote in the 1860 election, the secessionist candidates for the state convention swept all seven city wards and garnered a two-to-one margin of victory.[8]

Little suspense remained as the secession convention convened in Montgomery on the appointed day. Forsyth wrote Douglas that the state would "without doubt" adopt an ordinance of secession. He also noted that many conservatives did not even bother going to the polls—"looking upon secession as a foregone conclusion." The opening prayer of the convention set the tone for the gathering. The Reverend Basil Manly (a former president of the University of Alabama) left little doubt as to which side Providence favored, stating: "We thank Thee for all the hallowed memories connected with the establishment of the independence of the colonies, and their sovereignty as states, and with the formation and maintenance of our government, *which we had devoutly hoped might last*, unperverted and incorruptible, as long as the sun and moon endure." After unanimously passing a resolution stating that Alabama could not and would not submit to the Republican administration, the debate began on a proper course of action. On January 10, Mr. Yancey, chairman of a committee of thirteen (stacked seven to six in favor of the secessionists) reported an ordinance of secession to the full body. On the next day, the convention voted sixty-one to thirty-nine in favor of the ordinance.[9]

A leading Alabama history textbook concluded that there were basically three general reasons many Alabamians were in favor of secession: (1) a perceived loss of freedom; (2) the potential economic devastation resulting from the loss of slave property; and (3) racial fears and prejudices. It is interesting to note that Forsyth addressed all three of these concerns in one of his many letters to Senator Douglas. Forsyth confided to Douglas that "a quiet submission to Lincoln's administration would be taken and treated by the North as an unconditional surrender for all times to come." Furthermore, it was better to fight a "long and bloody war" than remain in the Union and "be stripped of 25 hundred millions of slave property." Finally, submission would result in the unthinkable prospect of having "turned loose among us 4,000,000 of free blacks."[10]

Delegates from Alabama joined five other Southern states (Texas did not arrive until a month later) in another convention held in Montgomery, which opened on 4 February 1861. This unique gathering actually had three functions. First, it was to draw up a provisional and, later, permanent constitution. Second, the body would serve as an electoral college to name a president and vice president. Finally, the convention would act as a provisional Congress of the Confederate States of America.[11]

Exactly one year prior, during the heat of the presidential nomination struggle, Forsyth had written a sarcastic rejoinder to the *Montgomery Advertiser,* in which he stated that, should the secessionists cause the election of a Republican and thus disrupt the Union, he would "quietly stay at home and mind [his] private business, and leave it to you and your friends to get the country out of the ugly scrape in which you had placed it."[12] Events in Charleston, South Carolina, and the call of the new Confederate government forced Forsyth to abandon any such thought and returned him to the center of national affairs. Immediately after secession, Southern state authorities began confiscating federal property on their now-independent soil. By the time of the formation of the Confederate States, Fort Sumter in Charleston and Fort Pickens in Pensacola were the most notable exceptions. Fort Sumter stood on a man-made granite island in the entrance to Charleston Bay. More of a political symbol than a military necessity, Fort Sumter nevertheless became a great concern for Confederate officials when the new government assumed responsibility (previously borne by South Carolina) for the military situation in Charleston.[13]

On 15 February 1861, the Confederate Congress passed a resolution authorizing President Jefferson Davis to appoint a three-man commission to be sent to Washington for the purpose of "negotiating friendly relations" between the United States and the Confederate States of America. This commission was also instructed to settle "all questions of disagreements between the two governments, upon principles of right, justice, equity, and good faith." On February 27, Davis sent word to the Confederate Congress of his appointment of Martin J. Crawford, Andre B. Roman, and John Forsyth for the task. Davis explained the political considerations involved in the composition of the commission. Roman, a former governor of Louisiana, had been a Whig and later a Constitutional Unionist supporter of John Bell. Crawford, a United States congressman, was a states' rights Democrat who had supported Breckinridge. Forsyth, in Davis's words, "had been a zealous advocate of the claims of Mr. Douglas." Davis believed that "the composition of the commission was therefore such as should have conciliated the sympathy and cooperation of every element of conservatism with which they might have occasion to deal."[14] The successful accomplishment of the mission to which the commissioners were dispatched would require, in the words of one historian, "sheer magic." According to President Davis's appointment letter, the commissioners were to attempt to accomplish the following: (1) secure Fort Sumter by negotiations; (2) negotiate the transfer of Fort Pickens; (3) ask for the Federal government's blessings for all property already seized; (4) secure recognition of Confederate independence; and (5) conclude treaties of amity and goodwill between the two nations.[15]

Crawford arrived in Washington on 3 March 1861. He called on President Buchanan, who was in his last full day of office. Buchanan refused Crawford an audience. When Forsyth arrived two days later, the situation regarding Fort Sumter was indeed tense. The previous December, Major Robert Anderson had moved his command from a weak Fort Moultrie to the stronger Sumter. Anderson's action set off patriotic outbursts of approval in the North and howls of protest in the South. Robert Barnwell Rhett Jr.'s *Charleston Mercury* termed Anderson's action as an "outrageous breach of faith" and advised patriotic women to begin rolling bandages. South Carolina artillery turned back an attempt to reinforce the fort in January of 1861. A fragile truce ensued whereby the Carolinians left Sumter alone as long as the Federal government did not try to bring reinforcements.[16] Such was the status when, on the day before Forsyth reached the federal capital, Abraham Lincoln delivered his first inaugural address. Most Southern newspapers reported the speech as a virtual declaration of war. Lincoln's assurances that "the power confided to me will be used to hold, occupy and possess the property and places belonging to the government" prompted the *Richmond Dispatch* to insist "the sword is drawn and the scabbard thrown away."[17]

By March 6, Forsyth and Crawford (not yet joined by Roman) made overtures through a third party to William Seward, the new secretary of state. Not wishing to recognize the Confederate government, Seward began a calculated strategy of delay. The Confederate commissioners wanted a signed pledge from Seward that no change would occur in the military situation at Fort Sumter during any period of delay. In turn, Forsyth and Crawford would not demand immediate recognition. Forsyth and Crawford obviously believed reports circulating that Fort Sumter would be evacuated in ten days. When several days passed without Seward's signature on the prepared pledge, the Confederate government, as well as its commissioners, began to smell a rat. On March 13, Forsyth and Crawford sent a formal letter (dated March 12) to Seward—via John T. Pickett, the commissioner's secretary—forcing the recognition issue. In this letter, the two commissioners explained that "the Confederate States constitute an independent nation, de facto and de jure" and, as such, requested Seward to "appoint as early a day possible, in order that they may present to the President of the United States the credentials which they bear and the objects of the mission with which they are charged."[18]

While awaiting a reply, Forsyth wrote to Confederate Secretary of War Leroy Pope Walker that the commissioners were "playing a game in which time is our best advocate." He believed that Lincoln's cabinet was torn over how best to respond to the commission's request. Wrote Forsyth: "There is a terrific fight in the cabinet. Our policy is to encourage the peace element in the fight, and at least blow up the cabinet on the question. The outside pressure in favor of peace grows stronger every hour." The commissioner confidently predicted that any delay would work in favor of the Confederate mission. On the next day, he communicated to South Carolina Governor Francis W. Pickens his belief that Fort Sumter would soon be evacuated. Regardless of Forsyth's optimism, the Confederate officials in Montgomery continued to grow restless. In a major change of policy, Toombs instructed the commission to relay to Seward an agreement to delay pressing for recognition in exchange for the *surrender* of the fort or at least an agreeable arrangement for a future surrender.[19] The Confederate policy thus shifted from retention of the status quo to a demand for full evacuation. The Confederates also wanted an answer to their March 13 letter by the 15th.

On March 15, two members of the United States Supreme Court—Samuel Nelson and John Archibald Campbell—became involved in the negotiations. Seward informed the two that Fort Sumter would indeed be evacuated within five days. Campbell relayed this information to the commissioners and asked them to hold off their demand for recognition for a few more days—a request to which they agreed. Again, on March 22, Forsyth expressed a confident air to Governor Pickens. In a telegram, the commissioner stated, "In spite of appearances, I believe I am not mistaken about Sumter. It will be evacuated if there is faith in Man."[20] On April 1, the fort had still not been vacated. Governor Pickens, apparently lacking "faith in man," telegraphed Campbell to find out the cause of the delay. Campbell went directly to Seward and found out that Lincoln, much like his Confederate counterparts, could change the terms of an agreement. Seward informed the commissioners that Lincoln would not resupply the fort *without first notifying* Governor Pickens.

After April 1, diplomatic conditions rapidly deteriorated. Forsyth and his colleagues began to function more as spies and purchasing agents than diplomats. The three sent reports of military activity in the Federal capital including troop and ship movements. Forsyth even communicated with Walker regarding the purchase of military supplies for the Confederacy. In a series of exchanges,

Forsyth and Walker argued over what was a fair price for rifles, Colt pistols, and three hundred tons of powder.[21]

Forsyth did manage to enjoy at least one pleasurable evening during his time in Washington. On April 4, he dined with Stephen A. Douglas, Salmon Chase (Lincoln's secretary of the treasury), Caleb Smith (secretary of the interior), and William H. Russell, a visiting correspondent of the *London Times*. In his diary (published two years later), Russell described Forsyth as a man "fanatical in his opposition to any suggestion of compromise or reconciliation." Russell, however, later referred to Forsyth as being "the most astute, and perhaps most capable of the gentlemen whose mission to Washington seems likely to be so abortive."[22] One can only speculate as to the conversation between Forsyth and Douglas. The Little Giant died less than nine weeks later.

By the first week of April, outside pressure was mounting on the Confederate government to insist that its commissioners press the recognition and evacuation issues. Politicians in the lower South grew increasingly impatient with what they saw as the feeble effort of Forsyth, Crawford, and Roman. On April 2, the *Savannah Republican* stated that "these men [Forsyth et al.] should require to know within five days whether the forts on our soil and justly belonging to us, are to be given up or whether we shall be compelled to take them by force of arms." On April 8, Seward finally answered the commissioner's March 12 letter. He disagreed with Forsyth and Crawford's contention that the Confederacy represented a "rightful and accomplished revolution." To the secretary of state, the Confederacy was a "perversion of a temporary and partisan excitement to the inconsiderate purposes of an unjustifiable and unconstitutional aggression upon the rights and authority vested in the Federal Government."[23] Seward concluded his reply with the assertion that he had no authority to recognize them as diplomatic agents or hold any other communications or correspondence with them.

Forsyth, Crawford, and Roman could not resist answering Seward's rejection. In a lengthy letter dated 9 April 1861, the commissioners accused Seward of bad faith, if not outright treachery, during the course of the negotiations. The commissioners expressed their belief that Seward, as secretary of state, had been speaking with some authority when he promised the evacuation of Fort Sumter. They concluded their bitter discourse with a prophetic statement: "Your refusal to entertain these overtures for a peaceful solution, the active naval and military preparations of the Government, and a formal notice to the commanding General of the Confederate forces in the harbor of Charleston that the President intends to provision Fort Sumter by forcible means if necessary, are viewed by the undersigned, and can only be received by the world, as a declaration of war against the Confederate States; for the President of the United States knows that Fort Sumter cannot be provisioned without the effusion of blood."[24]

Although the events of the final hours leading up to the actual firing on Fort Sumter need not be reexamined here, one question does deserve an answer— Were Forsyth and his fellow commissioners "duped" by Seward and the Lincoln administration? Historians such as Richard N. Current, who place the blame for the outbreak of the Civil War squarely on Jefferson Davis and the Confederate leadership, believe the commissioners knew all along that Seward was playing a devious game. On 2 April 1861, Secretary Walker wrote to General Pierre G. T. Beauregard that "the government [at Montgomery] has at no time placed any reliance on assurances by the government at Washington in respect to Fort Sumter."[25] According to proponents of this position, the commissioners thought they were using Seward, rather than he them. Indeed ten years after the fact, Forsyth himself told an author that the commissioners were willing "to play with Seward, to delay and gain time until the South was ready."[26]

Obviously, most Southerners did not share this view. Beginning with John A. Campbell, many Southern leaders claimed that, through their deception, Lincoln and Seward brought on the tragic war. On the day after the bombardment of Sumter began, Campbell wrote to Seward that no candid man "but will agree that the equivocating conduct of the administration . . . is the proximate cause of the great calamity."[27] Writing his memoirs years later, Jefferson Davis bitterly complained about the "absence of good faith" exhibited by the Lincoln administration. In the days just before and after the outbreak of hostilities, some Southerners were writing about the treacherous spirit of the Union government. One penman felt that the Lincoln administration had been "acting with duplicity, and whilst professing peace, has been secretly preparing for war." When Forsyth returned to Mobile, he made a speech from the balcony of the Battle House Hotel in which he blasted the conduct of the Federal administration and its agents. It is interesting to note that Forsyth (and many other Southerners) also accused Campbell of duplicity in his role as a mediator.[28]

Forsyth returned to a city worked into war preparation frenzy. Given the importance of Mobile as a major Southern port, its citizens were certain they faced imminent invasion. As part of a three-man "Committee for Defense," Forsyth appealed to Walker for arms and munitions. In a letter to Montgomery, Forsyth protested the removal of the state artillery from the city, since in so doing the only available field artillery pieces were lost. Forsyth's protest was "in the name of a defenseless community and millions of property at the mercy of the enemy." On 13 May 1861, he accepted the nomination of the Mobile Board of Alderman and the Common Council to fill the vacancy in the Mayor's office occasioned by the resignation of Jones M. Withers.[29] Withers, a West Point graduate and Mexican War veteran, accepted a commission in the Confederate army. As mayor of Mobile for the next six months, Forsyth found himself involved in problems common to all major Confederate communities. These problems can best be broken down into three categories: (1) city finances; (2) welfare of the citizenry; and (3) defense of the city.

Soon after Forsyth took office, a joint finance committee informed him that the financial condition of the city—"the revenues of which during times of peace and plenty is barely sufficient"—was now, in time of war, seriously lacking. The committee estimated that the immediate defense needs of the town would require at least fifty thousand dollars. Furthermore, the committee optimistically (but mistakenly) informed Forsyth that "the patriotism of our citizens will at once induce them to come forward cheerfully in support of a tax to raise the amount proposed for the defense of our beautiful city." The Board of Aldermen also authorized Forsyth to borrow from county funds, seize monies in accounts owned by citizens of the United States, and come up with his own revenue-producing and revenue-regulating measures. One measure that Forsyth submitted was a directive to local financial institutions to withhold payment of coupons on the city bonds issued in 1843 and due to mature on 1 July 1861.[30]

A major concern for Forsyth and the city of Mobile involved the use of Confederate treasury notes as payment for city taxes and fees. In June of 1861, the *Register* printed several letters and editorials concerning this issue. In one letter, an irate citizen complained that the Confederate government paid its obligations in Confederate treasury notes; however, since local banking institutions redeemed the notes at discounts ranging from 7 to 15 percent, local merchants were reluctant to accept them as payment for goods or services. Forsyth found himself involved in this financial dilemma in three different ways—as editor, mayor, and businessman. Editor Forsyth encouraged people to accept the treasury notes as they were backed by Southern cotton—"our grand staple which has as substantial a value as coin or bullion." Ironically, in the column next to this editorial, businessman Forsyth insisted that subscriptions to the *Register* be remitted in Mobile Bank bills or in gold. Mayor Forsyth, in September, asked the Board of Aldermen to pass a resolution or ordinance authorizing the receipt of Confederate treasury notes (at par value) for all taxes, licenses, and dues. Likewise, the city would use the same for all expenditures.[31]

Forsyth prepared a list of financial proposals for consideration by the Alabama house and senate. First, he wanted the lawmakers to repeal the act exempting goods imported from foreign countries from taxation. He believed the reason for the passage of the act (in February of 1861) no longer applied, and the city could gain much-needed revenue from its repeal. The mayor's second request involved the city's bonded debt. An act of 1843 required that certain tax revenues be deposited into a designated banking institution to pay bonds as they matured. Since Forsyth believed citizens of the United States held at least one quarter of this debt, he wanted the legislature to pass an act suspending the obligation to earmark this tax money during the continuance of the war. The third proposal asked the legislature to increase the rate of taxation on property within the city. This proposal was the only one of Forsyth's measures that did not pass the vote of the aldermen. Another scheme called for the issuance of checks (notes) in the denomination of five, ten, twenty-five, and fifty cents as well as one, two, and three dollars. These notes would be payable to the Mobile Savings Bank. Forsyth hoped this system would alleviate the inconvenience and "embarrassment" caused by the lack of coin in circulation. The fifth plan called for the suspension of the tax paid by the city to the state for the improvement of the Mobile harbor. Finally, should the war extend into 1863— when another major local bond issue was to mature—Forsyth wanted an act to allow the city to extend the maturity date to some period after the end of hostilities.[32]

Although finances were of critical importance, two other areas (themselves obviously related to finances) occupied the days of "His Honor the Mayor"— the welfare of the citizens and defense measures. Even during the earliest days of the war, many Mobile citizens found themselves facing economic hardships. One of Forsyth's first (unpopular) moves as mayor was to trim back the number of workers employed by the city. The laid-off laborers petitioned Forsyth and the aldermen to be rehired at lower wages. Forsyth later reported to the aldermen that "instances are not wanting, of women prostrate with disease and lying with hungry children around them in squalled apportionments, not only destitute of medical assistance, but of bread." In one case a white woman who was "indebted to some negroes in whose house she lies for the food that stands between her and starvation," asked him "if a human being can be left to starve in a Christian community." The mayor proposed a "free market for the poor," modeled after one he had recently seen in New Orleans. He also wanted to organize a "Mobile Relief Association" to address the plight of the needy.[33]

Another pressing concern was the defense of the vulnerable port city. On 4 January 1861, Governor Moore had ordered the occupation of Forts Morgan and Gaines on either side of the entrance to Mobile Bay. Most of the Confederate energy was spent increasing the capabilities of these installations to prevent the anticipated Union invasion. For the city itself, Major Danville Leadbetter, an engineer under Colonel William J. Hardee, planned field works at about a two and one-quarter mile curve from the courthouse. Leadbetter's plan included redoubts placed about a mile apart with intervening redans—the latter flanked by musketry and field guns. Mayor Forsyth's role in the early defense planning centered primarily on using his government connections to procure arms and supplies. In June 1861, the *Register* reported that Forsyth had obtained enough muskets, rifles, and percussion caps to equip a force of four thousand volunteers. In September, he expressed his concerns to Secretary Walker over the fact that there were less than fifty rounds of powder at the forts at the mouth of the bay. Forsyth wrote that "two hours of active fighting will exhaust the supply and then . . . Mobile is at the mercy of a naval power holding these forts and commanding the bay." He soon received a reply from acting Secretary of War Judah P. Benjamin (probably still angry over the Tehuantepec affair), assuring him that additional supplies were forthcoming. A year later, Governor John Gill Shorter was still complaining about the lack of men and materials available for Mobile's defense. Shorter felt the situation so grave that he sent word to President Davis that he hoped in the event of the fall of Mobile, the "order will be given that not one stone be left upon another." As far as the governor was concerned, the invading enemy should find "nothing but smoking and smoldering ruins to gloat over."[34]

Forsyth's brief term as mayor ended in December of 1861. During the early months of 1862, military affairs commanded the attention of the entire Forsyth clan. In March, editor Forsyth helped organize the Alabama 3rd Infantry Regiment Militia. In his public appeal for men, he opined, "Our homes, property, and liberties are all in danger—Nothing can save them but the prompt valor of the Sons of the South." Forsyth himself was named the commanding officer and given the rank of colonel. This group, more useful as a ceremonial outfit than an actual fighting force, was mustered out of service after only a few weeks in existence. Forsyth's oldest son John—by now sometimes referred to as "John Jr."—also attempted to serve. He enlisted as a private in the 3rd Regiment of Alabama Volunteers on April 16 for a three-year term. However, his health was such that he was forced to take a medical discharge after only a few weeks of service. His official medical record noted that the young man suffered from "original delicacy of constitution conjoined with exceedingly nervous disposition."[35]

It was the younger son Charles who had the most notable (and sometimes controversial) military career. The youngest Forsyth enlisted in April 1861 when the 3rd Alabama Infantry Regiment was organized in Montgomery. The 3rd Alabama, eventually under the command of Cullen A. Battle, became attached to the Army of Northern Virginia in April of 1862. Charles Forsyth was involved in many of the most famous battles of the war, including Antietam, Fredericksburg, Chancellorsville, Gettysburg, and Cold Harbor.[36]

After his short time as a military recruiter, Forsyth planned to help the war effort in a more familiar role as editor and commentator. Events in September 1862, however, pushed Forsyth once again away from the *Register* office and back into the national spotlight. This next opportunity came at the request of Forsyth's personal friend, General Braxton Bragg. During the first months of the war, Bragg held commands at both Pensacola and Mobile. By the summer of 1862, Union armies threatened Richmond in the east and held New Orleans, most of Tennessee and much of the Mississippi River. Two widely separated armies appeared to hold the fate of the Confederacy. The less famous of the two armies (Robert E. Lee's Army of Northern Virginia being the more famous) was badly disorganized in northern Mississippi. President Davis replaced its commander (General Pierre G. T. Beauregard) with Bragg on 20 June 1862.[37] In July, Bragg left a small force in Mississippi and moved the bulk of his army to Chattanooga to help defend eastern Tennessee from the advancing Union General Don Carlos Buell and the Army of the Ohio.

Stern, authoritative, and somewhat tyrannical, Bragg's sense of strict discipline was legendary. Perhaps more important, Bragg was also a favorite of President Davis. The Southern press, however, found little use for the arrogant general. Upset over the removal of the more personable Beauregard, members of the press reported that Bragg received the command only because of his insider status with the Confederate administration. On August 20, Bragg, tired of such media abuse, issued an order stating that "no person not properly connected with the army will be permitted to accompany it—whenever found within the lines, they will be arrested and confined." After one of his correspondents tested the new policy and was subsequently arrested, Samuel G. Reid of the *Montgomery Advertiser* wrote Bragg: "Allow me to say the arrest of our correspondent on the pretense of giving information to the enemy can only be regarded by all free-thinking men as another exhibition of that petty tyranny and vindictiveness for which you have gained an unenviable notoriety."[38]

With his army in Chattanooga, Bragg received new orders. Davis wanted him to invade Kentucky, thus drawing Buell out of Tennessee and, Davis hoped, "liberating" the Bluegrass State from its "Yankee oppression." Here Forsyth entered the story. By now, Bragg, realizing the importance of having his own side of a story in the newspapers, summoned Forsyth to help him engage in "psychological warfare" against the enemy. Bending his own rules, Bragg agreed to allow Forsyth to report the Kentucky campaign for four leading newspapers—the *Register*, the *Atlanta Confederacy*, the *Augusta Constitutionalist*, and the *Charlotte Courier*. Certainly Bragg intended to use his editor friend to enhance his own military reputation.[39]

Forsyth reached Atlanta on September 5 and Chattanooga three days later. Along with a dozen officers and commissary and quartermaster's clerks, Forsyth left to overtake Bragg's army, which now had a ten-day head start. So sick when he left Chattanooga that he could hardly ride, Forsyth's journey got steadily worse. Near Glasgow, Kentucky, a courier informed Forsyth's party of Union army activity in the area. The group took a detour but fell among a company of the 7th Regiment of Pennsylvania Calvary. Forsyth and his companions were taken prisoner. He was soon paroled but lost a "valuable" servant, two horses, his side-arms, and most of his clothes. Once Forsyth finally caught up with Bragg's army, he organized a corps of printers and obtained presses, types, and transports for a traveling newspaper office. He saw his work as important because "the soldiers want news and Kentucky, plunged in Yankee darkness, needs enlightenment."[40]

Forsyth's first major assignment was to compose a "Proclamation to the People of the Northwest." Although published (on September 26) under Bragg's name, historians agree Forsyth was most certainly the ghostwriter. The proclamation explained to the people of Kentucky the purpose of Bragg's presence. It began thus: "The Confederate Government is waging this war solely for self-defense—it has no designs of conquest, nor any other purpose than to secure peace and the abandonment by the United States of its pretensions to govern a people who have never been their subjects and who prefer self-government to a union with them." Bragg hoped that thousands of Kentuckians would rush to the support of the liberating army. Indeed, the army carried fifteen thousand extra rifles to arm any such converts. Forsyth reported that "Kentucky spirit is with us, but it halts in the flesh."[41]

From mid-September through the first of October, a stalemate situation existed in Kentucky. On September 30, from Bardstown, Forsyth wrote: "This army has been in quiet possession of this pretty Kentucky village for one week. The people, especially the fairer part of it, have been kind and hospitable, and the enemy has not ventured to appear in force to disturb us." General Buell held Louisville while Confederate General Kirby Smith seized the state capital at Frankfort (where Bragg planned to inaugurate Richard Hawes as Confederate governor). Northern criticism of Buell forced him to finally move against the rebels. Buell's and Bragg's forces met at Perryville on October 8. Although heavily outnumbered, Bragg's army made a strong showing—at one point pushing the Union left two miles off of the field and killing two generals in the process.[42] After heavy casualties to his forces (3,400 to his force of about 15,000), Bragg declined to fight the following day. Instead, the general ordered a retreat from Perryville and a withdrawal from the state of Kentucky. Buell pursued timidly but failed to attack the weakened, retreating Confederates.

This retreat from what seemed to many like a chance for a decisive victory produced a firestorm of controversy. In his official report that explained his decision, Bragg stated: "Ascertaining that the enemy was heavily re-enforced during the night, I withdrew my forces early the next morning to Harrodsburg and then to this point" (Bryantsville, Kentucky, from where the report originated). Never one to readily accept blame for a personal shortcoming, Bragg further stated that "the campaign here was predicated on a belief and the most positive assurances that the people of this country would rise in mass to assert their independence. No people ever had so favorable an opportunity, but I am distressed to add there is little or no disposition to avail of it." Several months after the incident, Bragg sent a private letter to President Davis. In this communication, he claimed that, although he did not want to rehash the results of the Kentucky campaign, nonetheless, he "knowing my position to be impregnable and failing to receive a burial of the whole matter," he was forced to "enter it with deep regret." He placed the blame for the bluegrass debacle squarely on his subordinates (particularly Generals Polk and Hardee) for not following his explicit orders.[43] This explanation notwithstanding, the Southern press savaged the controversial general for his withdrawal. Many of Forsyth's journalism colleagues refused to accept Bragg's claim of a successful campaign. The *Richmond Whig* complained that Bragg's grand invasion "has turned out to be simply a fizzle." The *Memphis Appeal* described Bragg's retreat as a "sad finale" to the movement that was promised to bring the redemption of Kentucky.[44]

It should be noted that Buell's actions received no less harsh condemnation in the North. A month after the Union general's failure to pursue Bragg's army, the United States War Department convened a military commission to investigate Buell's entire operation in Tennessee and Kentucky. During these proceedings, John Forsyth's name continued to come up. The military adjutant wanted to know why Buell's men paroled Forsyth, letting him return to Bragg's army in the service of the Confederacy. Buell was also asked if he had read and believed Forsyth's (inflated) reports of Bragg's troop strength. In one report, he commented that Bragg had in excess of forty thousand troops. The commission thought Buell failed to pursue because he believed these numbers.[45]

By the end of October 1862, Forsyth returned to Mobile determined to publish the "true policy and history" of Bragg's Kentucky campaign. His first installment, dated 30 October 1862, appeared in the *Register* on November 9. Forsyth opened his defense by stating that he had "a higher duty to the course of justice and truth to correct the multitudinous errors and misstatements which abound in the newspapers, and which give vent to the disappointment of those who are in a rage with a general because he did not realize their absurdly exaggerated expectations and perform impossibilities." He went on to demonstrate that sheer numbers dictated Bragg's strategy. Even a "succession of victories would have culminated in General Bragg's ruin." According to Forsyth, the aim of the campaign was to recruit loyal Kentuckians to the Confederate cause; however, "the 50,000 armed men did not come, and after a march of nearly 800 miles, General Bragg found the keystone of his entire plan of campaign dropped out. Abandoning all hope of aid, and disgusted with the failure of the Kentucky spirit, he turned his attention to Buell, who was advancing upon him in two heavy columns." Incredibly, Forsyth concluded his lengthy defense with several reasons he considered the campaign—even after the retreat—a resounding success: (1) Buell was forced to evacuate east Tennessee; (2) north Alabama was relieved of Federal occupation; (3) the Confederacy gained control of the Cumberland Gap; (4) Bragg took from eighteen to twenty thousand prisoners; (5) the army left Kentucky with more supplies than when they entered; and (6) the army won major battles at Richmond (Kentucky), Munfordsville, and Perryville. Like Bragg, Forsyth also sent a letter to Jefferson Davis trying to explain what had gone wrong. He informed the president that, "The people of Kentucky are subjugated and dared not take the arms we offered them to fight for their own liberty.[46]

Forsyth's explanation soothed the anger much like a spark soothes a cask of gunpowder. Bragg's (and now Forsyth's) most severe criticism now came from Kentuckians—incensed by what they perceived as Forsyth's implication that they were cowards. Governor-in-exile Hawes blasted Forsyth in the columns of the *Richmond Enquirer.* Hawes claimed Forsyth's account of the campaign was "written with singular power and adroitness and so replete with erroneous statements of assumed facts and distortions of many of the essential features of that movement, as to demand a reply." Governor Hawes felt that Bragg's mistakes (which he listed in great detail) outweighed any refusal of *some* Kentuckians to take up arms. According to Hawes, if Bragg had not retreated so rapidly, more Kentuckians would have soon come to his aid. In fact, there were moves underway to "raise companies, squadrons, and regiments, and that nearly the whole efforts were defeated by Bragg's sudden retreat." The withdrawal "came like a clap of thunder in a clear day and confusion and dismay was the result." Although the governor did admit "our rich men of Southern affinities loved their estates more than their liberties," he protested that Forsyth had ignored many "shining exceptions."[47]

Hawes's most serious charge directly questioned Forsyth's credibility. Forsyth had claimed in his report that Bragg's decision to pull out of Kentucky had near unanimous support from the general officers. According to the governor, this was simply not the case. He seemed to feel that Forsyth was going out of the way to defend his friend, regardless of the facts. Refusing to let this personal affront go unanswered, Forsyth responded that he "did not know what Governor Hawes saw or what he heard among the Kentuckians where he was, but there is no earthly doubt that in the tracks of the army's march, it met, save in the glorious women of the state, and except in the [few] brave men who came to its ranks, only frowning Unionists and timid friends." Although many in the press and Confederate government continued to hound Bragg, Forsyth steadfastly encouraged and defended his friend for the duration of the war.[48]

After two eventful war years, Forsyth spent the remainder of the conflict in a more traditional role for a Southern wartime editor. Probably his most important function during 1863–65 was his attempt to lift public spirits. In lieu of a well-organized propaganda effort on the part of the Confederate government, the maintenance of public morale devolved on a number of public and private agencies. The Confederate press played an important part in this effort. Editors such as Forsyth exerted a positive influence on the war effort in several ways: they praised heroic efforts of Confederate soldiers and civilians; rejoiced over Confederate victories (or at least minimized defeats); stressed the unanimity of war sentiment; glorified war in general and this war in particular; warned the public against overconfidence and apathy; inspired hatred and contempt for the enemy; spotlighted every enemy failure; and (especially as the war lingered) enlarged on the consequences of a Confederate defeat.[49] The pages of the *Register* show that Forsyth, at one time or another filled all these roles.

The peak of public morale in the Confederacy came at the beginning of the war. After the Confederate victory at Bull Run in July 1861, Forsyth had joined many of his fellow editors in extolling the glory and virtue of the effort. Comparing the defeated Union forces to the Spanish Armada, he believed that "the defeat at the Stone Bridge breaks the backbone on Lincoln's war power, for it overthrows the confidence of the people to whom he looks for support." During that heady summer, Forsyth had paused to reflect on the struggle. War, according to the editor, was a "great blessing to our people, morally and physically." It would "purify the nation, and it will come forth from it with a healthy and invigorated condition of the public mind."[50] Indeed, a musical number performed at the Mobile Theatre in 1861 by S. B. Duffield seemed to illustrate the typical feeling of the populace. The piece, entitled "Trust to Luck Alabama," featured the following verse:

Trust to Luck Alabama, prolong the loud shout,
Three cheers for our State, boys, she is out, she is out.
We have cut ourselves loose from the huckstering knaves
Who whine about negroes and of white men make slaves
Though enriched by the South, ranked traitors they stand
While sworn to befriend us, basest foes to our land.
Trust to Luck Alabama, prolong the loud shout
Three cheers for our State Boys, she is out, she is out.[51]

Sustaining this level of enthusiasm became much more difficult as the war dragged on, particularly after the disastrous summer of 1863—marred by the Confederate losses at both Vicksburg and Gettysburg. Although Forsyth and the *Register* still tried to put a positive spin on local and national events, the rapidly deteriorating conditions of the port city could no longer be glossed over. The city of Mobile faced several major problems during the final two years of the war. The first concerned the reluctance of the local population to assist in maintaining the city's defenses. When calls went out for volunteers to work on the extensive line of fortifications that the Confederate military officials deemed necessary, white citizens responded with apathy or outright indignation.[52] Even tougher was getting Mobilians to submit to new taxes to help pay for the fortifications. One innovative source was an occupation tax on professions ranging from physicians to jugglers. The *Register* warned that failure to respond to the defensive needs of the city would be "penny wise and pound foolish."[53]

Another problem was the shortage of basic staple items in the city. The federal blockade of Mobile—in effect since 25 November 1861—began to take a noticeable toll by 1863. Forsyth constantly railed against "extortioners" and profiteers who would undermine the Confederate cause for the sake of profit. In September of 1863 a bread riot, in which the women of Mobile marched down Dauphin Street breaking windows and taking what food they could find, made the pages of the *New York Times*. According to this account, the ladies, "rendered desolate by the sufferings," carried signs that read "Bread or Blood" and armed themselves with knives and hatchets. What ensued was "a most formidable riot by a long-suffering and desperate population." One eyewitness downplayed the incident, describing the group as a "motley crowd" of mostly barefooted women. This person only saw one store broken into with little damage or loss. He concluded that the women "are not well cared for, but many of them could care for themselves if they would, but are too lazy to work." Along with the serious shortages, the citizenry of, as well as the soldiers stationed near, Mobile increasingly began to face nuisance rules and regulations ranging from the rationing of sugar and molasses to a ban on "intoxicating liquors" to a prohibition of bathing in Mobile Bay. In the early fall of 1864, Mayor Robert H. Slough warned the Board of Aldermen and Common Council that many Mobilians would not be able to afford to purchase firewood for the winter.[54]

A final issue dealt with the manpower available to continue the war effort. As the war limped into its third year, citizens of Mobile, as well as much of the South, began to lose heart. In a letter to General Bragg, Dabury H. Maurey, a Confederate officer stationed in Mobile, complained at length about the able-bodied men in the city who were unwilling to support the cause. According to Maurey, if these men "had it in them the honest purpose of the militias of Petersburg, Richmond, and Stauton Bridge," the city could be easily defended from attack. He went on to claim that many Mobile men were already in contact with New Orleans cotton dealers and had "already made the arrangements to speculate largely in cotton on the arrival of the enemy." Along with a business class which was sometimes reluctant to serve, the Confederates had trouble hanging on to those already in service. The *Register* ran copies of "An Act to Aid the Confederate Government in Arresting Deserters and Others." In addition to the number of deserters and men absent from their units for various other reasons, Mobile's large foreign-born population required special legislation to determine their military status.[55]

During the fall of 1863, a personal matter distracted Forsyth from his editorial duties. By now, his son Charles had been promoted to full colonel and commanded a regiment in Rodes's Brigade of Hill's Division of the Army of Northern Virginia. The younger Forsyth had apparently served the Confederacy with valor and distinction. However, after Gettysburg, what editor Forsyth later described as "false and injurious reports" began to surface. A whispering campaign concerning Charles's leadership ability, and, in some cases, his bravery, turned into public gossip. Serious charges came out a year later, after a battle at Cedar Creek, Virginia. During this skirmish (on 19 October 1863), his regiment allegedly retreated in utter panic and confusion. Charles faced a military court martial for his conduct on that day. John Forsyth made a hasty trip to Richmond to be present for the trial. It is not known if he tried to use his influence in his son's favor. Interestingly, Charles was found guilty, only to have the sentence quickly reversed by President Davis. In the official letter of remittance, the Confederate secretary of war praised Charles Forsyth's "gallantry and efficiency displayed on many fields of battle." When he returned to Mobile, Forsyth, writing more as a father than an editor, penned a long, impassioned defense of his son's conduct.[56]

As the war wound to its close and the Confederacy neared collapse, Forsyth wrote to General Bragg that "we cannot win unless we keep up the popular heart." Trying to convey optimism, Forsyth nonetheless knew the difficulty of the times. Mobile's "hour of trial" came in August of 1864. On the morning of August 3, the *Register* reported that twenty-three federal warships lay anchored off the Mobile harbor. Expressing classic false hope, Forsyth wrote: "Were it not known that the enemy has no land force disposable for a combined land and naval attack on Mobile, we should conclude naturally that the city's time of trial was at hand." In case of attack, Forsyth confidently predicted that the Union fleet "will be checked and Mobile Bay will be strewed with the wreckage of many a Yankee man-of-war." On August 6, Union Admiral David G. Farragut (obviously not a *Register* subscriber) damned the torpedoes and entered Mobile Bay with his fleet. Forsyth had to admit that "the crisis which is to test the strength and earnestness of our people has at length arrived." The *Register* printed a proclamation from the mayor that stated that Mobilians must "defend the city to the last point of resistance. Let it not be said that Mobile is craven when we have the illustrious examples of Richmond,

Petersburg, and Charleston looking us in the face."[57] On August 21, Fort Morgan surrendered. The Union forces did not follow up the successful operation in Mobile Bay with an outright assault on the city. However, Farragut's control of the bay only exacerbated the hardships of the blockade.

Forsyth's last editorial of 1864 may have been his most controversial of the entire war. At last realizing the hopelessness of the Confederate cause, he wrote: "Today, after all our sacrifice, we find ourselves still sorely beset and hard pressed by our enemies, and the crisis of war, to all intelligent observers, near its culminating point."[58] However, realizing that defeat was at hand, and accepting it, was two different matters. Forsyth endorsed a final plan which, he felt, might turn the tide back in favor of the Confederacy. To the editor, the most pressing need of the South was plain—"We want more men with muskets in their hands to equalize the struggle with our enemies." Forsyth joined a small minority that favored enlisting slaves in the Confederate military. He obviously knew many disagreed with this idea, but, he rationalized, "Who can deny if we do not use our servants to fight for their masters, with a guarantee of their freedom, our enemies will so use them against us with the same guarantee?" In perhaps his most pessimistic statement of the entire war, Forsyth sadly noted that "if we are conquered, slavery is dead, and to secure our freedom and independence, we ought and must, whenever it becomes necessary, to lay the institution itself on the altar of sacrifice." Forsyth sent a copy of this editorial to Jefferson Davis. The president responded that the opinions contained therein were substantially his also. Davis wrote Forsyth that "it is now becoming daily more evident to all reflective persons that we are reduced to choosing whether the negroes shall fight for or against us, and that all arguments as to the positive advantages or disadvantages of employing them are beside the question, which is simply one of relative advantages between having their fighting element in our ranks or in those of our enemies."[59]

One way in which the Confederate press adversely affected public morale was in its creation of false hopes of a military success, whose failure to materialize led to disillusionment. Even though he understood the gravity of the situation, Forsyth continued to convey such false hopes until the very end. After returning to Mobile from Richmond in December of 1864, Forsyth claimed that General Lee was "the master of the city's defenses." He also boasted that "Grant is powerless beyond the Confederate entrenchments. His army is not so great as the public believes." In route to Mobile, he literally crossed the path of Sherman's "March to the Sea." Apparently not impressed, he noted, "We saw fewer signs of devastation than we expected." A few months later, Forsyth wrote, "Sherman's campaign has certainly been defeated by the unexpected energy and vigor with which the Confederate army was moved to the front." Likewise, "everything tends to confirm our prediction that General Lee will begin the spring campaign with a larger army by many thousands than has ever been marshaled under his banner."[60]

In April of 1865, with the sound of Union artillery fire on the eastern shore of Mobile Bay audible in the city, Forsyth wrote that "there is nothing in it that ought to disturb the nerves or ruffle the composure of any true Confederate." Looking forward to a "splendid victory to be achieved by the heroic generals and troops now assembled for the final blow," Forsyth predicted that "a few weeks of endurance and valor will save us."[61] One week later—exactly four years to the day from the firing on Fort Sumter—Mobile surrendered to Union forces. The long period of Reconstruction would determine if the giant struggle had indeed killed the giant nation.

8

"The Zenith of Today Is the Nadir of Tomorrow"

Only a few weeks after the surrender of Mobile, John Forsyth traveled to Montgomery. Walking along the streets of the defeated Confederacy's birthplace, the editor could not help but pause and reflect. Most likely thinking back on the Yanceyites, he wrote that "the doctrine of precipitation, which originally had the most prurient hot-bed in this capital, is quite abandoned as a political theory and would be expunged as a memory." Realizing that the postwar South would never be as it was before the great conflict, he waxed philosophically: "How times change, and men with them, in the world of transitory events and opinions. The zenith of today is the nadir of tomorrow."[1] Devastated by what Forsyth consistently claimed was an unnecessary war, the South entered into ten years of what he viewed as its nadir—Reconstruction.

The historiography of Southern Reconstruction centers on the actual motivation behind and response to the era's political programs. William Dunning, in his landmark *Reconstruction: Political and Economic,* tended to agree with Forsyth's assertion that Reconstruction represented a basic struggle of good versus evil (with the Republican regime personifying the latter). Walter Fleming, the author of the standard work on Alabama's Reconstruction experience, followed this same line of reasoning. Fleming (a student of Dunning at Columbia University) viewed the South as ready to return to the Union, only to succumb to the vindictive evils and lasting damage brought on by the Radical Republicans. In the 1950s and 1960s, revisions by scholars such as Kenneth Stampp, John Hope Franklin, and C. Vann Woodward appeared. To one degree or another, each of these writers saw some positive features in Reconstruction, which were sadly overturned by an unrepentant South. All of these works primarily examined the congressional (Radical) phase of Reconstruction.[2]

Newer works on Reconstruction tend to expand the focus back to the period of presidential Reconstruction. Eric L. McKitrick formulated what he termed the "shock of defeat" theory. According to McKitrick, the Southerners, overwhelmed with the loss, displayed an apathetic indifference. The ex-Confederates would have done anything President Johnson demanded, had the chief executive exhibited the needed leadership. Michael Perman disagreed. This historian felt that any sort of moderate Reconstruction policy faced certain doom due to the inherent opposition of former Confederates still in positions of leadership. In what may be considered the definitive work on the Reconstruction period, Eric Foner seemed to agree more with McKitrick. Foner noted that once it became clear to Southerners that Johnson favored a "white man's government," compromise and cooperation became increasingly rare.[3] John Forsyth typified the view of the Southerner as held by both McKitrick and Foner. Through the presidential and congressional phases of Reconstruction, one can see the transition of Forsyth's attitude—from optimistic cooperationist to bitter antagonist—reflected in his writings and actions.

Early on the morning of 12 April 1865, Union gunboats moved 8,000 men under the command of Major General Gordon Granger to the west bank of the Mobile River. These men were instructed to get into position to attack the city. Granger sent a message to Mayor Slough demanding the unconditional surrender of the city. By this time the Confederate military authorities and some of the leading Confederate sympathizers had fled the city, heading north on the Mobile and Ohio Railroad line. The Union conquerors placed "a sufficient number of gunboats directly in front of the city to give efficient protection to the loyal inhabitants." Fearing for the safety of the citizens, the mayor requested of General Granger that "for the sake of humanity, all the safeguards which you can throw around our people will be secured to them." At about noon, the mayor and a small delegation rode in a carriage under a white flag to formally turn over the port city. By 12:30 p.m., the Union flag once again flew over the courthouse.[4]

Forsyth was among the group that had fled the city in advance of the Union Army's arrival. Apparently with the idea of printing a paper behind the Confederate lines, and not wishing to leave anything of value for the detestable Yankees, he took along four power presses, all the ink and paper that could be transported, and nine employees. This effort was pretty much in vain for on May 4 General Richard Taylor (son of former President Zachary Taylor) surrendered the last active Confederate Army east of the Mississippi to General Edward R. S. Canby at Citronelle. An uncertain future replaced the hostility of war. Since the North insisted that there had been no Southern nation, there was no treaty to give guidance for a transitory period. The white citizens of the state, divided in the best of times, broke into more factions than ever before. In addition, some 439,000 of the state's former slaves became wards of the Bureau of Refugees, Freedmen, and Abandoned Lands. Estimates of Alabama's war dead ranged as high as 40,000. Additionally, much of the state's farmland, fledgling industry, and social structure lay in ruins. In Forsyth's words, "The land has been scared and furrowed by the iron plowshares of war." Many indeed gave themselves over to "sullen despair because of the present gloom."[5]

As early as 1863, President Lincoln had presented a plan of Reconstruction. Lincoln's plan assumed the future loyalty of the Confederates. The president offered pardons to Confederate supporters who would swear an oath to support the Constitution and the Union. When 10 percent of those eligible in a state did so, the state could form a new government (which would abolish slavery) and apply for readmission to the Union. When tragic events forced Andrew Johnson into the presidency, many in the South expressed outward anxiety. In 1864, Johnson had made a harsh proclamation: "Treason must be made odious and traitors must be punished and impoverished." At first, the Radical Republicans expressed confidence in Johnson. One such figure confidently testified, "I believe that the almighty continued Mr. Lincoln in office as long as he was useful and then substituted a better man to finish the job."[6]

Andrew Johnson came from the most humble of backgrounds—much more so than even Lincoln. Critical throughout his career of the "slaveocracy," he had risen through the political ranks as a spokesman for the common man. A strong unionist, Johnson had served as the military governor of Tennessee during the war. His conservative policies as well as his racist personal beliefs eventually put him in serious conflict with the Republican-controlled Congress. Although a strong believer in states' rights, Johnson felt the South had never legally left the Union, therefore, Congress had no authority over its "restoration"—Johnson disliked the phrase "Reconstruction."

When, on 29 May 1865, Johnson issued his version of a Reconstruction plan, most Southerners breathed a sigh of relief at the mildness of its terms. Southern states had only to repudiate secession and ratify the Thirteenth Amendment. The state leaders could then call for conventions for the purpose of setting up restored governments. The new president offered amnesty and pardon to participants in the late rebellion who would take a loyalty oath. Johnson did make exclusions for several classes of people—for example, major Confederate officials and owners of taxable property valued at more than $20,000. These special categories of people had to apply individually for amnesty. By the end of August, Forsyth had signed his loyalty oath that stated he would "faithfully defend the Constitution of the United States" and, furthermore, would "abide by and support all laws and proclamations which have been made during the existing rebellion with reference to the emancipation of slaves." On 21 June 1865, President Johnson appointed Lewis E. Parsons as provisional governor of Alabama. Johnson instructed Parsons to begin the voter registration process for a state convention, which would then complete the readmission process.[7]

After President Johnson's amnesty and restoration plans were underway, Forsyth's most pressing concern was to return to Mobile to reestablish his business. This was no easy task as, by this time, another person was publishing another newspaper out of his old office. One of General Granger's first orders after the occupation of Mobile granted E. O. Haile, a former Union officer, permission to print a "loyal" newspaper from 12 South Royal Street—the confiscated property of John Forsyth. The journal, named the *Mobile Daily News,* appeared on April 13, the day after the surrender. One can only imagine how Forsyth must have felt when he saw an issue of the *Daily News* (printed on the one press he had left behind) with the subtitle "*Late Advertiser and Register*" printed under its masthead. His anger must have grown only progressively worse as he perused the April 17 issue with bold headlines stating: "Glorious News . . . Surrender of Gen. Lee." After he complied with the amnesty process, Forsyth applied to General Canby to have his personal property returned. On June 9, Canby agreed, stating: "Unless the property is required for military purposes, its occupation by military authorities will be relinquished." After a few more weeks of legal wrangling, Forsyth and the *Register* returned to the Royal Street office in July.[8]

The bad feelings between Forsyth and Haile only intensified after an incident that involved the always-impetuous Charles Forsyth. Rumors were swirling around town that while Charles was serving the Confederacy on the battlefield, a young Cuban named De Viega was involved in less than patriotic activities with his young wife. Upon his return to Mobile, Charles got into a fight with De Viega in which he reportedly stabbed the Cuban suitor several times. Once again through the intervention of his notable father, Charles escaped prosecution. In the meantime, Mr. Haile had gone to New Orleans where he wrote a full account of the incident and had it placed in the *New Orleans Daily True Delta.* In his juicy (and somewhat embellished) report, Haile included many disparaging remarks about the Forsyth family in general. This, of course, evoked another response from Charles. The youngest Forsyth placed a card in the *Mobile Evening News* calling Haile a "Black Guard, a liar, and a coward." Naturally, this led to the obligatory duel—conducted in Magnolia

Park. Neither man was injured but Haile soon left the port city never to return. The entire chain of events made the front page of the *New York Times,* which used the story as an example of what was mockingly portrayed as the nature of "high-toned Southern gentlemen."[9]

Forsyth accepted the twin results of the war—defeat and the end of slavery. He began to use his influence to urge the speedy organization of an elected state government to replace the "quasi-military civilian regime." He wanted his fellow Mobilians to cooperate with Johnson's plan. Forsyth insisted "there is nothing in these [Johnson's] requirements of the government which any Southern man who means to remain in the United States should hesitate to accept." Certainly he did not mean that one necessarily had to like the results of the war. However, "The government of the United States, which is the conqueror in the war, has chosen to fix the terms by which Southern men shall be restored to the rights and privileges of citizenship. It is bootless for us to inquire into the reasonableness or justice of the terms."[10]

Forsyth also actively supported the call by Parsons for a state convention. Many diehard Confederates advocated a boycott of such a meeting as a protest against Reconstruction in general. Forsyth tried to squelch this movement, holding that "there has never been a period in the history of Alabama when it was more important than now for every good citizen to bear his part well and manfully in the business of government." It must be noted, however, that even at this early date, Forsyth betrayed his ulterior motive in advocating cooperation—a motive that seems to give credence to the McKitrick and Foner thesis. Cooperation offered the quickest return to white domination. Getting the "right" kind of man registered to vote determined "whether the government they [the convention delegates] institute shall be liberal, wise and conservative, or whether it shall be narrow, radical and burdensome."[11] By "narrow, radical, and burdensome," Forsyth meant a government that actively sought to elevate the freedmen to equal status with the whites.

Editor Forsyth appeared to be a model Reconstruction citizen during the summer of 1865. Perhaps no situation better typified this stance than his early relationship with the Freedman's Bureau. Congress had created the bureau on 3 March 1865 with General Oliver Otis Howard as its commissioner. In May, Howard appointed assistant commissioners to serve over each of the former Confederate states. The man chosen to lead the agency in Alabama was General Wager T. Swayne. Swayne was a native Ohioan with an excellent war record. At the Battle of Corinth, he received a field promotion for gallantry (later receiving the Congressional Medal of Honor). Swayne, the son of a United States

Supreme Court justice, lost a leg during later action in South Carolina. By March of 1865, his service to the Union won him a general's star. He was not yet thirty years old when he assumed command in Alabama.[12]

Although Swayne was later to be generally despised throughout the state, Forsyth, in the earliest days of Reconstruction, offered only praise. The editor described the general as "a just and sensible man, a gentleman and a soldier, who never understood that the duties of his office required him to harass and oppress the White citizens of the state and to set up the Black man as an idol of worship at the expense of the dignity and rights of the man of his own color." Although Swayne certainly instituted policies that many Mobilians found distasteful, Forsyth held that the general "performed his duty with the frankness of a soldier and the sensibility of a gentleman who respects life-long prejudices and who scorns to add to the humiliation of a people who have unreservedly succumbed to the decrees of the sword."[13]

One of Swayne's actions that directly linked him with John Forsyth involved the issue of black testimony in Mobile's city courts. Mayor Slough, in open defiance of Freeman Bureau directives, persisted in denying civil liberties to Mobile's black population. On several occasions, Slough ordered Mobile police to arrest all vagrants and announced that if "troublesome" blacks did not leave the city, they would be forced to labor on the streets. More disturbing to Swayne was Slough's refusal to allow black testimony in the mayor's court. In July 1865, Swayne received complaints that Slough dismissed several cases rather than hear the testimony of black men.[14] Swayne met with Provisional Governor Parsons to encourage the establishment of equal justice in Alabama's court system. Parsons rejected Swayne's proposal as "politically inexpedient." Within hours of receiving the governor's reply, Swayne moved on his own. He ordered state courts to admit black testimony. Refusal to comply would result in the dismissal of the offending court official.[15]

Mayor Slough stubbornly refused to be bullied by the bureau. Swayne wrote to Parsons regarding the need to replace Slough with "an honest man." Parsons this time agreed and gave Swayne a commission to be presented to the general's chosen replacement—John Forsyth. Swayne reported to General Howard that he chose Forsyth because the ex-Minister to Mexico was "more beloved by the colored people of Mobile than any other man in the city."[16] Swayne soon found out that securing the commission and delivering it were two different things. When Swayne reached Mobile, he discovered that Forsyth was at a pleasure resort on Mobile Bay. The assistant commissioner commandeered a "tug" and began to travel south on the bay where he encountered Forsyth and a party steaming north on another vessel. Swayne managed to get his boat turned and in pursuit of Forsyth. Forsyth's group, thinking the editor was about to be arrested, refused to stop. Swayne chased Forsyth for several miles before overtaking the slower craft and delivering the mayoral appointment.[17] In forty years of public service, Forsyth pursued many political objectives. This, however, was the only time one (literally) pursued him.

Forsyth now found himself in a delicate position. Although he wanted to cooperate with the bureau authorities, he did not want to appear to be disloyal to the Southern cause. In a lengthy letter to the Mobile Board of Aldermen and Common Council, the second-time mayor spelled out his reasons for accepting Swayne's commission. Forsyth felt that Mayor Slough's refusal to follow General Swayne's orders left Governor Parsons with a choice of replacing the wayward city official or placing Mobile under a Freedman's Bureau military court. Regarding Swayne's offer, Forsyth stated, "I did not feel at liberty, as a good citizen, to decline it. General Swayne's presence in Mobile whither he had come with the design of immediately establishing a military court, should I decline, made my duty clear and imperative in the matter."[18] Forsyth served as provisional mayor from August until December of 1865. In accordance with Swayne's wishes, he allowed the testimony of blacks in the mayor's court.

Governor Parsons set 31 August 1865, as election day for delegates to a state convention. The call, printed in the *Register*, stated that the election would be held "in the manner provided in the laws of Alabama on the 11th day of January, 1861; but no person can vote in said election, or be a candidate for election, who is not a legal voter as the law was on that day; and if he is excepted from the benefit of amnesty under the Presidential proclamation of the 28th of May, 1865, he must have obtained a pardon."[19] Thus, Alabama's new constitution would be written without any of the freedmen or many ex-Confederates.

President Johnson knew that until Northern public opinion became convinced that the South accepted the results of the war, Congress would not approve his restoration program. As several state conventions neared, the president urged governors to use their influence to secure the repudiation of ordinances of secession and the ratification of the Thirteenth Amendment. When the Alabama state convention convened in September of 1865, Forsyth used his newspaper for the same objectives. The editor urged the delegates to "declare the system of involuntary servitude at an end in this state, pronounce the ordinance of secession null and void, and abrogate all changes in the constitution, and all acts of the legislature made in Confederates times, which are contrary to the letter or spirit of the Constitution of the United States."[20]

Satisfied with the results of the Alabama gathering, President Johnson commented, "The proceedings of the convention have met the highest expectation of all who desire the restoration of the Union. All seems to be working well, and will result, as I believe, in a decided success."[21] The new state constitution went into effect without a vote of the people at large; the state held elections in early November; and the Alabama legislature convened on 20 November 1865. The first order of business for the new lawmaking body was the ratification of the Thirteenth Amendment. Forsyth and other Alabama editors made it clear that, in their opinion, this action did not grant Congress the power to legislate on the future state of Alabama's freedmen. The state legislature then selected Governor Parsons to serve the long term in the United States Senate and George S. Houston for the short term (Forsyth came in second to Houston for the latter position).[22]

John Forsyth must have looked back on the last eight months of 1865 with at least a little satisfaction. In an editorial that appeared just after the November state elections, he noted that "the whole world, including even our deadly political enemies, the Radicals of the North, have bared witness to the readiness and completeness of the submission of the South to the political decrees uttered by the sword in the late war. Indeed mankind has been surprised at the promptness with which the people have resumed their allegiance to a government they had sacrificed so much to throw off." Certainly events in the summer and fall of 1865 encouraged Southerners to look upon President Johnson as their ally and protector. Forsyth believed that the South should "gratefully acknowledge that the conditions and requirements he [Johnson] has put upon the South are not in the main unreasonable."[23] Forsyth's positive disposition soon faced a challenge, however, when the Republican-dominated Congress, which had not been in session since the end of the war, returned to the nation's capital.

In the eight months between his ascension to the presidency in April of 1865 and the opening of the Thirty-ninth Congress in December, Andrew Johnson attempted to revive state governments in the rebel states and to convince Northerners that these governments were worthy of restoration. The state elections of 1865—which Forsyth found so gratifying—actually guaranteed the failure of the presidential phase of Reconstruction. Johnson himself sensed that something had indeed gone awry: "There seems in many of the elections something like defiance, which is out of place at this time."[24] Northerners found it difficult to accept the hasty return of high-ranking ex-Confederates (such as former Confederate Vice President Alexander H. Stevens—elected to the U.S. Senate from Georgia) to the halls of government. This apparent lack of remorse filtered down to the local level. For example, when Forsyth's brief term as mayor ended, Mobilians elected former Confederate general Jones M. Withers as his replacement.

Even before the elections, Forsyth reported that many of his Northern friends had warned him about the type of people the South should elect as national representatives. Forsyth rejected such advice, insisting that "either the South is to be represented in the legislative counsels of the Union or it is not." He went so far as to theorize that if the South sent men to Congress who agreed with the Radical plan, they could not be true representatives. The "true course" was to "send men to Washington who actually represented the interests and sentiments of the Southern people, and then leave it to time and the good sense and good feeling of the North to determine whether or not it was in earnest when it took up arms and waged dire war to preserve the Union." From the opening gavel of the Thirty-ninth Congress, it was abundantly clear that the Republican majority (three to one in both houses) had serious misgivings about President Johnson's accomplishments and the suitability of the new Southern representatives. Clerk of the House Edward McPherson omitted the names of the newly elected Southern congressmen as he called the roll. The Congress proceeded to establish a Joint Committee on Reconstruction to investigate actual conditions in the Southern states and decide if they deserved immediate representation.[25]

A brief examination of the makeup of the Republican Party in the Thirty-Ninth Congress is in order here. Although the Dunning school saw radical leaders such as Charles Sumner and Thaddeus Stevens as vindictive opportunists, each had a long record of championing civil rights issues dating back before the war. The radicals had a clear ideological position, which in 1865 featured the call for black suffrage. They also had definite views on Reconstruction. Stevens, for example, believed the South was no more than a conquered territory that Congress could govern as it saw fit. Sumner claimed the rebels had committed "state suicide" and had thus reverted to territorial status. It must be noted that the majority of Congressional Republicans were moderates, led by men such as Lyman Trumbull and John Bingham.[26] While often blamed by critics of Reconstruction for the perceived evils that befell the South, the Radicals never controlled either house of the national legislature.

During the first few months of 1866, the South did little to convince the Radicals of any sincere repentance. The Alabama state legislature, having abolished slavery, nevertheless passed legislation designed to keep the freedmen in virtual servitude. These laws collectively became the basis of Alabama's future

black codes. A vagrancy law serves as a representative example. Defining a va-
grant as a runaway, common drunkard, "stubborn servant," or "any person who
habitually neglects his employment," the law called for an unusually large fine
of fifty dollars. If unable to pay, the offender could be sentenced to jail or hired
out for as long as six months until settling the debt. Regardless of his professions of a changed heart, Forsyth did not hesitate to write that "the Caucasian
is bound to be, as heretofore, the ruling race in the land. This it will be, in spite
of fanaticism, civil rights, or even 'political equality.'"[27]

Forsyth and his fellow Southerners began to realize that Reconstruction was
about to take a decided turn for the worse. On 9 April 1866, Congress passed
(over a presidential veto) a civil rights act. The act designated all persons born
in the United States (except Native Americans) as natural citizens and spelled
out the rights to which they were entitled, regardless of race. Forsyth complained that the action of the Radicals indicated a "wreckless determination to
push the war upon the Constitution and upon the cause of justice humanity
and fraternity to the very knife." As offensive as the act might have seemed,
Forsyth lamented that he and other Southerners—unrepresented in Congress—
were "yet only spectators of the great struggle between the powers of good and
evil."[28] Unsure of the constitutionality of their act, and annoyed with presidential vetoes, the Republicans began work on the Fourteenth Amendment to the
Constitution. Passed by Congress on 13 July 1866, this amendment prohibited
states from abridging equality before the law, called for a reduction in representation in proportion to the number of *male* citizens denied suffrage, prevented former Confederate officials who, before the war, had taken an oath of
allegiance to the United States and then supported the Confederacy, from holding state or national office, and repudiated the Confederate debt.

One year after the end of the war, Forsyth reevaluated the Reconstruction
process to date: "Looking back twelve months to the close of the late war, we
can imagine what will occur to the common sense of posterity—the Confederate States were overwhelmed, subdued, exhausted, prostrate at the feet of the
conquerors. State sovereignty—the great question of the war—was gone—lost
beyond recovery. African slavery was abolished. All, absolutely all, the North
had contended for was in its grasp." The editor, who only a few months earlier
had praised the speedy and just process of Reconstruction, now complained
that, owing to the ill-will of the Radical-dominated Congress, "a few hundred years hence it will be a marvel that men should have been so blind or so
stupid as not to perceive at once that this [Johnson's plan] was the course de-

manded, not only by magnanimity, but by every consideration of consistency and of true policy."[29]

The congressional elections of 1866 became a referendum on the Radical program. As Eric Foner noted, "For the first time in American history, civil rights for Blacks played a central part in a major party's national campaign." Just before the election, Forsyth embarked on a trip to New York City. While there, he sent letters back to the *Register* in which he reported on what he felt was the political pulse of the nation. At first, he got the impression that the North, tired of Reconstruction, would soon cast out the Radical element of Congress. Forsyth believed that "the popular sentiment of the North is unmistakably in favor of the admission to Congress of the Southern representatives" and that "the Radicals must yield that question, or suffer defeat in the coming election." As he journeyed in the North, Forsyth apparently liked what he encountered. At one point he noted: "I came here doubting if the Northern mind was yet ready to perform this great duty of patriotism and generous fraternity, and whether sufficient time had yet elapsed to restore the moral tone and clear away the mists of passions engendered by the war. My doubts are now yielding to what I see and hear."[30]

Forsyth's original plan called for him to go to Chicago to be present at the unveiling of the new tomb of Stephen A. Douglas. Sickness, however, prevented this leg of the journey. Remaining in New York, he began to realize that his earlier optimistic perceptions were perhaps premature. On 4 September 1866, Forsyth wrote that "the Radical party is unscrupulous and desperate, and will halt at nothing to retain their ill-used power." The Mobile editor believed civil war once again threatened the nation. He solemnly concluded, "I am not sure that the hot fever that bounds in the pulse of the body politic can be cured without much blood letting. The death of the president, freely talked of, would be the signal for civil war in the North." Forsyth clearly distinguished the coming civil war from the recently ended conflict, stating, "We have had our sectional war; the next one will be a civil war, with the North for its field, and the government divided and the people arrayed against each other."[31]

Forsyth saw the Fourteenth Amendment as the defining issue in the approaching elections. He carefully noted that the New York newspapers all reported that a Republican Congress would insist on the congressional plan of Reconstruction, including the notorious amendment. Particularly galling in the proposed amendment was the provision that barred certain former Confederates (including himself) from holding office. According to Forsyth, acquiescence to such a scheme meant "we of the South are to sell out Lee and Johnston and our best and truest citizens to disenfranchisement as the price of the recognition of our claims." Back in Mobile, he continued his opposition: "It is one thing to be oppressed, wronged and outraged by overwhelming force. It is quite another to submit to voluntary debasement." According to Forsyth, a line must be drawn as to just how far the South could be counted on to cooperate. In a challenging tone, the editor stated "if the Radicals insist on disunion, let them have it in this way." As far as his personal support for the amendment, he made it clear that "my hand shall wither before casting any vote in that direction."[32] Between October of 1866 and the following January, all ten Southern state legislatures that considered the amendment rejected it by overwhelming majorities. Alabama's final vote was seventy-one to nine against ratification.

After the congressional elections strengthened the Radical majorities in both houses of the Congress, Forsyth realized that presidential Reconstruction was only a fading hope. One week after the November election, he bitterly lamented that "on the 6th of the present month, ten states out of twelve proclaimed at the polls that their prostrate enemy, who laid down his arms eighteen months ago, is not sufficiently punished or adequately humiliated to satisfy their magnanimous souls." The simple message of the election was that "the perils of a continued disruption are to be encountered for the purpose of giving the Radicals the control of the government." The forlorn editor concluded, "We of the South can do no more than to pray for our country. We have no voice in shaping its destinies."[33]

On 2 March 1867, the Republican Congress—now with a mandate in favor of its radical policy—passed the first of four major Reconstruction acts. This act divided the ten "unreconstructed" states into five military districts, each commanded by an army general. Alabama was placed (along with Florida and Georgia) in the Third District, under the command of Major General John Pope. The act also laid out steps by which the former Confederate states might reenter the Union. Each state would hold elections (with black participation) for a state constitutional convention. A new constitution would have to provide for black suffrage. The completed document would then have to be ratified by a majority of registered voters. The state legislature would also have to ratify the Fourteenth Amendment.

To Forsyth and his colleagues, the "Military Act" was "a blow at the honor of the people who have gone down with the conquered banner, and who have nothing left in their desolation but their honor to console themselves withal." Self-pity aside, Forsyth understood the ramifications of the congressional action—white Republicans and freedmen would soon choose delegates to a crucial state convention. This reality forced a temporary change in strategy. Forsyth and other state leaders tried to court the black vote by convincing them that it was in their best interest to vote with their former masters. To this end, the Democracy of Mobile held a meeting on 19 April 1867—attended by both blacks and whites. According to Forsyth's glowing report in the next morning's edition of the *Register,* the "moral" taught by the gathering was that "the citizens of Mobile, without distinction of race, are prepared to meet squarely in the face, the dispensations of Providence, and the decree of war and political necessity in the present emergency." Rather than be led astray by the Radicals, Forsyth felt it was time to "let Southern men, Black and White, take care of themselves and spit in scorn and contempt upon all intermeddlers who seek their own vile advancement by trafficking in bad blood between them."[34]

Forsyth's new-found philosophy obviously centered more on a spirit of paternalism and manipulation than any sincere concern for the freedmen. The editor wanted the black populace to know their proper place in society. Thus, a few days after the unity meeting, he reminded his readers that "while the labor of the colored man is useful to the White, and the country needs it to develop its prosperity, it is still not absolutely indispensable. However, the dependence of the colored man upon the White is immovable and absolute. It is a question of bread with him, for he cannot live without employment."[35] Regardless of the ulterior motives, the short-lived policy of race reconciliation failed to provide fruitful results. In Mobile, blacks flocked to the Republican Party and even formed Union Leagues in the port city. Relations between the races reached low ebb in May of 1867 with the infamous "Pig Iron" Kelley Riot.

After the passage of the Reconstruction Act, several Northern politicians embarked on Southern tours to promote the Radical cause and enlist freedmen into the Republican Party. One such pilgrim was Congressman William D. Kelley of Pennsylvania. Nicknamed "Pig Iron" due to his support for protection of the Northern iron and steel industry, Kelley arrived in Mobile on May 14, having already addressed groups in Memphis and New Orleans. Kelley delivered a speech at 8:00 p.m. at the corner of Royal and Government Streets in downtown Mobile—literally just outside of John Forsyth's residence. In the speech, delivered to a mostly black crowd estimated by one paper to be as large as four thousand, Kelley emphasized the need for unity among the sections of the country. According to Kelley, the nation had to forget past differences that had so recently provoked the tragic war. Then, as one historian noted, "having urged his audiences to bury evil memories of the past, he began to recount them." The *Register* described the speech as "injudicious, insulting, and incendiary." During the speech, white hecklers from the back of the crowd tried to shout down the guest from the North. Kelley, perhaps a bit over-confident roared back: "Fellow citizens, I wish it to be understood that I have the Fifteenth United States Infantry at my back [he actually had the Fifteenth Infantry *band* at his back]; and if they are not enough to protect a citizen in the right of free speech, the United States Army can do it."[36]

Accounts of what happened next vary, depending on the source. As the Mobile police (conspicuously absent during most of the speech) attempted to arrest the troublemakers, shots rang out. The *Register* reported that "of the firing we know very little except for the general testimony that it was done chiefly by Negroes, who appeared to have provided themselves with arms for the occasion." The local Republican newspaper, the *Nationalist* reported that "a dense crowd of White men rushed toward the spot. In a minute or two firing commenced about simultaneously *from the windows of Hon. John Forsyth's house* and the windows above Brooks auction store, and the n.e. corner of Government and Royal. The firing soon became general, and quite a number of men were killed or wounded." The *New York Times* printed an account of the riot on its front page: "A large majority of the shots were fired by Negroes, as but very few of the White people were armed."[37]

The charge that shots came from Forsyth's house received serious scrutiny. Two days after the riot, the *Register* reported that "it is very generally reported on the streets among the colored population that our Mr. Forsyth fired at Judge Kelley from the east window of his house, which overlooked the speaker's platform and the general scene of the meeting." Five black men gave sworn testimony that shots came from the window in question. A sketch of the incident in *Harper's Weekly* showed men firing from nearby windows toward the speaker's stand. Authorities later determined that Forsyth was in another part of town attending a concert during the entire incident. The *Register* and, later, probably with great disappointment, the *Nationalist* both reported this fact. Rumors persisted that shots indeed came from the residence but, if true, they came from someone other than John Forsyth. Forsyth's son Charles ultimately became a suspect.[38]

Mobilians realized that the riot played into the hands of the Radical propagandists. National attention and condemnation might precipitate a military crackdown. The city leadership quickly moved to repudiate the violence. Two days after the riot, another biracial meeting took place, which adopted the following resolution: "We deeply deplore the unfortunate occurrences which took place at said [Kelley] meeting, and desire to express in strongest terms our disapprobation of them; second, we are of the opinion that the disturbances at said meeting were wholly unpremeditated and the result of accidental excitement, to which all assemblages are subject; third, in our opinion, our people are not disposed to impede in any manner the free exercise of speech to all and every class of persons." Forsyth himself felt that violence should be rejected—by blacks. Placing the blame on "a few turbulent and disorderly colored men who had gone to the meeting prepared for violence," he also issued a thinly veiled warning: "The Freedmen are occupying a position of great risk. They are in danger of being held responsible, as a class, for the atrocious outrages committed by some bad men among them. It is for their own sake that we advise them promptly and boldly to repudiate all sympathy with the mischief makers."[39]

The military authorities responsible for keeping the peace in Mobile did not accept the late proclamations of unity and peaceful intentions. On 23 May 1867, General Swayne removed Mayor Withers and the Mobile Chief of Police. A few days later, he also removed the entire Board of Aldermen and Common Council, as well as several other local officials. Swayne replaced Withers with Gustavus Horton. Horton (who had introduced Kelley at the recent meeting/riot) was one of only about a dozen Mobile men who had remained openly loyal to the Union through the secession crisis, formation of the Confederacy, and unsuccessful war. Reaction to the dismissals was predictably mixed. The *Register* termed the events a "revolution, but unlike ordinary revolutions, it had its source in the exercise of arbitrary power and not in the popular voice." The *Nationalist* expressed jubilation over "the removal of our disloyal city officials and the appointment of loyal men," which was "the first serious blow struck at disloyalty in our midst."[40]

John Forsyth, one of the aldermen who lost his position, could not quite understand the logic of the move. After all, the last time General Swayne deposed a Mobile mayor, he personally requested Forsyth as the replacement. Since that time, the editor had received the presidential pardon and, in his own opinion, had been "a better loyalist to my country and bore a truer and holier allegiance to the spirit of constitutional liberty than any Radical is or can bear." He asked a simple question: "If I was fit to be Mayor in a moment of crisis and responsibility in General Swayne's opinion, and afterward was pardoned and swore fealty to the government, how does it happen that I am not fit now to hold the humble office of a city alderman?"[41]

Forsyth spent the rest of 1867 trying to muster opposition to the calling of a new state constitutional convention. General Pope set October 1–4 as the date for the people of Alabama to decide the question. Forsyth warned, "The worst thing that could happen to these states is the election of a convention under the Radical plan—for these conventions are the designed instruments for the overthrow of our state constitutions and the framing of others to fasten the yoke of political slavery upon the Whites, and to make renegades, adventurers, and Negroes the masters of State Governments." Despite the best efforts of Forsyth and his fellow Democrats, the enfranchised people of the state voted in favor of holding a convention. The results of the election (in which blacks went to the polls in Alabama for the first time) showed 90,283 votes in favor of a convention and 5,583 against; 71,730 of the winning votes belonged to the freedmen.[42]

Beginning a trend that carried on through the end of Reconstruction, Forsyth and his *Register* staff became more blatantly racist in their attacks on the freedmen. Forsyth claimed that in siding with the Republicans, the freedmen had "sold themselves to strangers, separated from the Whites of their own country, and paved the way for a train of fearful evils to themselves in the future." The former cooperationist saved his most harsh criticism for his old friend General Swayne. In one lengthy editorial, Forsyth recounted his early faith in Swayne, only to find out that the Ohioan "carried the heart of a Black Republican of the blackest hue." Furthermore, Swayne had "set himself up as the nigger king of Alabama, and has drilled and trained, banded, and leagued his subjects together, under his orders and the direction of his miserable tools, to the end of Negro supremacy."[43]

General Pope set 5 November 1867, as the opening day of the state convention. The *Register* refused to print the call. One hundred delegates (ninety-six Republican, of which eighteen were black) met to change the nature of Alabama's government. The debates in the convention brought a not-so-well-hidden secret out into the open. Most native-born white Republicans, while radical on political and economic issues, remained very conservative on matters of racial equality. The convention leaders received word from Northern Radicals (backed by Generals Pope and Swayne) to avoid any "extremist" measures that might alienate Northern public opinion. Thus the proposed Republican constitution did not include such "extreme" measures as disenfranchisement, debt relief, land distribution, or a call for social equality.[44]

The next step on the road to reunion was the ratification of the new constitution by the people of the state at large. This election was to take place on 4–7 February 1868. According to the rules set up in the Reconstruction Act, the constitution had to be approved by a majority of *registered* voters in the state.

Realizing that his side did not have the power to numerically defeat the "menagerie constitution," Forsyth promoted a new strategy—register but do not vote. The old party stalwart explained: "Unless a majority of all the registered voters is polled, the constitution will be defeated and we shall have escaped a great danger and calamity. The object, therefore, is to keep a majority out of the ballot boxes, so that if a man deposits his vote *against* the Constitution, he virtually votes for it, because his vote will be counted in making up the necessary majority of the registered voters which must go in the box to secure the ratification."[45]

A more serious aspect of Forsyth's plan involved threats and intimidation directed at potential black voters. Calling the canvass "the most important election ever held in Alabama," he stated that it was time for the colored man to "choose between carpet bag speculators and unknown strangers, and their own Southern White people." In strikingly plain language, the *Register* warned that "every colored man who votes in the election for the thing they call a constitution makes his record as an enemy of his white fellow citizens." In another issue, Forsyth threatened that "the colored man will know too, that an election is not a thing done in a corner or in the secrecy of a league meeting, but in open day and before the eyes of all men. Every vote cast will be known and noted down on paper. The watchful eye of the White people will be upon the election as it transpires, and every colored voter will make his mark by his ballot, whether he is a friend or an enemy of his White neighbors."[46]

By 1 February 1868, voter registration in the state stood at 75,000 whites and 95,000 blacks. The people *who voted* were overwhelmingly in favor of the new constitution—the final tally was 70,812 for, 1,005 against. Statewide, only 6,702 whites voted in the election. Since adoption of the constitution required 85,000 votes (a majority of the registered voters), the Radical document failed. Apparently, intimidation affected the black turnout, as only 62,194 of the registered blacks went to the polls.[47] Even though his side won, Forsyth, true to his word, published a list of blacks (and a few whites) who voted in the election. For several days the Register contained the following warning: "We reprint and mean to keep it standing until the whole community becomes familiar with it, the names of the White men who sanctioned by their vote the infamous scheme to place the White people of the state under the political domination of Negroes." One Northern newspaper, reporting on Forsyth's list, blasted the editor in the strongest possible terms. In its view, the *Register* was the "most infamous of all papers edited by the most infamous of all scoundrels." As for Forsyth himself, the writer noted that "During the war, no man in the South gloated with more fiendish satisfaction over the fall of the Constitution, and with it the country." The Republicans, however, won in the long run as Congress, on 11 March 1868, passed a new Reconstruction Act that stipulated that constitutions could be (retroactively) ratified by a majority of *votes cast*.[48]

National issues once more prompted Forsyth to leave Alabama. In March of 1868, the well-traveled editor again became a field correspondent—this time from the halls of the United States Senate. On 24 February 1868, the United States House of Representatives impeached President Johnson. Forsyth sat in the visitor's gallery and sometimes walked on the Senate floor during most of Johnson's Senate trial. Beginning on 27 March 1868, Forsyth sent almost daily reports of the proceedings back to the *Register*. At first, he appeared confident of a Johnson victory: "Those nearest the President, and in the best condition to be well advised, are still confident of acquittal. They say that they have counted votes, and know they can rely upon the necessary seven Republicans to stand for justice and law in their Senatorial oaths and consciences." Still in Washington a month later, his mood appeared much more somber. On April 22, with rumors of a possible Republican coup circulating through the capital streets, Forsyth noted the "all but universal feeling that the revolution now in progress will culminate in another domestic war—this time not a sectional, but a civil war." On May 11, with the trial nearing an end, the observer from Mobile thought in terms of military action. He actually turned to handicapping the chances of a successful Republican military takeover: "In the event of a *coup d'etat* to seize and hold the government by force, I do not believe the Radicals would have the active sympathy of the army, especially the rank and file. Anti-Negro is a powerful sentiment in the ranks of the army." Due to a postponement of the final vote, Forsyth left Washington three days before the Senate failed to get the necessary two-thirds vote for conviction.[49]

While in Washington, Forsyth got to observe two other significant proceedings. The first was the congressional debate over the readmission of Alabama into the Union. Congress finally passed the readmission act on 25 June 1868. The second event was a ceremony marking the third anniversary of the assassination of Abraham Lincoln. This latter event touched off one of his lengthy reflections. Regarding Lincoln, Forsyth correctly stated that "probably no man ever lived who is so idolized by one, and so execrated by another party by his countrymen." Lincoln's death, the editor continued, could have certainly been avoided "had he been able to grasp the political problem as it stood in the spring of 1861." Managing to put himself in the political equation, Forsyth, for the first time, hinted that had Lincoln played his cards right, the South would have come back into the Union by their own choosing. He theorized: "If when the Confederate Commissioners [of which he was one] were in this city in March and April of that year, the administration had said, through them, to the wayward sisters, depart in peace, the experiment of secession would have broken down, and a truce, with guarantees to the South then deemed satisfactory, would have been the result—the restoring of the Union without blood." Stopping just short of commending John Wilkes Booth (referred to by Forsyth as a "patriotic monomaniac"), Forsyth opined that "political assassinations can never be justified in the code of morals, but they are an inseparable accompaniment of revolution and the tyrannical use of usurped power in certain of their stages."[50]

To John Forsyth and other long-time Democrats, Alabama's new government must have seemed very foreign. Both of the state's new United States senators were Union Army veterans. The new state senate contained thirty-two Republicans and only one Democrat. The house had ninety-four Republicans (of whom twenty-six were black) and three Democrats. Forsyth referred to Alabama's Republican governor, William Hugh Smith, as one who "writes himself Governor of Alabama, but is no more governor than the King of Dahomey."[51]

As the summer of 1868 approached, Forsyth, for the first time in eight years, geared up his press for a national campaign. In May, the *Register* contained a call for a "convention of the representatives of the Democratic and Conservative people of Alabama, who are opposed to radicalism in all its shapes." The purpose of this convention was to select delegates for the Democratic National Convention scheduled for July 4 in New York. Forsyth served as a delegate from Mobile County to the state meeting and then traveled to New York for the national gathering. According to this veteran of countless party assemblies, it was "no exaggeration to say that no political assemblage was ever convened in the country upon which interest more vast and enduring depended." These were strong words from a man who had also been at Charleston and Baltimore in 1860. He continued: "The constitutional conservatism of the nation meets at New York to enter its solemn protest against the vandalism which for seven years past has been battering down the free institutions under which this country has prospered for nearly a century." Although Forsyth earlier voiced support for General Winfield Scott Hancock as the party's nominee, once the convention selected Horatio Seymour as its standard-bearer, the party loyalist concluded that the former New York governor was "the strongest and best nominee that could have been made." Before going their separate ways, the convention delegates rewarded Forsyth's long service to the party with an appointment to the nine-man executive committee of the national Democratic Party.[52]

The Northern press recognized the feelings of the Southern delegates that had come to Tammany Hall. Under the headline "The Line Drawn," a writer in *Harpers Weekly* noted that "the late rebels and their friends" were "engaged in devising some method by which to persuade the country to renounce the victory it won in the war, and to entrust the government to those who had done the utmost to destroy it." The author went on to comment that "John Forsyth, one of the most malignant of rebels, and now one of the chief Democratic leaders of Alabama, spoke of the late rebel state governments as 'overturned by revolution, tyranny, and the sword.'"[53]

The Republicans, in the meantime, held their convention in Chicago on May 20–21. To the surprise of no one, the assembly chose General Ulysses S. Grant as its nominee. During the early days of Reconstruction, Forsyth surprisingly had printed nothing but praise for the victorious Union commander. In December 1865, Forsyth noted that "from the moment that he overwhelmed Gen. Lee with the irresistible force of numbers, wielded by his indomitable will and untiring perseverance, he dropped the character of military conqueror and all his utterances have been those of a patriot and statesman, who saw that the sword had finished its appointed work, and the policy of conciliation was the duty of the hour." In fact, Forsyth hoped Grant—"a Democrat in political faith and education, and a conservative in sentiment and principles"—might one day lead the Democratic national ticket. In 1865, Forsyth asked an interesting question regarding Grant: "Where could the Democratic conservatives of the nation find a worthier leader, or the restored United States a more honest President?"[54]

Both of the major party nominees ended their acceptance letters with an appeal for peace and unity. On 29 May 1868, Grant pleaded, "Let us have peace," while Seymour, in August, believed a Democratic victory would "restore our Union" and "bring back peace and prosperity to our land." Amidst this talk of future peaceful harmony, Forsyth wrote one of the most reprinted and attacked editorials of his entire career. Under the heading "The Campaign," Forsyth (after an obligatory attack on the Radical Congress) laid out his views on the future course of the South should the Radicals win in 1868. According to the *Register* editor, "The people of the South do not intend to submit to that permanent [Radical] rule, result as the Presidential election may." He went on to claim that the South had "only submitted to its indignities and insults so far because they have been waiting for the good sense and justice of the American people to relieve them from it and restore them to their civil rights in the November election." Was Forsyth predicting, and even supporting, another civil war—much as he had done in 1856 and 1860? Many Northerners apparently thought so. *Harper's Weekly* quoted at length from the above-mentioned editorial to demonstrate the violent nature of the unreconstructed Southerners. Forsyth, facing a strong national backlash, quickly retreated. In a printed rebuttal to the *Harper's Weekly* accusations, the Mobile editor claimed he had been quoted out of context. Forsyth claimed he had been speaking only of a scenario in which the Radicals might fraudulently steal the election away from the Democrats. Many in the North refused to accept this explanation, so Forsyth spent much of the fall campaign responding to his national critics.[55]

Despite the war of words and a campaign of violence and intimidation in the South (particularly from a newly active Ku Klux Klan), General Grant handily won the national contest. Referring to the late election, a despondent Forsyth lamented that "the whole system of barbarities and cruelties embodied in the Reconstruction program for the Southern states was invented for a simple object, and that object was accomplished on Tuesday last. It was to retain the power of the federal government in the Radical hands." In the same editorial, he made what turned out to be a prophetic statement: "God's ways are wiser than men's ways. Who knows but the apparent success may not be the very rock upon which the infamous party of Radicalism will be wrecked."[56] Although the party would win more national elections, Grant's terms in office indeed provided the foundation for the collapse of the Republicans in the South.

After Grant's election, a noticeable change took place in the nature of the editorial positions taken by Forsyth and the *Register*. More and more, the politically minded editor began to focus on economic concerns. Historian Michael Fitzgerald has pointed out the degree to which Reconstruction policy on the local level was affected by economic concerns. Fitzgerald has also demonstrated how economic matters divided the political alliance system among both the freedmen and the whites. The Democratic leadership of Mobile appeared to be treading water when it came to financial matters—hoping that the Reconstruction program would soon run its course and go away, at which time they would reenter the fray. When President Johnson left office, the reality that the Republicans would be around, at least for the near future, set in. After the election, a Union soldier stationed in Mobile wrote to his wife that the citizens "have arrived at the conclusion that they had better begin attending to their business [rather] than spending their time and money on torch light processions."[57]

Certainly John Forsyth did not all of a sudden become a champion of economic causes. On the contrary, he had promoted economic endeavors his entire career. Since the early 1840s he had advocated the diversification of the Southern economy, internal improvements such as government funding for railroads, and a more equitable tax system. He consistently called on Southerners to throw off their dependence on foreign (including United States' Northern) imports through a better system of education and, ultimately, manufacturing. In the 1850s, he was a lonely voice calling for Mobilians to raise their property tax rates to support the infant public school system. For years he had pushed for the improvement of Mobile's port as a method of benefiting from the lucrative trade opportunities with Cuba and Mexico.[58] The 1868 shift was not an awakening to economic concerns but rather a change from promoting such concerns for the good of the community to a pursuit of personal financial gain.

Two factors most likely led to this new emphasis. First was the general economic condition of the region. Financial depression gripped large parts of the state. As one correspondent noted about Mobile, "Times are mighty hard here—no money and very little business doing. The merchants all look bland." Those "bland-looking" merchants certainly could not afford to spend part of their limited cash on *Register* subscriptions or advertisements. Having lost a good part of his prewar business, Forsyth was forced to branch out in his business ventures. The second, and more noticeable, factor was his association with William D. Mann. Mann, a former Union Army officer, arrived in Mobile in 1866 as an Internal Revenue assessor. Many Mobilians saw him as the prototypical carpetbagger. Mann was determined to use his position, combined with newly acquired political and social contacts, to bolster his already sizeable personal wealth. One of his business ventures involved newspapers. He bought the *Mobile Times* and actually loaned money to Forsyth to help keep the *Register* afloat. This financial association soon led to the merger of the *Times* and the *Register* with Mann as owner/publisher and Forsyth retained as editor. Here began several years of unbridled economic promotions. The only problem was that many of these promotions involved ventures in which Mann and Forsyth stood to make a tidy profit. The *Register* began to promote city subsidies for a variety of projects ranging from railroads to harbor improvements, from new wharves to gaslights.[59] One project was particularly illustrative of the degree to which Mann, Forsyth, and the *Register* could be accused of a conflict of interest—the ill-fated Nicholson Pavement project.

In June of 1870, Mann and Forsyth advocated a plan by which the city of Mobile would invest a half-million dollars to pave some of the major city streets. A technique patented as "Nicholson Pavement," whereby treated wood was placed on the street and covered with tar, was to be employed. The conflict in this project stemmed from the fact that there was only one company in Mobile that was equipped to undertake such a project—the Mobile Paving Company. The paving company had been incorporated in March of 1868 and granted permission to use the Nicholson method. Mann was one of the major stockholders, having invested ten thousand dollars, while John Forsyth had been elected as a company officer.[60]

Opponents of the project presented many arguments against what they saw as a special interest boondoggle. First, many wondered if the city, already committed to the Grand Trunk Railroad, the New Orleans and Mobile Railroad, and harbor improvements (all backed by Forsyth and Mann), could afford any more bonded indebtedness. Second, the quality of the Nicholson paving came into question. Reports from several other cities questioned the long-term durability of such a method. The final argument struck directly at Forsyth. One critic wondered why the editor, who for his entire career had opposed taxing people in one part of the country for the benefit of the other part (i.e., protective tariffs), did not hold to the same principle when it came to local government. The question was thus raised: "In what respect does unequal taxation by the federal government differ from unequal taxation by a city government?" The implication in this question was clear—Forsyth had changed his tune because he stood to reap a financial windfall if the project progressed. Forsyth, of course, could not let these charges go unanswered. He argued that the city could not afford to pick one of the projects over another. In fact, expenditures such as the one for the harbor improvements made other improvements even more necessary. Regarding the increased taxes, he claimed, "Everyman will be willing to pay when he understands what he would gain by it as a citizen of Mobile." As to the conflict of interest insinuation, the editor stated that he had actually refrained from writing as much as he desired about the project just for that reason.[61]

The city set June 11 as the date for a referendum on the paving project. During the two weeks before the vote, Forsyth more than made up for his "silence" on the subject. In one editorial, he gave a long list of all who should vote for the paving venture and why. The young men of the city were urged to support it because after the "present generation of barnacles" died out they did not want to live "an oyster shell existence in a dead city." Firemen, draymen, workingmen, real estate owners, and even members of the various Mardi Gras societies were likewise implored to vote in favor of the paving. He went on to ask the citizenry to "shun the examples of the old fogies, and stand up for the improvements, enterprise, and public spirit." Perhaps the height of irony came in his claim that the paving project would "help everybody and hurt nobody except those who want to stop the spigot of city public expenditures except when it is allowed to run into their pockets."[62]

Apparently enough "barnacles" did want to stop the spigot because the referendum failed by a vote of 3,960 to 1,370 (74 percent opposed). Bitter over the defeat, Forsyth lashed out, furious over the fact that "improvements, progress, and civilization have suffered another defeat at the hands of the do-nothings." One can almost feel the frustrations of a tired warrior who noted that he had "wasted his life in a city held down and back in the race of progress." In a hint of the aggressive vindictiveness to come, Forsyth also complained that the referendum had gone down in a humiliating defeat largely because of the mobilization of the freedmen vote.[63]

While continuing to be involved in a number of business ventures, Forsyth once again centered his main efforts on political matters. His main focus now centered on restoring white rule to the South. As early as the summer of 1869, cracks had begun to appear in the Radical armor. Two distinct events seemed to threaten both the rights of blacks and the dominance of the Radical Republicans in the South. First was the growth of the amnesty/reconciliation sentiment in the North and, second, was the capture of two Southern state governments (Virginia and Tennessee) by a coalition of conservative Republicans and Democrats. By 1870, Alabama had elected a Democratic governor and, in 1871, the Democrats regained control of Mobile's city government. In the local election, the Republicans did not even enter an opposition ticket. After the victory by default, Forsyth crowed: "We have not met the enemy, yet they are ours."[64]

The year of 1872 appeared to hold great promise for Forsyth and the South. The Republican regime found itself besieged from all sides. The party, once on the outside, now experienced the problems of a ruling faction long in power—ambitions, jealousies, and fractional divisions. Additionally, the sense of a common danger, so prevalent during and just after the war, began to subside. The wartime idealism faded as new issues demanded attention. Newer party members, more pragmatic and opportunistic, did not share in the basic Radical philosophy. Finally, President Grant himself proved to be a tremendous weight on the Radicals. Americans had expected greatness from Grant as president because they had found greatness in him as a general. Repeated scandals and policy failures left many Republicans disillusioned with the great war leader.[65]

Despite what appeared to be a promising scenario, the year 1872 may have been Forsyth's lowest point, both personally and politically. Personal tragedy struck the Forsyth family early in the year. On 13 March 1872, Charles Forsyth met a violent death in a Royal Street saloon. A lengthy coroner's investigation could only conclude that "the cause of death was a pistol shot wound from a hand to the jury unknown." In a fairly crowded bar, no witnesses could actually give evidence as to what happened. One witness even speculated that the death might have been a suicide. Expressions of sympathy poured in from across the South. The *Memphis Gazette* offered a typical word: "The death of Col. Charles Forsyth is a great loss to Mobile, especially to its commercial circles. To the venerable and beloved Col. John Forsyth, we extend our sincere sympathy under an affliction which earth affords no consolation."[66] Charles left behind his wife Laura and three young children, Charles Jr., Elizabeth, and Margaret.

Fortunately for Forsyth's mental state (but not his physical condition), the upcoming presidential campaign diverted his mind from his personal grief. On 8 May 1872, he attended a meeting of the Democratic National Committee in New York. The committee set July 9 as the date for the national convention to be held at Baltimore. While en route to New York, Forsyth learned of the nomination of Horace Greeley by an upstart Liberal Republican convention in Cincinnati. The Liberal Republican movement began in Missouri where a coalition of Liberal Republicans and Democrats wrested control of the state from the regular Republicans. In January of 1872, the Missouri Liberals issued a call for a nominating convention to meet in Cincinnati. The Liberals wanted an alliance with Southern conservatives on the basis of home rule and amnesty in return for a Southern promise to accept the Reconstruction amendments and to enforce the basic rights of the freedmen. Forsyth warned Democrats to have nothing to do with the Cincinnati convention. His logic was fairly simple. If some Republicans and Democrats worked together, the election would pit "Grant against the field." If his own party remained separate, it would result in a "unified Democracy against the Republican tickets." He invoked the memory of the 1860 election—except this time the roles would be reversed.[67]

The nomination of Greeley, editor of the *New York Tribune,* presented a complicated dilemma for the Democrats. According to the *New York World,* Greeley was "the most conspicuous and heated opponent of the Democratic party that could be found in the whole country." Another Northern newspaper reported "Greeley has spit and stomped upon every principle of the Democracy during his entire life."[68] Forsyth himself commented that Greeley was "the most pronounced enemy of the Democratic party." The ill feelings were mutual, as Greeley once made the statement that "all Democrats might not be rascals, but all rascals are Democrats." Despite his dubious track record, Greeley did have a few redeeming qualities to the Democrats. Although he had certainly supported Radical positions on the Fourteenth and Fifteenth Amendments, he had called for amnesty for former Confederate officials and for an end to military rule in the South. Greeley felt that Reconstruction governments had done all they could and it was now time for the freedmen to take up their own cause. Additionally, the Democratic leadership knew that if the Liberal Republicans and the Democrats promoted rival tickets, a Republican victory appeared certain. Any chance of denying Grant a second term depended on the unity of the opposition.

The controversy soon engulfed the ranks of the Democratic faithful. The national committee was torn over what course to take regarding the upcoming national convention. Many wanted to "fall into the unopened arms of Cincinnati Republicans" and immediately endorse the Greeley nomination. Others, including Forsyth, wanted to take no action until the Democratic National Convention. Forsyth was receiving advice from back home to go ahead and embrace the Cincinnati ticket. Some actually suggested that the Democracy should not even hold a national meeting. He rejected this counsel, instead expressing the belief that the action of the Cincinnati group had actually strengthened the hand of the Democrats in that it required the endorsement of his party in order to be successful. Forsyth expressed this opinion directly to Greeley in a private interview on 10 May 1872. In a frank discussion, he told the New York editor, "The South would go for him, if we could do no better, to beat Grant; but we thought we could do better and were going to give it a fair trial." Since this was the first time he had personally met Greeley, Forsyth could not resist giving his readers a personal evaluation. He thought Greeley had in him "the stuff to make a 'bully' Democrat could we get him in proper training." He also felt it a shame that his Northern counterpart had not been born in the South because Greeley probably "would have slept with a cockade in his night cap and . . . been a 'red-hot' before-breakfast secessionist."[69]

The light-hearted personal reflection notwithstanding, Forsyth was greatly concerned over what he saw as a premature rush to "Greeleyism." His main concern appeared to be over the timing of the move: "If we do not wait for Baltimore to speak, we shall be cut up and shorn of our balance of power strength before the polling commences." Again, with what he saw as simple political logic, he pondered: "If a Democrat in Alabama may break ranks and run after Greeley, why may not a Democrat in Indiana . . . break ranks and run after Grant." To those who felt Greeley was the only possible candidate with national appeal, Forsyth once again suggested that General Hancock, who, in his words, was "the only great soldier who, when the war ended, remembered that the military was subordinate to the civil powers," would make a stellar choice.[70]

Forsyth returned to Mobile on 4 June 1872, but two weeks later journeyed back to New York, forgoing the Alabama State Democratic Convention. Before leaving, the editor wanted to make sure his views on Greeley received proper circulation. Questioning the wisdom of his own party, he believed the Democrats were squandering a great opportunity. He noted, "The late split in the Radical party *had* opened an opportunity for a brilliant victory by the Democratic party on its own broad and ancient principles, and with its own statesmen as candidates leading to that victory. We use the word *had* opened. But we do not believe that the path is *now* opened." In a rare moment of harsh public criticism of his beloved party, Forsyth complained that "the Democratic party has the numerical force but no longer the courage and the confidence to win victory single-handed." Again thinking back to 1860, Forsyth wanted the Democrats to, this time, stand firm over a divided Republican Party. His fear was that Greeley's nomination had the potential to do just the opposite. In words that would be difficult to revise, he wrote: "The *Register* is unalterably against Greeley, because as a representative of the great idea symbolized by the Cincinnati Convention, he is a dead failure, and if we follow him, we follow him to defeat and disgrace."[71]

This bold pronouncement opened him up to much scrutiny and ridicule. On 21 June 1872, he was in New York as one of the national Democratic leaders summoned to the so-called Fifth Avenue Hotel Conference. After several hours of debate, someone got the idea to poll each state to ascertain representative views. With Alabama being the (alphabetically) first state, Forsyth had to break the ice. Incredibly, he voiced what seemed to be enthusiastic support for the Greeley ticket. Newspapers from around the country had a field day at the Mobilian's expense. The *Paducah Kentuckian* (described by the *Register* as a "cheeky little paper") perhaps best asked the question on everyone's mind. Directly quoting his June 18 editorial, the Kentucky paper noted that "On June 20th, only two days later, the editor of the *Register,* Col. John Forsyth, is reported to have spoken at the Fifth Avenue Conference in favor of the Liberal movement, endorsed emphatically the Cincinnati ticket and platform, and pledged Alabama for Greeley and Brown by a large majority. Will the *Register* rise and explain?" A more prosaic version came from the *St. Louis Republican.* Under the heading "An Ancient Mariner Foundered," the Missouri newspaper waxed eloquently: "If any man doubts the strength of the political current now sweeping over this country and tossing the pure fabrics of politicians, let him note the ease with which it twirled the most stalwart of the old Democratic elements. While Col. John Forsyth was in New York attending the meeting of the Democratic National Committee, and trying to fend off the rising gale of Greeleyism by frequent letters to the New York press and to his own journal, the *Mobile Register,* the latter yielded to the prevailing influence and headed straight for the peaceful Horatian heaven."[72] Back home, a clearly embarrassed Forsyth could only defend his inconsistency by stating that he spoke for himself on June 18 and not for the state.

The Democratic National Convention did indeed nominate Greeley and also adopted the Cincinnati platform verbatim. Forsyth endorsed the nominee as the only way Southern votes would be "recorded against the radical administration" and because "between Grant and almost any nominee of the Democratic party, it cannot hesitate to choose." However, for the only time in his career, Forsyth openly rejected his party's platform, stating, in his opinion, that it contained "principles enunciated that we cannot conscientiously subscribe to even at the bidding of a Democratic convention." Although he did pledge to support the ticket, one can sense that it was to be a half-hearted effort. While he publicly promised to "take a stand by our Democratic brethren," he wanted his readers to know that "for the future of this course, we are free from responsibility."[73]

Forsyth did not attend the 1872 Democratic National Convention (the first such meeting he had missed since 1848—excepting the war years). Nearing age sixty, the editor was beginning to feel the physical strain of many personal and political battles. While the national convention was in progress, the *Register* printed the following notice: "Sunday night's train over the Mobile and Ohio Road once more carried our Editor-in-chief away from his post; this time for a protracted absence in the mountains of Virginia and other health-giving resorts. The unceasing strain and excitement of long political editorship have rendered Col. Forsyth temporarily unfit for duty at his desk." The ailing journalist did not return to Mobile until a week before the November election. The long silence seemed to underscore the lack of enthusiasm he felt for the Democratic ticket. In his own words, he returned "in the last days of the most momentous political conflict that has ever been fought on American soil."[74]

After the disastrous defeat in which Grant won 56 percent of the vote (the highest percentage for any candidate between 1828 and 1904), carried all but six of the Southern states, and led the Republicans to reclaim their two-thirds majority in the House and hold to a similar margin in the Senate, Forsyth could only wonder, "Have we a Republic?" He could also not resist pointing out that "We thought we saw something pretty clearly at the beginning of the late political flood [of support for Greeley], and it turns out that, in a measure at least, we did." He also somewhat sarcastically remarked that "nothing is more odious than the 'I told you so.'"[75]

The dejected journalist began to vent his pent-up frustrations and concerns. "The real defeat of the election is not of Mr. Greeley. It is a defeat of republican principles, a defeat of free government, a defeat of reconciliation between the States, a defeat of integrity and responsibility in the administration of the Federal Government." The election also seemed to unleash some of Forsyth's most virulent racial language. The defeat was the result of what happened "when 800,000 dummies were admitted to the ballot box." The freedmen, the "blind instruments of power," knew "just as little about the objects and efforts of their votes as so many oxen and mules." In a bitter conclusion, he complained "the Blacks were given the ballot to sustain the Radical party—to be its slaves—just what they are."[76] For John Forsyth, the first seven years after the war represented a personal low point. Political and financial disasters as well as personal grief sapped much of the spirit and strength out of the aging journalist. Although he would not live to see another Democratic president, his financial situation would continue to worsen, and he would never fully regain his health, one last zenith—the "redemption" of Alabama and the national Congress was approaching.

Conclusion

"We Never Doubted Where John Forsyth Stood"

The year 1873 marked the start of the decline of John Forsyth's editorial prominence. His health, which troubled him in the latter part of the previous year, never completely recovered. The ailing journalist increasingly found himself away from his beloved post. At the advice of his doctor, Forsyth, in the late spring, embarked on a trip to Europe. This journey, his first trip across the Atlantic since he had traveled as a boy with his father, was designed to get Forsyth away from the stress of the daily operation of the newspaper. In the editor's own words the respite would "give rest to a pate that has been used as a football so many years in the *Register* office." Apparently his physician had given him strict orders as to what he should and should not do while away. In one of his first letters home, he noted that while on the trip, he was "forbidden to think as well as to smoke."[1] Forsyth sent home a series of reports while on his European tour. His accounts were to be done "without strenuous effort," which would have defeated the trip's purpose. Thus the *Register* subscribers read about the style of dress in Liverpool ("Few Americans and certainly no Frenchmen would fail to observe the bad taste of women's dressing"), various public and private events, landscapes, and architecture. The vacationing journalist also gave his opinions on various aspects of life in London, Paris, Berlin, and Vienna.

Try as he might, Forsyth was not one who found it easy to relax. At every stop he seemed to be reminded of some issue or controversy he had left behind on the other side of the Atlantic. When he observed the neatly paved streets of even the smallest European towns, he could not resist a dig at Mobile: "I have not seen a town, great or small, since I left home that is unpaved. I am inclined to think that there is no town or city the size of Mobile in the civilized world that has not had the enterprise and good sense to consider health and comfort and beauty in covering its streets with some kind of pavement." When he saw the prevalence of industrial development between Paris and Berlin, he noted,

"I begin to entertain even a lively hope that somewhere within the next ten centuries our own slow little gulf city may feel the impulse of the steam genius of our age, and take step with the march of its generation."[2]

Certainly Reconstruction politics were never far from Forsyth's mind. While listening to a patriotic rendition in a London opera house, he could not help but ponder his own "political disabilities." He remorsefully noted that "It was not a little troubling to a poor devil to whom flag and country had been deprived by an act of a Radical Congress." While in Europe, he periodically received copies of the *Register*. Often, after such deliveries, he would go off on a tirade in reaction to what he had read. One such issue contained a call for immigrants to come to the South. Forsyth penned a response in which he stated he felt immigration "contains the germ of Southern rehabilitation in prosperity and power." Of course by immigration he, in effect, meant white, northern Europeans, who would "assure the preservation of the White civilization of our state, and to stay the tendency, backed by the force of Federal influences, to a enervated and accursed mongrelism." One illustration seems to perfectly typify Forsyth's futile attempt to unwind while on the grand tour. In September, he was on a train en route to Vienna. As the sun came up, he got his first glimpse of the beauty of the Austrian Alps. At about the same time, someone informed him that a fellow passenger in the next car had a fairly recent edition of the *New Orleans Picayune*. Forsyth jumped from his seat and literally ran to find the gentleman. For the next couple of hours, he "devoured the '*Pic*' and left the Alps for a more convenient season." Forsyth began the return voyage on 18 October 1873. He was reported to be in New York on the last day of the month. He pronounced a somewhat ambivalent benediction on the entire experience: "I have seen a good deal, and learned some things, I hope, and having come, I am glad that I came. But I am satisfied not to repeat the visit." Apparently the trip did not fulfill its purpose as the *Register*, in November, noted that, "Owing to extreme fatigue incident on a long trip," Forsyth would be out of the office for a while longer.[3]

Although clearly no better physically, when Forsyth returned to the states he was temporarily bolstered by what he sensed was a revolution in the political currents. Before returning to Mobile, he traveled from New York to Milwaukee. While there, he was present for an election in which "the Radicals heard thunder and smelled brimstone all along the borders of Wisconsin." The state Democratic Party regained the governorship and the state legislature. Forsyth saw this as a sign that "signalized the broken power of a nightmarish party." He used this victory as an opportunity to lecture those who, he felt, had sold out the Democrats in the last presidential election. "When a political party throws down its flag and fears its own principles, it confesses its failure and deserves to become what it makes itself."[4]

Even though the Radical Republicans fared well in the 1872 presidential and congressional elections, momentum clearly began to shift away from their cause. Several reasons explain this phenomenon. First, the national debate of 1872 succeeded in articulating and advertising the idea of reconciliation. Some Radical editors actually praised timid enforcement of the new Reconstruction measures as "discretion and forbearance." Reconciliation between the sections took precedence over reconciliation between the races. Second, the Radicals appeared to lose their political nerve when it came to the freedmen. As one historian noted, "the cause of the Negro seemed to appeal more to people's sense of drama when the blacks were yet to be bought and sold than when they were involved in politics and patronage." Black suffrage, according to Forsyth, had "enabled the Radical party to hold the power of the Federal Government in its hands for a few years." However, he continued, by 1874, it was the "retributive force that is pulling down about Radical hands the political structure it helped to build up."[5]

As the 1874 state and congressional off-year elections drew near, the Democrats in Alabama smelled the blood of a wounded opposition. Forsyth and his *Register* staff determined to pull no punches to make this campaign a success. One almost gets the idea that Forsyth—his health now noticeably failing—realized this campaign might be his last. On 4 July 1874, the *Register* announced the kick-off of the summer and fall campaign season. Under the headline "To Your Tents White Men," Forsyth issued a call for a "Democratic, Conservative, and White Man's Convention of Mobile County," to be held on July 14. The purpose of the meeting was to select delegates for a state Democratic convention. During the campaign, his columns became more openly hostile to black citizens than ever before. In the aforementioned July 4 editorial, Forsyth recruited "all upon whom nature has conferred a white face and a white blood to be defended from the contamination of miscegenation, and the damning disgrace of subordination to race inferiority." Even more blatantly racist was his urging that "all turn out and answer to the roll call of White supremacy over the black monkey mimics of civilization." The *Register* published large advertisements for the coming county convention under the headlines of "Let White Men Unite" and "White Men Should Govern the State."[6]

The state convention assembled on 29 July 1874, in Montgomery. The delegates concerned themselves with three items of business. First, the conclave nominated General George S. Houston as the Democratic candidate for governor. Second, candidates were nominated for two at-large congressional vacancies. Since west Alabama had no representation, the body named Burwell B. Lewis of Tuscaloosa to fill one of the positions. In the agreed-on system of rotation, Mobile normally would have received the nomination for the other spot, but two names were presented from the city—John Forsyth and C. C. Langdon. On the first ballot, Forsyth received twenty-five votes to Langdon's seven. Forsyth asked that his name be taken out of consideration, but on the second ballot, he garnered an increased vote total. This split among two Mobile candidates paved the way for the defeat of both and guaranteed that Forsyth would never sit in the United States Congress. The body elected General William H. Forney of Calhoun to the remaining seat.[7]

The third item of business—the adoption of a state platform—went off more smoothly. As Forsyth stated, "In the present aspect of Southern politics, the one overwhelming need of release from Negro government is so absorbing a question, that it is not easy to think of any other." The convention delegates did not spend much time in divisive debate because, as Forsyth observed, "when a man's dwelling is in flames, the paramount interest of the moment is to save it from destruction, and all questions of its subsequent economy are intuitively postponed for a calmer occasion."[8]

On August 18, Mobile's Democracy gathered across from Bienville Square for a large ratification rally. The *Register* contained a description of the lively scene: "Long before 8 o'clock a dense crowd assembled around the stand, and was constantly augmented by the arrival of club after club, with nearly every member on the roll in its ranks. Several transparencies, with appropriate and inspiring transcriptions, were seen in the long line as it rapidly moved to the place of assemblage. Barrels of tar, torches, fireworks, and other modes of illumination were displayed along the streets." County Democratic committee chairman Price Williams nominated Forsyth to serve as president of the meeting. Forsyth made the opening address and, according to one account, "although he said he was physically unable to speak, he made one of his most telling speeches." In the oration, Forsyth spoke of a revived Democracy and the "glad tidings of Democratic victories." He went on to recount Radical shortcomings and confidently predicted a November victory.[9]

The next step in the redemption process was another Mobile County Democratic meeting—this time to nominate a slate of candidates for local and state offices. Although he was obviously in poor physical health by this time, the assembly elected Forsyth as one of its nominees for the state legislature. Surprisingly, Forsyth accepted the nomination. The local Democracy held yet another ratification meeting/celebration. At this gathering, Forsyth made one of his last public speeches for the cause of the Democratic Party. According to one observer, the aging editor was "met with a rousing and gratifying reception, several minutes having elapsed before the cheering and demonstrations of those present had sufficiently subsided for him to proceed." Forsyth took this opportunity to defend his long record as a Democrat and to once more lash out at the Republican Congress. On the former issue, Forsyth, perhaps weary of people questioning his party loyalty, recounted his many years of party service and sarcastically commented that he "thought about asking some gentleman to give him a certificate showing that he, the speaker, was a Democrat." Regarding the latter issue, Forsyth observed that "since the Southern representatives were driven from the Congress of the United States, that body has been adopting injudicious and tyrannical measures." Furthermore, he concluded, "The North does not know enough of liberty to govern well."[10]

Forsyth could not physically take part in the last two months of the campaign. In October 1874 illness again forced him to take a leave of absence from his editorial duties. On October 20 the *Register* reported that he was "gradually gaining strength" and (expressing confidence in a November victory) "will doubtless be ready to take his seat in the General Assembly in a few weeks." One negative bit of information came out regarding Forsyth during the campaign. The *Register* noted a rumor that "some persons will not vote for John Forsyth for the legislature because that gentleman, when Mayor, allowed Negro evidence in his court."[11] Even Forsyth's long advocacy of Southern causes during nine years of Reconstruction did not win forgiveness from some "unreconstructed" Mobilians.

During the last week before the election, the Mobile Democracy could scarcely control its glee. By now aware of Democratic triumphs in other parts of the nation, the time of Alabama's redemption seemed close at hand. On 31 October 1874 (Forsyth's sixty-second birthday), the city of Mobile witnessed jubilant demonstrations on the corner of Government and Royal Streets. This location—the same as the Kelley Riot seven years earlier—placed the excited mobs just outside of the house in which the ailing Forsyth remained bedridden. Under the glare of Roman candles and sky rockets, a long procession of "honest White men" paraded down Government Street. One large sign read "For the *Register*, the White man's paper." At least one sign proclaimed "For Col. John Forsyth."[12] The Democratic leadership around the state realized they had the necessary votes to oust the Republicans.

John Forsyth could not have been emotionally prepared for the results of the November 3 election. Large headlines in the *Register* the day after the tally proclaimed, "The Strike For Freedom," "White Supremacy Sustained," and "The White Men as a Unit." The lead editorial triumphantly noted that "the returns from all parts of the Union show great gains for the Democratic party," and "it appears that the Democratic and Conservative ticket [including Forsyth] is elected by a handsome majority." The news from other states was just as "glorious." Massachusetts, South Carolina, New York, Florida, Louisiana, Pennsylvania, Virginia, and Georgia all experienced great Democratic victories.[13]

As the dust settled, Forsyth and the Democrats truly reveled in their good fortune. Several facts from the late elections bore out the devastating nature of the Republican Party's first great catastrophe in their twenty-year history. The Democrats captured the United States House of Representatives for the first time since the beginning of the Civil War. A Republican majority of 111 became a Democratic majority of 79. The new House contained 182 Democratic and 103 Republican members. Long excluded from the deliberative body, the Confederate leaders returned with a vengeance. Of the 107 House members elected in the new Southern or border state delegations, 80 had served in the Confederate army—including 35 former Confederate generals.[14] In the Senate, the Democrats cut the Republican majority in half. Nationwide, the Democrats won 19 gubernatorial races.

Forsyth pronounced his own benediction on Reconstruction: "In the new light of deliverance and of blessed liberty that has dawned upon the people, the *Register* wishes to propose two questions: First—IS THERE A DEMOCRATIC PARTY IN THE UNITED STATES? Second—Have not the people endured enough of contumely humiliation, wrongs, public devastation and private impoverishment to say to the carpet-bag emissaries and incendiaries of Radicalism and their leading domestic abettors 'THUS FAR SHALT THOU GO AND NO FARTHER'?" Forsyth, who never doubted the correctness of his own course of action, noted with satisfaction that "the State of Alabama is Democratic in every branch, and that the people of the United Sates are at last come to their senses."[15]

After the election of 1874, John Forsyth quickly disappeared from the public eye. He did make a brief physical recovery, as the *Register* of November 21 reported that the "Hon. John Forsyth left the city last night for Montgomery to take his seat in the Legislature." On November 24, Forsyth made an appearance in the lower chamber. One legislative correspondent described Forsyth as "the only member of the House who has a national reputation" but whose "feebleness at the time may prevent his taking an active part in the discussions of the House." The house membership offered Forsyth the position of speaker "as a slight recognition of his life-long service in the cause of the principles of his party and the defense of the people of the state."[16] Although declined due to the "feebleness of his health," this offer must have brought great satisfaction to Forsyth, who, in his first stint in the state legislature, had been routinely referred to as a "Douglas traitor." Forsyth had indeed won the appeal of time.

Forsyth's health continued to decline after 1874. Rarely was his name mentioned on the pages of the *Register* nor was he listed in the numerous local and state Democratic gatherings. In 1875, his doctors pronounced him on the verge of "nervous prostration" and ordered "total cessation of all mental labor." Forsyth turned over the sole charge of the paper to Thomas Cooper DeLeon and abandoned the office for an extended rest. Many editorials attributed to Forsyth during this period were actually penned by DeLeon, who noted, "The most enjoyed compliment ever paid me by the press anywhere, was its copying my editorials and their ascription to him [Forsyth]." Forsyth stayed away for nearly a year and then briefly returned to Mobile. According to DeLeon, Forsyth had "lost all his fire and much of his zest for his loved game—politics."[17]

One last controversy marred Forsyth's final months at the *Register*—one that dealt not with politics, but finances. In the decade after the end of the war, the *Register* changed ownership four times. In 1870, William D. Mann was forced to sell the business to Isaac Donovan in order to settle an outstanding debt. In 1872, Donovan was caught in the same trap. Having made a bad investment in Grand Trunk Railroad bonds, he likewise had to give up sole ownership of the enterprise. A business corporation under the name of the Register Printing Association (with Donovan as president) assumed control. In 1874, Forsyth, who had been retained as editor-in-chief during each of these transfers, became co-owner of the *Register* for the last time. Forsyth formed a partnership with John L. Rapier to publish the newspaper under the name "Forsyth and Rapier."[18]

The business continued to struggle financially. Forsyth complained, "Southern people do not sustain their newspapers as it is in the popular interest to do." After the Panic of 1873, many Southern newspapers indeed went out of business. The *Register*, while still acclaimed across the South for its strong editorial stands, struggled mightily to stay financially solvent. A final embarrassment came to Forsyth in the form of a lawsuit filed against him by his partner, Rapier. In April of 1876, Rapier filed a complaint in the Mobile Chancery Court that brought several charges against the senior partner. Rapier claimed that in 1874, just after he and Forsyth agreed to a partnership plan, Forsyth announced plans to go to New York to accept a job with another newspaper. Apparently, some of Forsyth's "political friends" talked him out of the move by promising to raise six thousand dollars to invest into the *Register*. With this financial backing supposedly assured, Rapier signed on to the partnership. The promised funds never materialized, but the *Register* and its owners limped ahead for the next two years. In the suit, Rapier contended that while he had invested over twenty-eight hundred dollars of his own capital into the company, "Forsyth, in fact had no money and could only contribute his skill and talents as an editor." Although he certainly recognized that Forsyth was the main drawing card of the paper, his "skill and talents" alone could not hold off the *Register*'s numerous creditors. Rapier asked the court to dissolve the partnership and appoint a receiver to handle the business end of the company until the debts could be paid. On 25 April 1874, the court issued a subpoena ordering Forsyth to appear in court.[19]

Forsyth wasted little time in responding to the charges. The promise of the funds was never, in his opinion, a precondition of the partnership agreement. Additionally, he felt that the *Register* had made enough money over the previous two years (according to his estimate, at least eight thousand dollars per annum) to pay the bills. He blamed Rapier, who as business manager "has had entire control of the books, receipts, and expenditures." With better business oversight, the company should have not only have satisfied its creditors, but "left a large surplus as profits."[20]

On May 17, the court dissolved the two-year-old partnership. In addition, the presiding judge appointed Joseph Hodgeson to act as receiver over the liquidation of assets. The *Register* was basically bankrupt and Forsyth's dream of owning the newspaper was once again crushed. Creditors rushed forward to demand their share of the soon to be liquidated property. The Gulf City Paper Company led the way with an outstanding claim of five thousand and thirty-five dollars. Forsyth and Rapier both realized that even during this difficult time, there was no way to ever balance the ledgers unless the *Register* stayed in business. All during the Chancery proceedings, the proud journal never missed an issue. Perhaps aware that they were reaching the point of no return, Forsyth and Rapier entered into some type of negotiations. On June 29, the former partners signed a paper that stated, "The proceedings in Chancery now pending . . . may be dismissed, as they have arrived at a satisfactory settlement of their partnership affairs out of court." The court accepted their decision and vacated all its previous orders and dismissed the immediate claims of the various creditors.[21] Rapier and Company, with Forsyth retained as editor, would publish the *Register.* John L. Rapier owned the newspaper until his death in 1905. He spent most of next decade trying to straighten out the financial plight of the business. Forsyth's editorial career now existed in name only. Although the *Register* masthead proudly bore his byline, the old editor was seldom present. Once more seeking rest and solitude, he journeyed to the western Alleghenies, but, in the spring of 1877, obviously near death, abruptly returned home.

John Forsyth died on 2 May 1877. The *Register* of the next day (its columns draped in black) printed a lengthy obituary. Retracing Forsyth's career, the article concluded that the late editor, "stricken down by the insidious enemy, disease, spent his last strength in battling with Alabama's foes; and stretched upon the field he helped to win, was cheered by the cry of victory, bore to his ears." At 10:30 a.m. on May 4, Forsyth's body was taken from his residence to the Christ Church where "a large congregation of Mobile citizens was assembled to testify by their presence, their love and respect for the honored dead." Rev. A. J. Drysdale read the Episcopal burial service. After the singing of "Rest Spirit Rest" (reportedly Forsyth's favorite hymn), a funeral cortege traveled to the Magnolia Cemetery where the final interment took place. In an fitting twist, the Alabama Press Association convention happened to be meeting in Mobile when Forsyth died. The entire group attended the funeral to pay final respects to its most distinguished member.[22]

For the next several days, the *Register* reprinted tributes to Forsyth that had appeared in newspapers across the nation. The *New York Sun* reported that "for a whole generation his name has been familiar among the journalists of the country; he has been regarded as a leader by a large portion of the Southern press, and he has often exercised a measure of control over popular opinion and in matters of policy that no other Southern editor has equaled since the days of Father Ritchie." The *Atlanta Constitution* noted that "Colonel Forsyth was not only what is technically called a fluent and vigorous writer, but genius added to observation imparted to his style a classical brilliancy not often found in editorial writing." Referring to the recent end of Reconstruction, the *New York World* stated, "His loss will be sincerely felt; but he lived to see the victory of justice and the law, and to know that the land he loved was reaping the harvest of his unfaltering fidelity to her best interests." Even his old adversaries at the *Montgomery Advertiser* admitted, "His loss will be keenly felt not only in the state, but throughout the Union where he was so well and favorably known. For to his marked ability he added great personal worth and a high character for integrity and devotion to principle."[23]

Forsyth's fame quickly faded. On 31 October 1912, the city of Mobile recognized the centennial of his birth. After several speeches and resolutions, the crowd dispersed and John Forsyth's name once again vanished from the public consciousness. As one historian later noted, "John Forsyth was one of the more notable Southern journalists of the nineteenth century. Probably no man in the history of Alabama devoted more energy to what he determined the political and economic course the state should follow—only to be forgotten in the process." This assertion is basically correct, as modern history texts rarely mention the Mobile editor. The most recent, comprehensive textbook on Alabama history has only two (one-sentence) references to Forsyth—as Douglas's campaign manager and, later, as a commissioner to the Lincoln administration. Perhaps one example best typifies the historical amnesia regarding Forsyth. A recent article about Mobile's Magnolia Cemetery highlighted prominent citizens buried within its grounds. The article (properly) listed Braxton Bragg, former Alabama governor John Gayle, and author Augusta Evans Wilson, among others. John Forsyth was nowhere to be found on the list. The sad irony of this omission was that it came on the front page of the *Mobile Register*.[24]

Forsyth's contemporaries often expressed the idea that he did not receive just recognition. In 1872, the *Montgomery Advertiser* stated "there is no position the state could confer upon him that he would not richly deserve for long, exacting, and important service in the most arduous and responsible of all professions." Two years later, the *Tuscaloosa Times* claimed, "he has rendered long, faithful, and splendid service to the South, and to the cause of the party of which he is a leading ornament and support. He deserves recognition at the hands of the party, for his fidelity and valuable services, and will adorn by his talents and virtue, any office within its power to bestow." The *Montgomery Advertiser* once concluded about Forsyth, "we trust the day may yet come when Alabama may have it in her power to manifest her appreciation of his abilities and high character."[25] Since over 125 years have passed since Forsyth's death, and the day for which the *Advertiser* wished never arrived, what then is the final evaluation of John Forsyth? Any such assessment must weigh both the criticisms and praises heaped on Forsyth by his contemporaries.

His numerous critics usually based their concerns on one of three issues—family connections, personal motivations, or political causes. The longest lasting criticism centered on his illustrious family ties. Dating back to his editorial beginnings in 1837, Forsyth had to constantly answer the charge that he was the son of privilege, living off of the name of his famous father. Even death could not free him of this association. Nearly every obituary notice printed in out-of-state newspapers began with the obligatory reference to John Forsyth Sr. Some, like the *New York Herald,* could not help making a final comparison of the two men: "The son inherited much of the talent of the father, though without the readiness of the elder for public speaking."[26] Throughout his lifetime, John Forsyth Jr. never repudiated or spoke unfavorably about his father, yet at the same time, he made a conscious effort to seldom invoke his family name, even when doing so would have been to his advantage. This may explain why Forsyth rarely mentioned anything about his own immediate family. In forty years of editorial writing, one is hard pressed to find even a passing comment concerning his wife or children. An exception is when, on more than one occasion, he wrote in defense of his son Charles. While it is true that Forsyth's first public office came as a favor from Andrew Jackson to his father, his subsequent positions came as a result of personal merit or at least as political favors earned through his own efforts. The charge that his father set him up in the newspaper business also appears unfounded as John Forsyth Sr. held little esteem for the journalism profession in general. The newspaper venture may actually have been the not so hidden attempt of an ambitious son to distance himself from his famous father.

The second criticism, at first glance, appears more serious. Many felt that Forsyth used his newspaper merely for political and/or economic gain. Indeed, a few weeks after his death, one of his political associates commented, "The editorial profession was with him not a chosen and darling vocation, but merely a means to an end, and that his goal was political office." This writer also noted, "No professional journalist ever showed less penchant for composition." This charge seems very odd when one considers the context of the day. Criticism of a nineteenth-century editor for being a partisan politician is much like faulting a priest for being overly religious. From his first day at his desk until he took his last breath, John Forsyth never claimed to be anything other than a voice for the Democracy. Furthermore, he made it clear that the *Register* was his own voice. Once in 1860, someone referred to the *Register* as a "Douglas Organ." A response appeared quickly: "If the *Register* is an organ in any sense, it is the organ of Mr. Forsyth. It has never received an impulse from anyone else."[27]

If financial gain was Forsyth's driving ambition in his operation of the *Register,* it was definitely an unfulfilled ambition. Although the *Mobile Register* gained national prominence and notoriety for its editorial stance during Forsyth's long tenure, commercial success never followed. In actuality, Forsyth's devotion to his editorial career probably prevented him from pursuing other avenues of monetary gain. The talented penman had ample chances to branch out in his writing. One correspondent speculated that Forsyth could have made a tidy profit by writing accounts of his experiences in Mexico, or about the Charleston convention of 1860, or even a travel guide–style account of his European adventure. Additionally, the editor had at least one chance to leave Mobile to accept higher paying employment elsewhere. As we have seen, he turned down an offer to become editor-in-chief of the *New York Herald*—with a salary of over seven thousand dollars per year. His explanation, if sincere, casts doubts as to his economic greed. He stated, "Having abided with my people in the days of adversity—it was my wish, if my life should be spared, to be with and among them, when time and justice, and their own manly courage should work out their deliverance from the baleful toils and snares of miscalled Radical reconstruction."[28] Obviously, Forsyth did stand to reap economic gains from some of the projects and causes he promoted in his newspaper. However, it must also be noted that even when such ventures failed (i.e., the Nicholson paving fiasco), and he no longer stood to gain anything, he never stopped championing the same course of action. There is no question Forsyth promoted railroads in the 1870s while owning stock in the railroad companies. Obviously a conflict of interest charge can legitimately be raised. However, one must also note that Forsyth promoted railroads in Columbus in the 1840s when he owned no stock. Promoting developments such as street paving, harbor improvements, gaslights, and railroads were consistent themes during Forsyth's career.

A final criticism concerns the positions Forsyth took on a variety of key political issues. More often than not he found himself on the losing side of political contests or policy struggles. In Mexico, his protectorate scheme was pushed aside by President Buchanan's plan of land acquisition. His support of Stephen A. Douglas went against the vast majority of his own state party. His early acceptance of Reconstruction earned him the reputation of being a cooperationist. His record in presidential politics was certainly less than stellar. Forsyth was not on the winning side in a presidential election after 1856. In his own Democratic Party, he had not supported the eventual presidential nominee since he backed Franklin Pierce in 1852. His opposition to Greeley's nomination in 1872 was the last of his losing political causes. His contemporaries often found humor in Forsyth's ill-fated stances. Once in 1869, commenting on unfounded rumors that Forsyth was about to switch his allegiance to the Republican Party, the [Republican controlled] *Mobile Nationalist* mockingly stated, "We sincerely hope not, for he brings disaster to every cause he advocates."[29]

Had Forsyth died in 1872, one might be tempted to consider his career of political advocacy a disappointing failure. However, by 1874, with the great war fading into bitter memory, and Reconstruction having nearly run its course, many of Forsyth's contemporaries came to (perhaps grudgingly) realize that he had been correct on many of the positions that he had championed during the previous four decades. The best example of this reevaluation was his course of action in 1860–61. His support of Douglas and opposition to immediate secession—easily the most unpopular stances of his long career—came to be accepted by many of his former adversaries as a most prudent course. In 1866, after the brutal finality of defeat, Forsyth stated that he could not deny himself the "pride and pleasure" of hearing his former political enemies admit their mistakes. One of his most vocal critics confided to Forsyth that "Those men at the South who had the sagacity to comprehend and appreciate the statesman-ship of Douglas and the far-reaching scope of his doctrines, and the nerve to advocate and defend them, were the wisest men among us, and deserve most of the public esteem. We were honest, and meant our county good, but were all wrong." Forsyth took comfort in the fact that "Time was an appellate judge."[30]

What then is a fitting epitaph for John Forsyth? Although seldom remembered today, Forsyth was a giant of nineteenth-century journalism. He was recognized in both North and South as a dominant journalistic and political figure. One New York writer spoke for many when he noted about Forsyth "His death will leave a void in the councils of the party in his state and in the ranks of Southern journalism which it will be hard to fill." John Forsyth deserved such respect then and he deserves our study today. Forsyth must be held up as an example of one who, right or wrong, stuck to his beliefs and party. His old adversaries at the *Mobile Times* summed up this idea: "However much others differed with John Forsyth in his political course through life, none can deny him the mead of steady devotion and principle and firm adherence to conviction." When, in 1874 Forsyth got ownership of the *Register* for the final time, he was asked if his editorial position would be modified. His response was swift and sure: "Its [the *Register*'s] principles were fixed long ago, and they are engraved upon the body of the times within whose sphere and epoch it has lived. I have no changes to make." Enemies of the *Register* could certainly argue against the positions that Forsyth took, but they suffered credibility problems when they questioned the consistency of the one taking them. The *Vicksburg Herald*, in 1872, perhaps expressed this quality best when its editor simply stated, "We never doubted where John Forsyth stood."[31]

Two decades before his death, in a speech given to Mobile's Franklin Society, Forsyth presented a good summary of his journalistic philosophy. In closing the long talk, he said, "How noble the influence that belongs to the conductor of a Press who sways it only for his country's good—who can measure the perilous mazes of that untrodden path, where the mere partyist never dares to enter." He concluded this speech with an illustration that compared the editor's pen to a sword. It was the unique privilege of the editor "to be able with one hand to wield the universal armor of truth and with the other to smite its enemies." From 1837 to 1877, John Forsyth used his pen as a sword for the Democracy. We must be careful not to base our evaluation of Forsyth strictly on the results of his many battles. A. W. Dillard, a long-time acquaintance of Forsyth, offered this final word on the editor's career: "The leader of a forlorn hope, whether he succeeds or not, is entitled to the tribute of praise due to courage."[32]

Notes

Introduction

1. *Mobile Daily Commercial Register,* 11 Dec. 1837. (Note that during John Forsyth's long association with the *Register,* given various mergers and reorganizations, its name went through several changes. In chronological order, it was called the *Mobile Daily Commercial Register and Patriot,* the *Mobile Register and Journal,* the *Mobile Daily Register,* and the *Mobile Daily Advertiser and Register.* Hereafter, the paper will be cited as the *Mobile Register.*) See also *New York Times,* 3 May 1877; *Mobile Register,* 11 Dec. 1837; and Carl R. Osthaus, *Partisans of the Southern Press: Editorial Spokesmen of the Nineteenth Century* (Lexington: University of Kentucky Press, 1994), 1. Throughout this work the word "Democracy" is used in its nineteenth-century connotation—to refer to a political party.

2. J. Mills Thornton, III, *Politics and Power in a Slave Society* (Baton Rouge: Louisiana State University Press, 1978), 40.

3. Avery O. Craven, *The Growth of Southern Nationalism, 1848–1861* (Baton Rouge: Louisiana University Press, 1953), 275; Brayton Harris, *Blue and Gray in Black and White: Newspapers in the Civil War* (Washington, D.C.: Brassey's, 1999), ix; *Atlanta Constitution,* 4 May 1877; and Osthaus, *Partisans,* 1, 11, and 4.

4. See Michael W. Fitzgerald, *Urban Emancipation: Popular Politics in Reconstruction Mobile, 1860–1890* (Baton Rouge: Louisiana State University Press, 2002).

5. *Mobile Register,* 11 Dec. 1837.

Chapter 1

1. Jeannie Forsyth Jeffries, *A History of the Forsyth Family* (Indianapolis, Ind.: William H. Burford, 1920), 49.

2. George Washington, General Orders, 11 Sept. 1779, George Washington Papers, Series 3g, letter book 4, Library of Congress (it should be noted that Lee was acquitted "with honor" on all eight charges); and George Washington to Robert Forsyth, 5 Sept. 1779, George Washington Papers, Series 3b, letter book 9, Library of Congress.

3. *Annals of the Congress of the United States, 1789–1824,* 1st Cong., 1st sess., 87–89; and 3rd Cong., 1st sess., 74.

4. For biographical sketches of John Forsyth Sr., see Allen Johnson and Dumas Malone, eds., *Dictionary of American Biography,* 11 vols. (New York: Charles Scribner's Sons, 1959), 3: 533–35; John E. Findling, *Dictionary of American Diplomatic History* (Westport, Conn.: Greenwood Press, 1980), 174; and Samuel Flagg Bemis, ed., *The American Secretaries of States and Their Diplomacy,* 18 vols. (New York: Pageant Book Co., 1958–70), 4: 301–43. There are several valuable (undated) newspaper clippings that contain biographical sketches of John Forsyth Sr. in the John Forsyth Papers, Hargrett Rare Book and Manuscript Library, University of Georgia, Athens.

5. Alvin Laroy Duckett, *John Forsyth, Political Tactician* (Athens: University of Georgia Press, 1962), 5–6.

6. Ibid., 10.

7. Bemis, *American Secretaries of States,* 302.

8. Johnson and Malone, *Dictionary of American Biography,* 533. For a complete account of John Forsyth Sr.'s foreign tenure, see Duckett, *John Forsyth,* 42–80.

9. James F. Cook, *Governors of Georgia* (Huntsville, Ala.: Strode Publishing, 1979), 113.

10. Ibid., 114; Johnson and Malone, *Dictionary of American Biography,* 534; Duckett, *John Forsyth,* 162; and *Speech of the Hon. John Forsyth of Georgia on the Subject of the Removal of the Public Deposits. Delivered in the Senate of the United States, January, 1834* (Washington, D.C.: F. P. Blair, 1834), 22.

11. Findling, *Dictionary of American Diplomatic History,* 174; and Johnson and Malone, *Dictionary of American Biography,* 534–35.

12. See Duckett, *John Forsyth,* 198–202; and Johnson and Malone, *Dictionary of American Biography,* 535.

13. Findling, *Dictionary of American Diplomatic History,* 174; Duckett, *John Forsyth,* 185–87; and John Forsyth, *Address to the People of Georgia* (n.p., 1840), 4.

14. B. F. Riley, *Makers and Romance of Alabama History* (n.p., n.d.), 87. Note that hereafter, any reference to John Forsyth, unless otherwise specified, refers to John Forsyth Jr.

15. Luther N. Steward Jr., "John Forsyth," *Alabama Review* 14 (Apr. 1961): 99; and Duckett, *John Forsyth,* 182. See also Andrew Jackson to John Forsyth [Sr.], 29 Sept. 1835, Appointment Papers of the Department of State: Applications and Recommendations for Public Office, 1829–1836, National Archives.

16. As the *Mobile Register* reached anniversaries and milestones, it printed various histories. See, for example, "Ourselves at 75," *Mobile Register* 31 Jan. 1895, "History of the *Register,*" *Mobile Register,* 2 Sept. 1907, and "A History of the *Mobile Register,*" *Mobile Register,* 30 June 2002. It is interesting to note that the various accounts over the years disagree as to when the *Register* originated. Notice that the 1895 article celebrates the 75th anniversary of the paper, which would make its date of origin 1820. The current *Register* has the words "Since 1813" on every nameplate.

Chapter 2

1. For the best overall summaries of antebellum Mobile, see Harriet E. Amos, *Cotton City: Urban Development in Antebellum Mobile* (Tuscaloosa: University of Alabama Press, 1985), 1–47.

2. Information condensed from Mobile City Directories, 1837 and 1839.

3. *Mobile Register,* 1 Sept. 1837; and Thaddeus Sanford Papers, Delaney Historical Reference Collection, University of Mobile, Mobile, Alabama (hereafter referred to as Delaney Collection).

4. *Mobile Register,* 11 July 1838 and 4 May 1840.

5. Ibid., 1 June 1837 and 1 Mar. 1837.

6. Burton W. Folsom II, "Party Formation and Development in Jacksonian America: The Old South," *Journal of American Studies* 7 (Dec. 1993): 217; and Charles Grier Sellers Jr., "Who Were the Southern Whigs?" *American Historical Review* 59 (Jan. 1954): 336–37.

7. See Thomas Alexander et al., "Who Were the Alabama Whigs?" *Alabama Review* 16 (Jan. 1963): 5–19.

8. William Warren Rogers et al., *Alabama: The History of a Deep South State* (Tuscaloosa: University of Alabama Press, 1994), 142; Thornton, *Politics and Power,* 38; and *Mobile Register,* 10 Nov. 1840.

9. Clement Eaton, *A History of the Old South* (New York: MacMillan, 1949), 281; Edward Pessen, *Jacksonian America* (Urbana: University of Illinois Press, 1969), 201; and Richard L. McCormick, *The Second American Party System: Party Formation in the Jacksonian Era* (Chapel Hill: University of North Carolina Press, 1966), 3–4.

10. *Mobile Register,* 18 July 1838.

11. Richard L. McCormick, *The Party Period and Public Policy: American Politics from the Age of Jackson to the Progressive Era* (New York: Oxford University Press, 1986), 120.

12. Eaton, *History of the Old South,* 281; Pessen, *Jacksonian America,* 202; Robert Remini, *Andrew Jackson and the Course of American Democracy, 1833–1845* (New York: Harper and Row, 1984), 132–41.

13. Arthur C. Cole, *The Whig Party in the South* (1913; reprint, Gloucester, Mass.: Peter Smith, 1962), 71–72.

14. Eaton, *History of the Old South,* 284.

15. Grady McWhiney, "Were the Whigs a Class Party in Alabama?" *Journal of Southern History* 23 (Nov. 1957): 522.

16. Thornton, *Politics and Power,* 40.

17. Pessen, *Jacksonian America,* 202; Marvin Meyers, *The Jacksonian Persuasion* (New York: Vintage, 1957), 13–14.

18. Major L. Wilson, *The Presidency of Martin Van Buren* (Lawrence: University of Kansas Press, 1984), 69; and *Mobile Register,* 19 May 1841.

19. For the standard accounts of Jackson and the bank war, see Arthur M. Schle-

singer Jr., *The Age of Jackson* (Boston: Little, Brown, and Co., 1945), 74–102; Bray Hammond, *Banks and Politics in America* (Princeton: Princeton University Press, 1957), 369–450; Remini, *Andrew Jackson and the Course of American Democracy,* 161–78; and Pessen, *Jacksonian America,* 122–48.

20. *Mobile Register,* 2 Feb. and 1 Jan. 1838.

21. Ibid., 26 Sept. 1838 and 27 Feb. 1840.

22. Ibid., 26 Sept. 1838.

23. Ibid., 6 Nov., 7 Sept., and 9 Nov. 1839.

24. Amos, 151–52.

25. *Mobile Register,* 2 Feb. 1838; Wilson, *Presidency of Martin Van Buren,* 56; and Thornton, *Politics and Power,* 35.

26. Wilson, *Presidency of Martin Van Buren,* 56.

27. *Mobile Register,* 2 Feb. 1838.

28. Wilson, *Presidency of Martin Van Buren,* 49–51.

29. Sellers, "Who Were the Southern Whigs?" 340–41; and Meyers, *Jacksonian Persuasion,* 11.

30. *Mobile Register,* 6 Aug. 1838.

31. Thornton, *Politics and Power,* 35; and Rogers et al., *Alabama: The History,* 144.

32. *Mobile Register,* 18 Jan. and 28 July 1838.

33. Ibid., 9 Mar. 1841 and 28 July 1838.

34. Wilson, *Presidency of Martin Van Buren,* 60–61.

35. *Mobile Register,* 23 Jan. 1838.

36. Wilson, *Presidency of Martin Van Buren,* 123 and 79.

37. *Mobile Register,* 21 Apr. 1838.

38. Ibid., 14 May 1840.

39. Duckett, *John Forsyth,* 214–15. See also *Mobile Register,* 19 May 1840.

40. *Mobile Register,* 19 May 1840; *Baltimore American and Daily Commercial Advertiser,* 5 May 1840.

41. Theodore Henley Jack, *Sectionalism and Party Politics in Alabama, 1819–1842* (Menasha, Wis.: George Banta, 1919), 68; Wilson, *Presidency of Martin Van Buren,* 191; Thornton, *Politics and Power,* 48; *Mobile Register,* 16 Nov. 1840; and *Washington Democratic Review,* 7 June 1840.

42. *Richmond Enquirer,* 11 May 1840.

43. Schlesinger, *Age of Jackson,* 279; see *Mobile Register,* 18 and 21 Nov. 1840.

44. Ibid., 2 June and 13 May 1840.

45. Ibid., 13 May, 16 Sept., and 7 Oct. 1840.

46. Ibid., 10 Nov. and 16 Nov. 1840.

47. Ibid., 25 Feb., and 1, 12, and 17 Mar. 1841.

48. Ibid., 4 Mar. and 1 Apr. 1841.

49. Ibid., 12 Apr. 1841.

50. For a complete text of the resolution and schedule of the services, see the *Mobile Register,* 14 Apr. 1841.

51. Milo B. Howard Jr., "The General Ticket," *Alabama Review* 19 (July 1966): 165–66; and Rogers et al., *Alabama: The History,* 143.

52. *Mobile Register,* 27 Nov. 1840.

53. Quoted in Jack, *Sectionalism,* 75.

54. Rogers et al., *Alabama: The History,* 143; and Thornton, *Politics and Power,* 42.

55. *Mobile Register,* 19 May 1841.

56. Howard, "The General Ticket," 174.

57. *Mobile Register,* 25 Aug. and 22 Sept. 1841.

58. Ronald P. Formisano, *The Birth of Mass Political Parties* (Princeton: Princeton University Press, 1971), 128.

59. James Roger Sharp, *The Jacksonians Versus the Bank: Politics in the States after the Panic of 1837* (New York: Columbia University Press, 1970), 107.

Chapter 3

1. T. Sanford et al. to John Forsyth, 19 May 1841, printed in *Mobile Register,* 25 May 1841; John Forsyth Sr. to T. Sanford et al., printed in *Mobile Register,* 25 May 1841.

2. *Mobile Register,* 26 May 1841.

3. *Columbus Times,* 11 Nov. 1841. For samples of tributes, see *Washington Daily National Intelligencer,* 23 Oct. 1841, and *Baltimore American,* 22 Oct. 1841.

4. *Mobile Register,* 1 Dec. 1841.

5. *Savannah Georgian,* 18 June 1849.

6. Court of Ordinary Minutes: Muscogee County, 1838–51, 128, Georgia State Department of Archives, Morrow, Georgia.

7. *Columbus Enquirer,* 14 Dec. 1842.

8. Inventories and Appraisals: Muscogee County, Book 4, 1839–43, 560–64, Georgia State Department of Archives, Morrow, Georgia.

9. Court of Ordinary Minutes: Muscogee County, 1831–58, 128, Georgia Archives; *Milledgeville Southern Recorder,* 8 Aug. 1843.

10. Annual Return Books: Muscogee County, Book B, 1843–48, 35, 296, 405, and Book C, 1848–53, 60, Georgia Archives; see John Forsyth to James A. Butts, 31 Aug. 1850, John Forsyth Papers, Georgia State Department of Archives, Morrow, Georgia.

11. Summerville was a community of well-to-do Mobilians who could afford to build residences away from the unhealthy downtown area. People who are familiar with modern Mobile would recognize this as the Spring Hill Avenue area near the Bragg-Mitchell home.

12. *Columbus Times,* 29 Jan. 1845.

13. Ibid., 15 Oct. 1845; *Savannah Georgian,* 18 June 1849.

14. *Mobile Register,* 10 June 1845; see *Columbus Times,* 18 June 1845.

15. *Columbus Times,* 1 Apr. and 11 Mar. 1846; 16 May 1848.

16. Ibid., 23 July 1845.

17. Ibid., 15 Apr. 1846 and 27 Aug. 1845.

18. Ibid., 9 July 1845. Milledgeville was the Georgia state capital during the period covered in this chapter.

19. As is true for most topics dealing with antebellum sectionalism, the best source for background information on the Mexican War is David M. Potter, *The Impending Crisis, 1848–1861* (New York: Harper and Row, 1976), 1–50.

20. James D. Richardson, ed., *A Compilation of the Messages and Papers of the Presidents, vol. 3* (Washington: Bureau of National Literature and Art, 1897), 2288.

21. Richardson, *Messages and Papers,* 2292.

22. *Columbus Times,* 13 May 1846.

23. Ibid., 13 May 1846. See also Wilbur G. Kurtz, "The First Regiment of Georgia Volunteers in the Mexican War," *Georgia Historical Quarterly* 27 (Dec. 1943): 305.

24. Governor's Letter Book, 1843–1846, 702, 708, Georgia State Department of Archives; Gordon Smith, *History of the Georgia Militia, 1783–1861. Vol. 3: Counties and Commanders, Part 2* (Milledgeville, Ga: Boyd Publishing, 2001), 299–301.

25. *Columbus Times,* 18 and 9 July 1845.

26. *Milledgeville Union Recorder,* 16 June and 3 June 1846; *Columbus Times,* 24 June 1846.

27. Forsyth to *Columbus Times,* 3 July 1846. Note: Forsyth's letters often appeared in the paper up to three weeks after they were written. To ensure chronological clarity, I am citing the date they were written.

28. Forsyth to *Columbus Times,* 3 and 10 July 1846.

29. Kurtz, "Georgia Volunteers in the Mexican War," 313; Forsyth to *Columbus Times,* 10 July 1846.

30. Forsyth to *Columbus Times,* 11 and 14 July 1846.

31. Ibid., 20 July 1846.

32. Ibid., 24 July 1846.

33. Ibid.

34. Ibid., 31 July 1846.

35. Ibid.

36. Ibid.

37. Ibid., 1 and 6 Aug. 1846.

38. Ibid., 13 Aug. 1846.

39. Ibid., 14 Aug. 1846.

40. Ibid., 24 and 26 Aug. 1846.

41. Ibid., 29 Aug. 1846.

42. Ibid., 1 Sept. 1846.

43. Ibid., 5 Sept. 1846.

44. Ibid., 14 and 18 Sept. 1846.

45. Ibid., 8 Oct. 1846.

46. Kurtz, "Georgia Volunteers in the Mexican War," 311–12.

47. *Milledgeville Southern Recorder,* 1 June 1847.

48. Horace Montgomery, "The Crisis of 1850 and Its Effect on Political Parties in Georgia," *Georgia Historical Quarterly* 24 (Dec. 1940): 294–96.

49. Ibid., 294.

50. *Congressional Globe,* 29th Cong., 1st Sess., 1217, University of South Alabama Microfilm collection, Mobile, Alabama.

51. Donald E. Ferenbacher, *The South and Three Sectional Crises* (Baton Rouge: Louisiana State University Press, 1980), 35.

52. Augustus Baldwin Longstreet, *A Voice From the South: Comprising Letters from Georgia to Massachusetts and to the Southern States* (Baltimore: Samuel E. Smith Printers, 1848), 59.

53. Fehrenbacher, *The South and Three Sectional Crises,* 26, 35.

54. *Columbus Times,* 11 July 1848.

55. Ibid., 14 Nov. 1848.

56. Ibid.

57. Forsyth to Howell Cobb, 10 Nov. 1848, in Ulrich Bonnell Phillips, ed., "The Correspondence of Robert Toombs, Alexander H. Stephens, and Howell Cobb," *Annual Report of the American Historical Association* (1911): 136.

58. *Columbus Times,* 28 Nov. 1848.

59. Ibid., 5 Dec. 1848.

60. *Savannah Georgian,* 18 June 1849.

61. *Columbus Times,* 12 Feb. 1850.

62. Ibid., 19 Feb. 1850; *Augusta Constitutionalist,* 2 Aug. 1850.

63. Benning to Cobb, 29 Mar. 1850, in R. P. Brooks, ed., "Howell Cobb Papers," *Georgia Historical Quarterly* 5 (Sept. 1921): 37–38.

64. *Columbus Times,* 9 Apr. 1850; Anthony Gene Carey, *Politics, Slavery, and the Union in Antebellum Georgia* (Athens: University of Georgia Press, 1997), 162.

65. Dallas Tabor Herndon, "The Nashville Convention of 1850," *Publication of the Alabama Historical Society, Transactions* 5 (1904): 216–17.

66. *Columbus Times,* 18 June 1850.

67. Montgomery, "The Crisis of 1850," 314–15; see *Milledgeville Southern Recorder,* 27 Aug. 1850, and *Augusta Chronicle and Sentinel,* 28 Aug. 1850.

68. See Montgomery, "The Crisis of 1850," 312–14 for resolutions.

69. Richard Harrison Shyrock, *Georgia and the Union in 1850* (Durham: Duke University Press, 1926), 285–86.

70. *Columbus Times,* 10 Aug. 1850.

71. Ibid., 10 Sept. 1850.

72. Ibid., 28 Sept. 1850.

73. Ibid., 22 Oct. 1850; Brian G. Walton, "Georgia's Biennial Legislatures, 1840–1860 and the Elections to the U.S. Senate," *Georgia Historical Quarterly* 61 (Summer 1977): 147.

74. Montgomery, "The Crisis of 1850," 318; Carey, 168.

75. Montgomery, "The Crisis of 1850," 322.

76. *Columbus Times,* 1 Apr. 1851; *Montgomery Advertiser,* 7 Nov. 1860.

77. *Columbus Times,* 31 June 1851.
78. Ibid., 16 July 1851.
79. Walton, "Georgia's Biennial Legislatures," 149.
80. *Mobile Register,* 5 Jan. 1853.

Chapter 4

1. "History of the *Register,*" *Mobile Register,* 2 Sept. 1907; Thomas M. Owen, *History of Alabama and Dictionary of Alabama Biography* (Chicago: S. T. Clark, 1921), 598; and *Mobile Register,* 2 Sept. 1907.

2. Thornton, *Politics and Power,* 349. For discussions of the nature of national politics as related to state concerns, see William E. Gienapp, *The Origins of the Republican Party, 1852–1856* (New York: Oxford University Press, 1987), 5–7; and William J. Cooper Jr., *The South and the Politics of Slavery, 1828–1856* (Baton Rouge: Louisiana State University Press, 1978), xiii–xiv.

3. Roy Franklin Nichols, *The Democratic Machine, 1850–1854* (New York: AMS Press, 1967), 30–40.

4. *Mobile Register,* 13 Mar. 1856.

5. Holman Hamilton, *Prologue to Conflict: The Crisis and Compromise of 1850* (Lexington: University of Kentucky Press, 1964), 189.

6. Frank Haywood Hodder, "The Railroad Background of the Kansas-Nebraska Act," *Mississippi Valley Historical Review* 12 (June 1925): 4; James M. McPherson, *Battle Cry of Freedom* (New York: Ballantine Books, 1988), 121; and Potter, *The Impending Crisis,* 203.

7. Hodder, "The Railroad Background of the Kansas-Nebraska Act," 4–5, 10; Grace Lewis Miller, "The Mobile and Ohio Railroad in Antebellum Times," *Alabama Historical Quarterly* 7 (Spring 1945): 50; James H. Lemly, *The Gulf, Mobile and Ohio* (Homewood, Ill.: Richard D. Irwin, 1953), 308–9; George Fort Milton, *The Eve of Conflict* (Boston: Houghton Mifflin Co., 1934), 10; and Potter, *The Impending Crisis,* 121. For the text of the bill, see *Congressional Globe,* 31st Cong., 1st sess., 904; for Forsyth's early view of Douglas, see *Mobile Register,* 29 Sept. 1855.

8. Quoted in McPherson, *Battle Cry of Freedom,* 121.

9. For concise summaries of the Kansas-Nebraska legislative process, see James M. McPherson, *Ordeal By Fire: The Civil War and Reconstruction* (New York: Alfred Knopf, 1982), 86–91; and Potter, *The Impending Crisis,* 145–76. For a complete treatment, see James C. Malin, *The Nebraska Question, 1852–1854* (Ann Arbor: Edwards Brothers, 1953).

10. *Mobile Register,* 6 Nov. 1855.

11. Quoted in Roy F. Nichols, "The Kansas-Nebraska Act: A Century of Historiography," *Mississippi Valley Historical Review* 43 (June 1956): 188.

12. Quoted in Michael F. Holt, *The Political Crisis of the 1850s* (New York: W. W. Norton, 1978), 145.

13. *Mobile Register,* 6 Nov. and 9 Oct. 1855.

14. *Congressional Globe,* 33rd Cong., 1st sess., 281–82; see also Potter, *The Impending Crisis,* 163.

15. Thornton, *Politics and Power,* 350–52; Potter, *The Impending Crisis,* 202; and Holt, *Political Crisis of the 1850s,* 151.

16. *Mobile Register,* 16, 21, and 23 Sept. 1855. For detailed reports, see letters that appeared in ibid., 6 and 9 Oct. 1855.

17. *Congressional Globe,* 33rd Cong., 1st sess., appendix, 769.

18. *Mobile Register,* 6 Nov. 1855.

19. Ibid., 1 Apr. and 6 Nov. 1855.

20. Ibid., 24 Oct. 1855.

21. Ibid., 18 Mar. 1856.

22. Ibid., 1 Apr. 1856.

23. Potter, *The Impending Crisis,* 175–176.

24. *Mobile Register,* 6 and 9 Oct. 1855.

25. Ibid., 11 Dec. 1855.

26. Cooper, *The South and the Politics of Slavery,* xi; Anthony Gene Carey, "Too Southern to Be Americans: Proslavery Politics and the Failure of the Know-Nothing Party in Georgia, 1854–1856," *Civil War History* 41 (Mar. 1995): 24; and Michael F. Holt, "The Politics of Impatience: The Origins of Know Nothingism," *Journal of American History* 60 (Sept. 1973): 311.

27. Tyler Anbinder, *Nativism and Slavery: The Northern Know Nothings and the Politics of the 1850s* (New York: Oxford University Press, 1992), ix; McPherson, *Ordeal By Fire,* 83; Anbinder, *Nativism and Slavery,* ix; and Potter, *The Impending Crisis,* 246.

28. McPherson, *Ordeal By Fire,* 82; Potter, *The Impending Crisis,* 241; and Alan Smith Thompson, "Mobile, Alabama, 1850–1861: Economic, Political, Physical, and Population Characteristics," Ph.D. diss., University of Alabama, 1979, 263–64.

29. *Mobile Register,* 14 Feb. 1856.

30. Robert L. Robinson, "Mobile in the 1850s: A Social, Cultural, and Economic History," M.A. thesis, University of Alabama, 1982, 67.

31. Quoted in Ray Allen Billington, *The Protestant Crusade, 1800–1860* (New York: Macmillan, 1938), 291.

32. Quoted in Allan Nevins, *Ordeal of the Union,* 2 vols. (New York: Charles Scribner's Sons, 1947), 2: 329.

33. William J. Cooper Jr., *Liberty and Slavery: Southern Politics to 1860* (New York: Alfred A. Knopf, 1983), 247.

34. Rogers et al., *Alabama: The History,* 162, 167.

35. Holt, "Politics of Impatience," 312–13.

36. Potter, *The Impending Crisis,* 250.

37. *Mobile Register,* 15 Dec. 1855 and 16 Feb. 1856.

38. Ibid., 11 Dec. 1855; 13 and 15 Feb. 1856.

39. Ibid., 11 Dec. 1855; 21 and 16 Feb. 1856.

40. Cooper, *The South and the Politics of Slavery,* 369; Potter, *The Impending Crisis,* 259; Carey, "Too Southern to Be Americans," 33; and Thornton, *Politics and Power,*

359–60. For the text of the 1856 American party platform, see Arthur M. Schlesinger Jr., ed., *History of American Presidential Elections, 1789–1968,* 2 vols. (New York: Chelsea House, 1971), 2: 1041–43.

41. *Mobile Register,* 13 Feb. 1856.

42. Rogers et al., *Alabama: The History,* 169; Michael D. Pierson, "'All Southern Society Is Assailed by the Foulest Charges': Charles Sumner's 'The Crime Against Kansas' and the Escalation of the Republican Anti-Slavery Rhetoric," *New England Quarterly* 58 (Mar. 1995): 535; and Gienapp, *Origins of the Republican Party,* vii–viii; and McPherson, *Ordeal By Fire,* 89.

43. Pierson, "'All Southern Society,'" 535–36; and McPherson, *Ordeal By Fire,* 85.

44. Quoted in Eric Foner, *Free Soil, Free Labor, Free Men* (Oxford: Oxford University Press, 1970), 234.

45. *Mobile Register,* 11 July 1856.

46. William E. Gienapp, "The Crime Against Sumner: The Caning of Charles Sumner and the Rise of the Republican Party," *Civil War History* 25 (Summer 1979): 224; *Mobile Register,* 5 June and 24 July 1856; and David Donald, *Charles Sumner and the Coming of the Civil War* (New York: Alfred A. Knopf, 1960), 311.

47. *Mobile Register,* 6 Jan. and 13 Mar. 1856.

48. See McPherson, *Battle Cry of Freedom,* 119; Holt, *Political Crisis of the 1850s,* 142; and Larry Gara, *The Presidency of Franklin Pierce* (Lawrence: University Press of Kansas, 1991), xii.

49. *Mobile Register,* 19 Apr. 1856.

50. See, for example, *Mobile Register,* 16 May 1856; ibid., 6 May 1856.

51. McPherson, *Battle Cry of Freedom,* 157.

52. For the complete text of the official correspondence, see *Mobile Register,* 26 June 1856.

53. *Mobile Register,* 10 and 13 June 1856.

54. Ibid., 29 June, 1, 13, and 11 July 1856.

55. Ibid., 24 July 1856.

56. Ibid., 29 July 1856.

57. *New York Times,* 6 Oct. 1856.

Chapter 5

1. Donathan C. Olliff, *Reforma Mexico and the United States: A Search for Alternatives to Annexation, 1854–1861* (Tuscaloosa: University of Alabama Press, 1981), 65; Paul Neff Garber, *The Gadsden Treaty* (Gloucester, Mass.: Peter Smith, 1959), 175–76; 25 Members of Congress to the President of the United States, 22 Apr., 1854; and C. C. Clay and Benjamin Fitzpatrick to Franklin Pierce, 24 Apr., 1854, General Records of the Department of State, "Applications and Recommendations for Public Office," Series 967, roll 17, RG 59, National Archives; and *New York Times,* 10 May 1859.

2. Marcy to Forsyth, 16 Aug. 1856, in William R. Manning, ed., *Diplomatic Cor-*

respondence of the United States: Inter-American Affairs, 1831–1860, 12 vols. (Washington: Carnegie Endowment for International Peace, 1932–39), vol. 9 (hereafter cited as *Diplomatic Correspondence*); John Bassett Moore, ed., *The Works of James Buchanan,* 10 vols. (New York: Antiquarian Press, 1960), 10: 253; Richard N. Sinkin, *The Mexican Reform, 1855–1876: A Study in Liberal Nation Building* (Austin: Institute of Latin American Studies, 1979), 5, 96; and Wilfred Hardy Calcott, *Church and State in Mexico, 1827–1857* (New York: Octagon Books, 1965), 25.

3. Brian Hamnett, *Juárez* (New York: Longman Press, 1994), 1; Sinkin, *The Mexican Reform,* 7; Charles A. Hale, *Mexican Liberalism in the Age of Mora, 1821–1853* (New Haven: Yale University Press, 1968), 1; John Mason Hart, *Revolutionary Mexico: The Coming and Process of the Mexican Revolution* (Berkeley: University of California Press, 1987), 77; Florencia Mallon, *Peasant and Nation: The Making of Post-colonial Mexico and Peru* (Berkeley: University of California Press, 1994), 31, 33; and Hart, *Revolutionary Mexico,* 55.

4. Sinkin, *The Mexican Reform,* 26–27; David A. Brading, "Liberal Patriotism and the Mexican Reforma," *Journal of Latin American Studies* 20 (May 1988): 30.

5. Sinkin, *The Mexican Reform,* 119; Jasper Ridley, *Maximilian and Juárez* (New York: Ticknor and Fields, 1992), 7; Robert J. Knowlton, *Church Property and the Mexican Reform, 1856–1910* (Dekalb: Northern Illinois University Press, 1976), 219; and Walter V. Scholes, "A Revolution Falters: Mexico 1856–1857," *Hispanic American Historical Review* 32 (Feb. 1952): 11.

6. Hale, *Mexican Liberalism,* 1; Hart, *Revolutionary Mexico,* 77; and Scholes, "A Revolution Falters," 14–15.

7. Sinkin, *The Mexican Reform,* 29; Olliff, *Reforma Mexico,* 44.

8. Richard A. Johnson, *The Mexican Revolution of Ayutla, 1854–55* (1939; reprint, Westport, Conn.: Greenwood Press, 1974), 44; Sinkin, *The Mexican Reform,* 31; and Jan Bazant, "Mexico From Independence to 1867," in Leslie Bethell, ed., *The Cambridge History of Latin America,* 8 vols. (Cambridge: Cambridge University Press, 1985), 7: 452.

9. Sinkin, *The Mexican Reform,* 34–35; Gilbert M. Joseph and David Nugent, eds., *Everyday Forms of State Formation: Revolution and the Negotiation of Rule in Modern Mexico* (Durham: Duke University Press, 1995), ix; and Olliff, *Reforma Mexico,* 57.

10. Bazant, "Mexico From Independence to 1867," 453; and Scholes, "A Revolution Falters," 5.

11. Forsyth to Marcy, 25 Aug 1856, Despatches of United States Ministers to Mexico, University of Southern Mississippi Microfilm Collection, Hattiesburg (hereafter cited as Despatches). Forsyth to Antonio de la Fuente, 20 Oct. 1856, Records of Foreign Service Posts, "Notes to Mexican Foreign Offices," vol. 188, RG 84, National Archives II, College Park, Md. (hereafter cited as "Notes to Mexican Foreign Offices").

12. *Mexican Extraordinary,* 29 Oct. 1856, Despatches.

13. Forsyth to Marcy, 8 Nov. 1856, in *Diplomatic Correspondence;* see also Thomas

Schoonover, *Dollars over Dominion: The Triumph of Liberalism in Mexican–United States Relations, 1861–1867* (Baton Rouge: Louisiana State University Press, 1978), xviii–xix; and W. Dirk Raat, *Mexico and the United States: Ambivalent Vistas* (Athens: University of Georgia Press, 1992), 84–85.

14. Olliff, *Reforma Mexico*, 11. See also Jürgen Buchenau, *In the Shadow of the Giant: The Making of Mexico's Central American Policy, 1876–1930* (Tuscaloosa: University of Alabama Press, 1996), 11.

15. Report of an Interview between Mr. Forsyth and Sr Lerdo de Trjada, at the National Palace, Dec. 16th 1856, "Notes to Mexican Foreign Offices"; and Forsyth to Marcy, 19 Dec. 1856, in *Diplomatic Correspondence*.

16. Forsyth to Marcy, 15 Jan. and 2 Feb. 1857, in *Diplomatic Correspondence*. For a complete text of the terms of the loan provisions, see Forsyth to Marcy, 10 Feb. 1857, in *Diplomatic Correspondence*.

17. Donathan C. Olliff, "Mexico's Mid-Nineteenth Century Drive for Material Development," *SECOLAS Annals* 8 (1977): 23. See also Buchenau, *In the Shadow of the Giant*, 11.

18. Marcy to Forsyth, 3 Mar. 1857, in *Diplomatic Correspondence*.

19. Philip Shriver Klien, *President James Buchanan: A Biography* (University Park: Pennsylvania State University Press, 1962), 130–31.

20. Cass to Forsyth, 3 Mar. 1857, in *Diplomatic Correspondence*.

21. Forsyth to Cass, 4 Apr. 1857, in *Diplomatic Correspondence*.

22. Forsyth to Cass, 10 Apr. and 5 May 1857; and Appleton to Forsyth, 17 June 1857, in *Diplomatic Correspondence*.

23. Cass to Forsyth, 17 July 1857 (nos. 27 and 28), in *Diplomatic Correspondence*.

24. Forsyth to Cass, 15 Sept. 1857, in *Diplomatic Correspondence*.

25. Ibid.

26. Cass to Forsyth, 17 July 1857, in *Diplomatic Correspondence*.

27. Ibid.

28. Forsyth to Cass, 15 Sept. 1857, in *Diplomatic Correspondence*.

29. James Morton Callahan, *American Foreign Policy in Mexican Relations* (New York: MacMillan, 1932), 244; A. L. Diket, "Slidell's Right Hand: Emile La Sere," *Louisiana History* 4 (Summer 1963): 180–81; Amos Aschbach Ettinger, *The Mission to Spain of Pierre Soulé, 1853–1855* (New Haven: Yale University Press, 1932), 129–30; and Robert E. May, *The Southern Dream of a Caribbean Empire: 1854–1861* (Baton Rouge: Louisiana State University Press, 1973), 156–57.

30. Forsyth to Cass, 29 Sept. 1857, in *Diplomatic Correspondence*.

31. For Benjamin and la Sére's charges against Forsyth, see Benjamin and la Sére to Buchanan, 19 Sept. 1857, in *Diplomatic Correspondence;* for the administration's response to these charges, see Cass to Forsyth, 20 Oct. 1857, in *Diplomatic Correspondence;* for a concise summary of the bickering between Forsyth and these two agents, see May, *Southern Dream of a Caribbean Empire*, 157–58.

32. Benjamin and la Sére to Buchanan, 19 Sept. 1857, in *Diplomatic Correspondence*.

33. John Preston Moore, "The Correspondence of Pierre Soule: The Louisiana Tehuantepec Company," *The Hispanic American Historical Review* 32, no. 1 (Feb. 1952): 65–68.

34. Benjamin and la Sére to Buchanan, 19 Sept. 1857, in *Diplomatic Correspondence;* see also Diket, "Slidell's Right Hand," 194.

35. Forsyth to Cass, 24 Nov. 1857, in *Diplomatic Correspondence.*

36. Ibid.

37. Forsyth to Stephen A. Douglas, 1 Oct. 1857, Stephen A. Douglas Papers, University of Chicago Library (hereafter cited as Douglas Papers).

38. Cass to Forsyth, 17 Nov. 1857, in *Diplomatic Correspondence.*

39. Forsyth to Cass, 17 Dec. 1857, in *Diplomatic Correspondence.* For a summary of these events, see Sinkin, *The Mexican Reform,* 77–79.

40. For a brief summary, see Michael C. Meyer et al., *The Course of Mexican History* (New York: Oxford University Press, 1999), 367–69; and Tulio Halperin Donghi, *The Contemporary History of Latin America* (Durham: Duke University Press, 1993), 128–30.

41. Forsyth to Cass, 18 Nov. 1857 and 14 Jan. 1858, in *Diplomatic Correspondence.*

42. Olliff, *Reforma Mexico,* 96–97.

43. Forsyth to Cuevas, 27 Jan. 1858, and Forsyth to Cass, 29 Jan. 1858, in *Diplomatic Correspondence.*

44. Forsyth to Ocampo, 30 Jan. 1858, in *Diplomatic Correspondence.*

45. Olliff, *Reforma Mexico,* 99; *El Heraldo* (Mexico City), 23 Jan. 1858, cited in Olliff, *Reforma Mexico,* 98.

46. James Buchanan, *Mr. Buchanan's Administration on the Eve of the Rebellion* (New York: D. Appleton, 1866), 260–61; Mares, cited in Olliff, *Reforma Mexico,* 99; and Forsyth to Cass, 30 Jan. 1858, in *Diplomatic Correspondence.*

47. Forsyth to Cuevas, 22 Mar. 1858, in "Notes to Mexican Foreign Offices."

48. Cuevas to Forsyth, 5 Apr. 1858, in *Diplomatic Correspondence.*

49. Forsyth to Cuevas, 8 Apr. 1858, and Cuevas to Forsyth, 12 Apr. 1858, in *Diplomatic Correspondence.*

50. Forsyth to Cass, 16 Apr. and 2 May 1858, in *Diplomatic Correspondence.*

51. Forsyth to Cuevas, 22 May 1858, in "Notes to Mexican Foreign Offices"; Cuevas to Forsyth, 25 May 1858, in *Diplomatic Correspondence.*

52. Forsyth to Cuevas, 17 June 1858, Cuevas to Forsyth, 18 June 1858, Forsyth to Cuevas, 21 June 1858, in *Diplomatic Correspondence.* For a complete text of Buchanan's message, see Fred L. Israel, ed., *The State of the Union Messages of the Presidents,* 2 vols. (New York: Chelsea House, 1966), 1: 984.

53. See Forsyth to Cass, 1 July 1858, in *Diplomatic Correspondence.*

54. Cass to Forsyth, 15 July 1858, in *Diplomatic Correspondence.*

55. Forsyth to Cass, 31 Aug. 1858, in *Diplomatic Correspondence.*

56. Ibid., 1 Aug. 1858.

57. Forsyth to Lanzas, 26 Aug., 14 and 18 Oct. 1858, "Notes to Mexican Foreign Offices."

58. Ibid., 20 Oct. 1858.

59. Ibid.

Chapter 6

1. *New York Times,* 9 Feb. 1859.

2. See, for example, *New York Times,* 18 Jan., 23 Apr., and 9 Feb. 1859; *Mobile Register,* 14, 18, 20, and 21 May 1859; and *New York Times,* 10 May 1859; John Forsyth to Stephen A. Douglas, 26 Mar. 1859, Douglas Papers.

3. *Mobile Register,* 12 June 1859.

4. J. E. D. Younge, "The Conservative Party in Alabama, 1848–1860," in *Studies in Southern and Alabama History,* ed. George Petrie (Montgomery: Alabama Historical Society, 1904), 137–41; and William Warren Rogers et al., *Alabama: The History of a Deep South State* (Tuscaloosa: University of Alabama Press, 1994), 156.

5. John Witherspoon Dubose, *The Life and Times of William Lowndes Yancey,* 2 vols. (Birmingham: Roberts and Son, 1892), 2: 320–21.

6. Donald B. Johnson, comp., *National Party Platforms, 1840–1956* (Urbana: University of Illinois Press, 1978), 23–27; Thomas Hudson Mckee, ed., *The National Conventions and Platforms of All Political Parties, 1789–1905* (1906; reprint, New York: AMS Press, 1971), 88–91; Potter, *The Impending Crisis,* 262; and Younge, "The Conservative Party in Alabama," 143.

7. John Forsyth to William F. Samford, 5 Oct. 1859, in *Letters of Hon. John Forsyth, Of Alabama, Late Minister to Mexico, To Wm F. Samford, Esq., In Defence of Stephen A. Douglas* (1859), 10 (hereafter cited as *Letters of John Forsyth*); and *Mobile Daily Commercial Register,* 18 Nov. 1859.

8. Potter, *The Impending Crisis,* 337, 402; Robert W. Johannsen, "Stephen A. Douglas, *Harpers Magazine,* and Popular Sovereignty," *Mississippi Valley Historical Review* 45 (Mar. 1959): 606–31; William B. Hesseltine, ed., *Three Against Lincoln: Murat Halstead Reports the Caucuses of 1860* (Baton Rouge: Louisiana State University Press, 1960), 5; and Robert W. Johannsen, "Douglas at Charleston," in *Politics and the Crisis of 1860,* ed. Norman A. Graebner (Urbana: University of Illinois Press, 1961), 64–67.

9. During the election campaign of 1860, Ultra newspapers often printed lengthy samples of Forsyth's earlier writings. For examples, see *Montgomery Weekly Advertiser,* 30 Oct. 1860 and 7 Nov. 1860. For speculation concerning Forsyth's motivations in supporting Douglas, see *Montgomery Weekly Advertiser,* 28 Mar. 1860.

10. *Mobile Register,* 8 Feb. 1860.

11. *The Douglas Doctrine of Popular Sovereignty in the Territories; Its Counterpart. By a Missourian* (St. Louis, Mo.: R. U. Kennedy & Co., 1860).

12. Forsyth to Samford, 5 Oct. 1859, *Letters of John Forsyth,* 10; and *Speech of Mr. Forsyth of Mobile on the Senatorial Question, In the House of Representatives in the Alabama Legislature, November 29, 1859,* John Forsyth Papers, Historic Mobile Preservation Society.

13. *Mobile Register,* 25 Feb. 1860.

14. Benjamin Fitzpatrick to C. C. Clay, 30 Aug. 1859, Clement C. Clay Papers, Perkins Library, Duke University, Box 3, Folder 3.

15. John Forsyth to Stephen A. Douglas, 31 Mar. 1859, Douglas Papers; Forsyth to Samford, 13 Sept. 1859, *Letters of John Forsyth*, 3–4; Forsyth to Douglas, 31 Mar. 1859, and Douglas to Charles A. Lanphier, 1 Oct. 1859, Douglas Papers; and *The* [Washington, D.C.] *Federal Era,* 8 Dec. 1859.

16. *Mobile Register,* 27 Jan. 1860 and 9 Dec. 1859.

17. Ibid., 17 Jan. 1860. See also Kenneth Stampp, *America in 1857* (New York: Oxford University Press, 1990), 292–93.

18. *Montgomery Weekly Advertiser,* 23 May 1860; and Forsyth to Douglas, 26 June 1859.

19. Ollinger Crenshaw, *The Slave States in the Election of 1860* (Baltimore: Johns Hopkins University Press, 1945), 250; and Lewy Dorman, *Party Politics in Alabama from 1850 through 1860* (Wetumpka, Ala.: Wetumpka Printing Co., 1935), 148; *Mobile Register,* 2 July 1859; Forsyth to Douglas, 30 July 1859, Douglas Papers; and *Mobile Register,* 16 July and 26 Aug. 1859.

20. *Mobile Register,* 31 July, 3 Aug., and 3 July 1859. For a good sample of Forsyth's campaign rhetoric, see Forsyth to Douglas, 30 July 1859, Douglas Papers.

21. *Mobile Register,* 7 Aug. 1859.

22. Forsyth to Douglas, 4 Aug. 1859, Douglas Papers.

23. Durward Long, "Political Parties and Propaganda in Alabama in the Presidential Election of 1860," *Alabama Historical Quarterly* 25 (Spring 1963): 120.

24. *Montgomery Weekly Advertiser,* 3 Mar. 1858.

25. Reprinted in the *Mobile Register,* 6 Dec. 1859.

26. *Charleston Mercury,* 13 Oct. 1859.

27. Forsyth to Douglas, 4 Feb. 1860, Douglas Papers. For a text of Forsyth's speech to the Alabama House, see *Mobile Register,* 24, 25, and 28 Feb. 1860.

28. Dorman, *Party Politics in Alabama,* 154.

29. Quoted in the *Mobile Register,* 16 Dec. 1859.

30. Dubose, *William Lowndes Yancey,* 443–44; and Forsyth to Douglas, 10 Jan. 1860, Douglas Papers.

31. *Mobile Register,* 4 Feb. 1860; and Thornton, *Politics and Power,* 387–88.

32. *Proceedings of the Democratic State Convention Held in the City of Montgomery Commencing Wednesday, January 11, 1860* (Montgomery: Shorter and Reid, 1860), 24–26.

33. *Mobile Register,* 12 and 24 Feb. 1860.

34. Ibid., 10 Feb. 1860 (my emphasis).

35. Forsyth to Douglas, 31 Jan. 1860, Douglas Papers (my emphasis).

36. Forsyth to Douglas, 9 and 4 Feb. 1860, Douglas Papers.

37. Hesseltine, ed., *Three Against Lincoln,* 36.

38. Forsyth to Douglas, 6 Jan., 4 Feb., and 5 Apr. 1860, Douglas Papers.

39. Lindsey S. Perkins, "The Democratic Convention of 1860," in *Anti-Slavery and Disunion, 1858–1861,* ed. J. Jeffry Aver (New York: Harper and Row, 1963), 172;

For an excellent summary of the opposing factions at the convention, see Johannsen, "Douglas at Charleston," 76–77, and Perkins, "The Democratic Convention of 1860," 173–75; Hesseltine, ed., *Three Against Lincoln,* 12.

40. Perkins, "The Democratic Convention of 1860," 184; Thornton, *Politics and Power,* 383; and Phillip G. Auchampaugh, "The Buchanan-Douglas Feud," *Illinois Society Journal* 25 (Apr. 1932): 37.

41. Perkins, "The Democratic Convention of 1860," 184; and *Charleston Daily Courier,* 25 Apr. 1860.

42. Hesseltine, ed., *Three Against Lincoln,* 3.

43. Mckee, *The National Conventions and Platforms,* 108; Johannsen, "Douglas at Charleston," 82; and Hesseltine, ed., *Three Against Lincoln,* 79–80.

44. Johannsen, "Douglas at Charleston," 85–86. See Halstead's accounts of days seven through ten of the convention in Hesseltine, ed., *Three Against Lincoln,* 108–9.

45. *Mobile Register,* 15 May 1860; and Forsyth to Douglas, 9 May 1860, Douglas Papers.

46. *Montgomery Weekly Advertiser,* 23 and 30 May 1860; and Dubose, *William Lowndes Yancey,* 475.

47. *Montgomery Weekly Advertiser,* 23 May 1860.

48. Hesseltine, ed., *Three Against Lincoln,* 185–86; and James Leonidas Murphy, "Alabama and the Charleston Convention of 1860," in *Studies in Southern and Alabama History,* ed. George Petrie (Montgomery: Alabama Historical Society, 1905), 164. For the Yanceyite point of view, see *Address of the Democracy of Alabama to the National Democratic Convention at Baltimore, June 18th, 1860.* Published by the Democratic Party of Alabama.

49. Douglas to William A. Richardson, 20 June 1860, Douglas Papers, Perkins Library, Duke University; *Charleston Daily Courier,* 21 June 1860; and Hesseltine, ed., *Three Against Lincoln,* 215–17.

50. Hesseltine, ed., *Three Against Lincoln,* 215–17, 244, 250; and Thornton, *Politics and Power,* 396.

51. Robert W. Johannsen, *Stephen A. Douglas* (New York: Oxford University Press, 1973), 771–72; and Roy Franklin Nichols, *Disruption of American Democracy* (New York: Collier Books, 1948), 316.

52. J. J. Seibels to Fitzpatrick, 23 June 1860; and Gabriel B. Duval to Fitzpatrick, 25 June 1860, Benjamin Fitzpatrick Papers, Southern Historical Collection, Wilson Library, University of North Carolina, Chapel Hill, Box 1, Folder 6; Fitzpatrick to Wm. Ludlow of New York, and others, Benjamin Fitzpatrick Papers, Alabama Department of Archives and History, Montgomery, Box 44, Folder 1.

53. *Montgomery Weekly Advertiser,* 20 June 1860; and Waldo W. Braden, "The Campaign for Memphis, 1860," in *Anti-Slavery and Disunion, 1858–1861,* ed. J. Jeffry Aver (New York: Harper and Row, 1963), 230. Henry S. Foote was a Tennessee Douglas leader, while Jere Clemens led the Bell effort in Memphis.

54. Forsyth to Douglas, 30 Oct. 1860, Douglas Papers.

55. *Mobile Daily Advertiser,* 6 Nov. 1860; Lionel Crocker, "The Campaign of

Stephen Douglas in the South, 1860," in *Anti-Slavery and Disunion, 1868–1861,* ed. J. Jeffry Aver (New York: Harper and Row, 1963), 276.

56. Johannsen, *Stephen A. Douglas,* 803.

57. For complete Alabama county returns, see Dorman, *Party Politics in Alabama,* 176–77.

58. See Thornton, *Politics and Power,* 390–91, and 382–83.

59. Forsyth to Douglas, 5 Apr. 1860, Douglas Papers; and Thornton, *Politics and Power,* 392–93.

60. Nichols, *Disruption of American Democracy,* 313. It is interesting to note that "bolters" from several other states were seated by the committee.

61. *Wilmington Journal,* 28 June 1860.

62. For a detailed explanation of this argument, see Thornton, *Politics and Power,* 396.

63. Ibid.; and Nichols, *Disruption of American Democracy,* 320.

Chapter 7

1. Forsyth to Douglas, 28 Dec. 1860, Douglas Papers.

2. Letter dated 22 Nov. 1860 in *New York Times,* 7 Dec. 1860.

3. Belmont to Forsyth, 19 Dec. 1860, in *Letters, Speeches, and Addresses of August Belmont,* privately published, 1890; and John Forney, *Eulogy Upon the Hon. Stephen A. Douglas, Delivered at the Smithsonian Institute.* Washington, July 3, 1861. Philadelphia: Ringwalt and Brown Printers, 1861; and Percy Scott Flippin, *Herschel V. Johnson of Georgia. State Rights Unionist.* Richmond: Dietz Printing Co., 1931.

4. See, for example, *Montgomery Weekly Advertiser,* 22 Feb., 28 Mar., 23, 30 May, and 20 June 1860.

5. *Columbus* [Georgia] *Times,* 13 May 1850; *New York Evening Post,* 6 Oct. 1856, quoted in George Fort Milton, *The Eve of Conflict: Stephen A. Douglas and the Needless War* (1934; reprint, New York: Octagon Books, 1963), 240; *Mobile Register,* 1 Apr. 1856; and *Montgomery Daily Mail,* 15 Oct. 1860. For the best summary of Forsyth's position on the secession issue, see *Mobile Register,* 14 Feb. 1860.

6. Quoted in Dwight Lowell Dumond, *Southern Editorials on Secession* (Gloucester, Mass.: Peter Smith, 1964), 269.

7. Malcolm C. McMillan, *The Alabama Confederate Reader* (Tuscaloosa: University of Alabama Press, 1963), 3–4; William H. Brantley Jr., "Alabama Secedes," *Alabama Review* 7 (July 1954): 168–69; Ralph A. Wooster, *The Secession Conventions of the South* (Princeton: Princeton University Press, 1962), 51–52; Rogers et al., *Alabama: The History,* 183; and *Montgomery Weekly Advertiser,* 28 Nov. 1860, quoted in Younge, "The Conservative Party in Alabama," 160.

8. William L. Barney, *The Secessionist Impulse: Alabama and Mississippi in 1860* (Princeton: Princeton University Press, 1974), 253; Wooster, *Secession Conventions,* 52; and Barney, *The Secessionist Impulse,* 253.

9. Forsyth to Douglas, 28 Dec. 1860, Douglas Papers; William R. Smith, *The History and Debates of the Convention of the People of Alabama, Begun and Held in the*

City of Montgomery, on the Seventh Day of January, 1861 (1861; reprint, Spartanburg: The Reprint Company, 1975), 20 (my emphasis), 30, 76–77, and 118.

10. Rogers et al., *Alabama: The History,* 184–85. For a historiographical discussion of this topic, see Ralph A. Wooster, "The Secession of the Lower South: An Examination of Changing Interpretations," *Civil War History* 7 (June 1961): 117–27; and Forsyth to Douglas, 28. Dec. 1860, Douglas Papers.

11. Albert N. Fitts, "The Confederate Convention," *Alabama Review* 2 (Apr. 1949): 83.

12. *Mobile Register,* 14 Feb. 1860.

13. Ludwell H. Johnson, "Fort Sumter and Confederate Diplomacy," *Journal of Southern History* 26 (Nov. 1960): 442.

14. *Journal of the Congress of the Confederate States of America, 1861–1865,* 7 vols. (Washington, D.C.: Government Printing Office, 1904–5), 1: 55; *The War of the Rebellion: A Compilation of the Official Records of the Union and Confederate Armies,* 127 vols. (Washington, D.C.: Government Printing Office, 1880–1901), series 1, vol. 51, part 2: 8 (hereafter cited as *Official Records*); and Jefferson Davis, *The Rise and Fall of the Confederate Government* (1881; reprint, New York: Sagamore Press, 1958), 246.

15. W. A. Swanberg, *First Blood: The Story of Fort Sumter* (New York: Charles Scribner's Sons, 1957), 220; *Official Records,* series 1, vol. 51, part 2: 8; and Johnson, "Fort Sumter," 447.

16. Quoted in Emory Thomas, *The Confederate Nation, 1861–1865* (New York: Harper and Row, 1970), 69; and McPherson, *Battle Cry of Freedom,* 264–66.

17. Quoted in Dumond, *Southern Editorials,* 475.

18. Johnson, "Fort Sumter," 450–451; and Davis, *The Rise and Fall of the Confederate Government,* 676.

19. Forsyth to L. P. Walker, 14 Mar. 1861, in *Official Records,* series 4, vol. 1: 165; Forsyth to Pickens, 15 Mar. 1861, Papers of F. W. Pickens, Library of Congress Manuscript Division, Container 2, Jan. 31, 1861–Feb. 1, 1863 (hereafter referred to as Pickens Papers.); and Johnson, "Fort Sumter," 454.

20. Forsyth to F. W. Pickens, 22 Mar. 1861, Pickens Papers.

21. Crawford, Forsyth, and Roman to Toombs, 3, 5 and 6 Apr. 1861 in *Official Records,* series 1, vol. 1: 286–87; *Official Records,* series 4, vol. 1: 212–13.

22. William H. Russell, *My Diary North and South* (1863; reprint, Philadelphia: Temple University Press, 1988), 60–61, 63.

23. Quoted in Richard N. Current, "The Confederates and the First Shot," *Civil War History* 7 (Dec. 1961): 360; and Davis, *The Rise and Fall of the Confederate Government,* 677.

24. For a full text of this letter, see Davis, *The Rise and Fall of the Confederate Government,* 681.

25. Quoted in Current, "The Confederates," 359.

26. Samuel W. Crawford, *The Genesis of the Civil War* (New York: F. P. Harper 1887), 333.

27. Crawford to Seward, 13 Apr. 1861, quoted in Davis, *The Rise and Fall of the Confederate Government,* 685.

28. Jones Withers to Francis Levert, Levert Family Papers, Southern Historical Collection Manuscripts Department, Wilson Library, University of North Carolina, Chapel Hill, Box 3, Folder 31 (hereafter referred to as Levert Papers); Thomas C. DeLeon, *Four Years in Rebel Capitals* (1892, reprint; Spartanburg: The Reprint Company, 1988), 55. See also Thad Holt Jr., "The Resignation of Mr. Justice Campbell," *Alabama Review* 12 (Apr. 1959): 106–7; and James M. McPherson, "The Career of John Archibald Campbell: A Study of Politics and The Law," *Alabama Review* 19 (Jan. 1966): 58. Campbell returned to Mobile under at least one threat of lynching. Apparently, all was either forgotten or forgiven as the United States Courthouse in Mobile today bears his name.

29. Forsyth et al. to L. P. Walker, 4 May 1861, in *Official Records,* series 1, vol. 52, part 2: 85; and City of Mobile: Alderman's Minute Books, Book 4, 1857–61, 441, Mobile Municipal Archives, Mobile, Alabama (hereafter cited as Alderman's Minutes).

30. Alderman's Minutes, 450–57. For an excellent discussion of Confederate banking and taxation practices, see Walter L. Fleming, *The Civil War and Reconstruction in Alabama* (New York: Columbia University Press, 1905), 162–74.

31. *Mobile Register,* 16 and 28 June 1861 (On 1 June 1861, the *Register* consolidated with the *Mobile Advertiser.* The name was changed to the *Mobile Advertiser and Register.* However, as the paper was always referred to as the *Register,* note references remain the same); Alderman's Minutes, Book 4, 473.

32. Ibid., Book 5, 7–9.

33. Ibid., Book 4, 446 and 475; Book 5, 18.

34. *Official Records,* series 1, vol. 1: 327–28; James L. Nichols, "Confederate Engineers and the Defense of Mobile," *Alabama Review* 12 (July 1959): 182–83; *Mobile Register,* 30 June 1861; and *Official Records,* series 1, vol. 6: 738–39, 744: and John Gill Shorter to Jefferson Davis, 22 Oct. 1862, in John Gill Shorter Papers, Alabama Department of Archives and History, Montgomery.

35. John Forsyth, "Volunteers for the War," 2 Mar. 1862, Alabama Confederate Regimental History File, Alabama Department of Archives and History, Box 1, Folder 2; Stewart Sifakis, *Compendium of the Confederate Armies: Alabama* (New York: Facts on File Books, 1992), 57; and Compiled Service Records of Confederate Soldiers Who Served in Organizations from Alabama, National Archives, Washington, D.C., RG 109, Series M311, Roll 105 (hereafter referred to as Compiled Service Records).

36. Sifakis, *Compendium,* 56–57; and Compiled Service Records, M311, Roll 105.

37. Grady McWhiney, "Controversy in Kentucky: Braxton Bragg's Campaign of 1862," *Civil War History* 6 (Mar. 1960): 5; and McPherson, *Ordeal by Fire,* 288.

38. J. Cutler Andrews, *The South Reports the Civil War* (Princeton: Princeton University Press, 1970), 232–37.

39. Ibid., 241. See also Stanley F. Horn, *The Army of Tennessee: A Military History* (New York; Bobbs-Merrill Company, 1941), 177.

40. *Mobile Register,* 14 Oct. 1862.

41. See Horn, *The Army of Tennessee*, 177; and McWhiney, "Controversy in Kentucky," 24. For the full text of the Proclamation, see *Mobile Register*, 15 Oct. 1862; *Mobile Register*, 22 Oct. 1862.

42. Ibid.; and McPherson, *Ordeal of the Union*, 290. For Forsyth's romanticized account of the battle, see *Mobile Register*, 18 Oct. 1862.

43. *Official Records*, series 1, vol. 16: 1088; and Braxton Bragg to Jefferson Davis, 22 May 1863, Braxton Bragg Papers, Perkins Library, Manuscript Collections, Duke University (hereafter referred to as Bragg Papers).

44. Quoted in Andrews, *The South Reports the Civil War*, 248.

45. For a transcript of the military inquiry, see *Official Records*, series 1, vol. 16: 331–85.

46. *Mobile Register*, 9 and 16 Nov. 1862; and Forsyth to Jefferson Davis, 26 Oct. 1862, John Forsyth Papers, Delaney Collection.

47. Hawes's letter appeared in the *Charleston Mercury* as well as the *Richmond Enquirer.* Forsyth printed the entire letter in the *Mobile Register*, 5 Dec. 1862; *Mobile Register*, 5 Dec. 1862. See also Grady McWhiney, *Braxton Bragg and Confederate Defeat*, 2 vols. (Tuscaloosa: University of Alabama Press, 1969), 1: 332–33.

48. *Mobile Register*, 5 Dec. 1862. See also Thomas Lawrence Connelly, *Autumn of Glory: The Army of Tennessee, 1862–1865* (Baton Rouge: Louisiana State University Press, 1971), 20; See Judith Lee Hallock, *Braxton Bragg and Confederate Defeat*, 2 vols. (Tuscaloosa: University of Alabama Press, 1991), 2: 89, 216, and 231. After his death in 1876, Bragg was buried in Mobile's Magnolia Cemetery. His grave is near that of Forsyth.

49. J. Cutler Andrews, "The Confederate Press and Public Morale," *Journal of Southern History* 32 (Nov. 1966): 448. See also Donald E. Reynolds, *Editors Make War: Southern Newspapers in the Secession Crisis.* Nashville: Vanderbilt University Press, 1970.

50. *Mobile Register*, 24 June and 14 Aug. 1861.

51. Historic American Sheet Music Collection, Perkins Library, Duke University.

52. For specific examples of problems in the defense of Mobile, see Arthur W. Bergeron, *Confederate Mobile* (Jackson: University Press of Mississippi, 1991), 45–91.

53. Quoted in Bergeron, *Confederate Mobile*, 47.

54. For the effects of the blockade, see Earl W. Fornell, "Mobile During the Blockade," *Alabama Historical Quarterly* 23 (Spring 1961): 29–43; *Mobile Register*, 9 and 28 Oct. 1863; *New York Times*, 1 Oct. 1863; E. Orear to Carrier Orear, 5 Sept. 1863, Eldridge Virgil Weaver III Collection, Special Collections Division, Tulane University; General Orders, No. 49 and 34; Special Order, No. 117, Department of Alabama and West Florida: General and Special Orders, 1861–65. RG 109, Box 1, National Archives, Washington, D.C.; and R. H. Slough to Hon. Boards of Alderman and Common Council, 20 Sept. 1864, Mobile City Records, Delaney Collection.

55. Dabury Maurey to Braxton Bragg, 14 July 1864, Bragg Papers, Duke University; *Mobile Register*, 9 Oct. 1863. For a more general discussion of the problem of disloyalty in Alabama, see Hugh C. Bailey, "Disloyalty in Early Confederate Alabama,"

Journal of Southern History 23 (Nov. 1957): 522–28; and *Official Records,* series 4, vol. 1: 1127.

56. Charles Forsyth, *History of the Third Alabama Regiment, C.S.A.* (Montgomery: Confederate Publishing Company, 1866), 20–21. See also *Official Records,* series 1, vol. 27: 594–95. For another account of the events at Cedar Creek, see *Official Records,* series 1, vol. 43: 548; Special Order No. 293, Compiled Service Records, RG 109, Series M311, Roll 105; and *Mobile Register,* 8 Jan. 1865.

57. *Official Records,* series 1, vol. 52, part 2: 808; and *Mobile Register,* 3, 6, and 11 Aug. 1864.

58. Ibid., 31 Dec. 1864.

59. Ibid.; and Davis to Forsyth, 21 Feb. 1865, in *Official Records,* series 4, vol. 3: 1110.

60. Andrews, "Confederate Press," 453; and *Mobile Register,* 28 Dec. 1864 and 1 Apr. 1865.

61. Ibid., 5 Apr. 1865.

Chapter 8

1. *Mobile Register,* 1 Aug. 1865. This letter was also printed in the *New York Times,* 20 Aug. 1865.

2. For classic works of historiographical significance, see William Archibald Dunning, *Reconstruction: Political and Economic, 1865–1877* (1907; reprint, New York: Harper and Brothers, 1962); John Hope Franklin, *Reconstruction After the Civil War* (Chicago: University of Chicago Press, 1964); Kenneth Stampp, *The Era of Reconstruction, 1865–1877* (New York: Vintage Books, 1965); and C. Vann Woodward, *Origins of the New South, 1877–1913* (Baton Rouge: Louisiana State University Press, 1951).

3. Eric L. McKitrick, *Andrew Johnson and Reconstruction* (Chicago: University of Chicago Press, 1960), 8–9; Michael Perman, *Reunion Without Compromise: The South and Reconstruction, 1865–1868* (Cambridge: Cambridge University Press, 1973), 10–11; and Eric Foner, *Reconstruction: America's Unfinished Revolution, 1863–1877* (New York: Harper and Row, 1988), 292–94. For an examination of the historiography of Reconstruction as it applies specifically to Alabama, see Robert Reid, "Changing Interpretation of the Reconstruction Period in Alabama History," *Alabama Review* 27 (Oct. 1974): 263–81.

4. H. K. Thatcher to Hon. Gideon Welles, 12 Apr. 1865, Gordon Granger to E. R. S. Canby, 13 Apr. 1865, R. H. Slough to Gordon Granger, 13 Apr. 1865, *Official Records of the Union and Confederate Navies in the War of the Rebellion,* 22 vols. (Washington, D.C.: Government Printing Office, 1908), 22: 92–94.

5. *Mobile Evening News,* 10 Oct. 1865; "Terms of Capitulation," in Richard Taylor Papers, Perkins Library, Duke University; Elizabeth Bethel, "The Freedman's Bureau in Alabama," *Journal of Southern History* 14 (Feb. 1948): 49; and *Mobile Register,* 1 Aug. 1865.

6. Foner, *Reconstruction,* 177–78.

7. Amnesty/Proclamation Oaths, Probate Court of Mobile County, Alabama, File 36, 1287; and Rogers et al., *Alabama: The History,* 230–31.

8. *Mobile Daily News,* 12 and 17 Apr. 1865. See also Elizabeth M. Lavanna, "South Alabama Newspapers in the Nineteenth Century," Master's thesis, University of Alabama, 1983, 182–83.

9. *Mobile Evening News,* 2 Sept. and 10 Oct. 1865; *New York Times,* 2 Nov. 1865. For a good account of the events of the summer of 1865, see Ralph Poore, "Alabama's Enterprising Newspaper. The Mobile Register and Its Forbearers, 1813–1991," unpublished manuscript, Mobile Public Library, Mobile, Alabama.

10. John Kent Folmar, "Reaction to Reconstruction: John Forsyth and the *Mobile Advertiser and Register,* 1865–1867," *Alabama Historical Quarterly* 37 (Winter 1975): 248; and *Mobile Register,* 21 July 1865.

11. *Mobile Register,* 28 July 1865.

12. For the organizational process of the Freedman's Bureau, see John and LaWanda Cox, "General O. O. Howard and the 'Misrepresented Bureau,'" *Journal of Southern History* 19 (Nov. 1953): 427–31. Kenneth B. White, "Wager Swayne: Racist or Realist," *Alabama Review* 31 (Apr. 1975): 94–95. See also Richard L. Hume, "The Freedman's Bureau and the Freedman's Vote in the Reconstruction of South Alabama: An Account by Agent Samuel S. Gardner," *Alabama Historical Quarterly* 37 (Apr. 1975): 217; and John B. Meyers, "The Alabama Freedmen and the Economic Adjustments During Presidential Reconstruction, 1865–1867," *Alabama Review* 26 (Oct. 1973): 252–54.

13. *Mobile Register,* 21 Sept. and 12 Aug. 1865.

14. Peter Kolchin, *First Freedom: The Response of Alabama's Blacks to Emancipation and Reconstruction* (Westport, Conn: Greenwood Press, 1972), 7; and Joseph E. Brent, "No Compromise: The End of Presidential Reconstruction in Mobile, Alabama, January–May, 1867," *Gulf Coast Historical Review* 7 (Fall 1991): 50–52.

15. White, "Wager Swayne," 95. For the full complaint, see "Petition of Colored Citizens, Mobile, Aug. 2, 1865, Records of the Bureau of Refugees, Freedmen and Abandoned Lands, Reel 23, M809, National Archives, Washington, D.C.

16. Swayne to Parsons, 11 Aug. 1865, Swayne to Howard, 21 Aug. 1865, Records of the Assistant Commissioner for the State of Alabama, Bureau of Refugees, Freedmen, and Abandoned Lands, 1865–1870, reel 2, University of South Alabama Library Microfilm Collection (hereafter cited as Bureau Records).

17. Fleming, *The Civil War and Reconstruction in Alabama,* 430.

18. Forsyth to the Honorable Board of Alderman and Common Council, *Transcription of City Documents, Mobile, Alabama* (W. P. A. Municipal and County Records Project, 1939), 99–102, Mobile Municipal Archives, Mobile, Alabama.

19. *Mobile Register,* 10 Aug. 1865.

20. Donald G. Nieman, "Andrew Johnson, the Freedman's Bureau, and the Problem of Equal Rights, 1865–1866," *Journal of Southern History* 44 (Aug. 1978): 403–4; and *Mobile Register,* 13 Sept. 1865.

21. Quoted in McKitrick, *Andrew Johnson and Reconstruction,* 167.

22. John B. Meyers, "The Freedmen and the Law in Post-Bellum Alabama, 1865–1867," *Alabama Review* 23 (Jan. 1970): 60; and *Mobile Register,* 1 Dec. 1865.

23. *Mobile Register,* 9 Nov. 1865. See Foner, *Reconstruction,* 190–91.

24. Quoted in Foner, *Reconstruction,* 197.

25. *Mobile Register,* 29 Oct. 1865; and Foner, *Reconstruction,* 239.

26. Foner, *Reconstruction,* 228–39.

27. *Mobile Register,* 25 Oct. 1865.

28. Ibid., 8 Aug. 1865.

29. Ibid., 9 May 1866.

30. Foner, *Reconstruction,* 267; and *Mobile Register,* 4 Sept. 1866.

31. *Mobile Register,* 7, 11, and 12 Sept. 1866.

32. Ibid., 13 and 21 Sept. 1866.

33. Ibid., 15 and 9 Nov. 1866.

34. Ibid., 12 Mar. and 29 Apr. 1866.

35. Ibid., 7 May 1867.

36. Sarah Woolfork Wiggins, "The 'Pig Iron' Kelley Riot in Mobile, May 14, 1867," *Alabama Review* 23 (Jan. 1970): 45–48; and *Mobile Register,* 15 May 1867.

37. *Mobile Register,* 15 May 1867; *Mobile Nationalist,* 16 May 1867, my emphasis; and *New York Times,* 15 May 1867.

38. *Mobile Register,* 16 May 1867; *Harper's Weekly,* 1 June 1867; and *Mobile Nationalist,* 23 May 1867. For the grand jury report to the Mayor's Court, see *Mobile Register,* 16 June 1867.

39. *New York Times,* 17 May 1867; and *Mobile Register,* 18 May 1867.

40. Ibid., 23 and 24 May, 1867. Third Military District Headquarters, Special Order 27, 22 May 1867, in Charles Augustus Ropes Dimon Papers, Perkins Library, Duke University. See also Billy G. Hinson, "The Beginning of Military Reconstruction in Mobile, Alabama, May-Nov., 1867," *Gulf Coast Historical Review* 9 (Fall 1993): 67–71; Harriet E. Amos, "Trials of a Unionist: Gustavus Horton, Military Mayor Of Mobile During Reconstruction," *Gulf Coast Historical Review* 4 (Spring 1989): 134, 140; and *Mobile Register,* 5 June 1867.

41. *Mobile Register,* 13 June 1867.

42. Ibid., 27 Sept. 1867; and Rogers et al., *Alabama: The History,* 244.

43. *Mobile Register,* 8 and 25 Oct. 1867. See also Michael Perman, *The Road To Redemption: Southern Politics, 1869–1879* (Chapel Hill: University of North Carolina Press, 1984), 77–81.

44. Loren Schweninger, "Black Citizenship and the Republican Party in Reconstruction Alabama," *Alabama Review* 29 (Apr. 1976): 86–87; and Rogers et al., *Alabama: The History,* 245.

45. *Mobile Register,* 3 Feb. 1867.

46. Ibid., 1 and 4 Feb. 1868.

47. Rogers et al., *Alabama: The History,* 246–47. See also Loren Schweninger, "Alabama Blacks and the Congressional Reconstruction Act of 1867," *Alabama Review* 31 (July 1978): 196–97.

48. *Mobile Register*, 11 Feb. 1868; Clipping in Reconstruction Papers, Delaney Collection (n.p., n.d.); and Bethel, "The Freedman's Bureau in Alabama," 82.

49. *Mobile Register*, 4 and 27 Apr., 18 May 1868. For a concise summary of the final impeachment proceedings, see McPherson, *Ordeal By Fire*, 530–33.

50. *Mobile Register*, 20 Apr. 1868.

51. Rogers et al., *Alabama: The History*, 249–50; and *Mobile Register*, 23 July 1868.

52. *Mobile Register*, 27 May, 27 June, 21 and 23 July 1868.

53. *Harpers Weekly*, 11 July 1868.

54. For details of the Republican nomination process, see John Hope Franklin, "Election of 1868," in Arthur M. Schlesinger Jr., ed., *History of American Presidential Elections, 1789–1968*, 2 vols. (New York: Chelsea House, 1971) 2: 1247–66; and *Mobile Register*, 16 Dec. 1865.

55. *Mobile Register*, 22 July 1868; *Harper's Weekly*, 12 Sept. 1868, quoted in the *Mobile Register*, 23 Sept. 1868. See, for example, Forsyth's letter to the *Cincinnati Enquirer*, printed in the *Mobile Register*, 26 Sept. 1868, and to the *Milwaukee Sentinel*, printed in the *Mobile Register*, 14 Oct. 1868.

56. *Mobile Register*, 5 Nov. 1868.

57. Fitzgerald, *Urban Emancipation*, 134–35; and John D. Wilkins to Wife, 15 Nov. 1868, in John Darragh Wilkins Papers, Perkins Library, Duke University (hereafter cited as Wilkins Papers).

58. *Columbus Times*, 26 Mar. and 5 Nov. 1845; and *Mobile Register*, 25 Jan. 1856. For the best summary of Forsyth's economic positions, see *The North and the South: A Lecture Before the Franklin Society of Mobile, May 2, 1854, By John Forsyth* (Mobile: Thompson and Harris Printers, 1854).

59. Wilkins to Wife, 8 Nov. 1868, Wilkins Papers. For an interesting biography of William D. Mann, see Andy Logan, *The Man Who Robbed the Robber Barons. The Story of Colonel William D'Alton Mann: War Hero, Profiteer, Inventor, And Blackmailer Extraordinary* (New York: Norton, 1965). *Mobile Register*, 4 and 17 Mar., 16 Apr., 6 and 15 May 1869; and Fitzgerald, *Urban Emancipation*, 135–39.

60. Incorporation Records, Miscellaneous Book G, Probate Court of Mobile County, Alabama, 657–58.

61. *Mobile Register*, 1 June 1870.

62. Ibid., 8 June 1870.

63. Ibid., 12 and 14 June 1870.

64. See James M. McPherson, "Grant or Greeley? The Abolitionist Dilemma in the Election of 1872," *American Historical Review* 71 (Oct. 1965): 44; and *Mobile Register*, 7 Dec. 1871.

65. William Gillette, *Retreat from Reconstruction, 1869–1879* (Baton Rouge: Louisiana State University Press, 1979), 56–57.

66. The complete coroner's report was printed in the *Mobile Register*, 16 Mar. 1872; see also *Mobile Register*, 21 Mar. 1872.

67. McPherson, *Ordeal By Fire*, 568; McPherson, "Grant or Greeley," 47; and *Mobile Register*, 24 Mar. 1872.

68. Quoted in Gillette, *Retreat from Reconstruction,* 62–63.

69. *Mobile Register,* 13 and 15 May 1872.

70. Ibid., 23 May 1872.

71. Ibid., 18 June 1872.

72. Ibid., 28 June 1872.

73. Ibid., 11 July 1872.

74. Ibid., 16 July and 27 Oct. 1872.

75. Ibid., 10 Nov. 1872.

76. Ibid.

Conclusion

1. *Mobile Register,* 3 Oct. and 28 Sept. 1873.

2. Ibid., 23 and 3 Oct. 1873.

3. Ibid., 1 and 6 Aug., 16 Sept., 18 and 8 Oct., and 15 Nov. 1873.

4. Ibid., 13 Nov. 1873.

5. Gillette, *Retreat from Reconstruction,* 71–72, 238–39; and *Mobile Register,* 12 July 1874.

6. Ibid., 4 July 1874. See also Perman, *Road to Redemption,* 156–58; and *Mobile Register,* 14 July and 16 July 1874.

7. *Mobile Register,* 1 Aug. 1874.

8. Ibid., 5 Aug. 1874.

9. Ibid., 19 Aug. 1874.

10. Ibid., 24 Sept. and 2 Oct. 1874.

11. Ibid., 20 and 3 Oct. 1874.

12. Ibid., 31 Oct. 1874.

13. Ibid., 4 Nov. 1874.

14. Gillette, *Retreat from Reconstruction,* 249–52.

15. *Mobile Register,* 5 and 4 Nov. 1874.

16. Ibid., 21 and 24 Nov. 1874.

17. *Centennial Remembrance Book of Col. John Forsyth,* 21, John Forsyth Papers, Mobile Public Library, Mobile, Alabama.

18. *Mobile Register,* 25 June 1889, 11 Oct. 1887, and 2 Sept. 1907.

19. Ibid., 27 Mar. 1874; and *Rapier vs. Forsyth,* filed 22 Apr. 1876, case 3535. Circuit Court Records, Mobile County, Alabama. University of South Alabama Archives, Mobile (hereafter referred to as Circuit Court Records).

20. Circuit Court Records, 3 May 1876.

21. Ibid., 29 June 1876.

22. Ibid., 3, 4 and 5 May 1877.

23. For these and other tributes, see *Mobile Register,* 6–8 May 1877.

24. Folmar, "Reaction to Reconstruction," 265; see Rogers et al., *Alabama: The History,* 181 and 192; and *Mobile Register,* 9 Nov. 1999.

25. Quoted in *Mobile Register,* 17 May 1872, 21 July 1874, and 17 Mar. 1872.

26. *New York Herald,* 3 May 1877.

27. *Mobile Register,* 27 May 1877 and 14 Jan. 1860.

28. Ibid., 27 Mar. 1874.

29. *Mobile Nationalist,* 14 July 1869.

30. *Mobile Register,* 5 Sept. 1866.

31. *New York Herald,* 3 May 1877; *Mobile Register,* 6 May 1877, 27 Mar. 1874, and 17 July 1872.

32. Forsyth, *The North and the South,* 20; and *Mobile Register,* 27 May 1877.

Bibliography

Primary Sources

Manuscript Collections

Alabama Department of Archives and History, Montgomery, Alabama.
    Confederate Regimental History File.
    Benjamin Fitzpatrick Papers.
    John Forsyth Papers.
    Andrew B. Moore Papers.
    John Gill Shorter Papers.
Cook Library. University of Southern Mississippi, Hattiesburg, Mississippi.
    Despatches of United States Ministers to Mexico. General Records of the Department of State: Applications and Recommendations for Public Office, 1797–1924. National Archives, Washington, D.C. (microfilm).
Delaney Historical Reference Collection, University of Mobile, Mobile, Alabama.
    City of Mobile, Records File.
    John Forsyth Papers.
    Reconstruction Papers.
    Thaddeus Sanford Papers.
Georgia State Department of Archives, Morrow, Georgia.
    Annual Return Books: Muscogee County, Georgia, Book B (1843–48) and Book C (1848–53).
    Court of Ordinary Minutes, Muscogee County, Georgia, 1838–51.
    Governor's Letter Book, 1843–46.
    Inventories and Appraisals: Muscogee County, Georgia, 1831–58.
    John Forsyth Sr. Papers.
Hargrett Rare Book and Manuscript Library, University of Georgia, Athens, Georgia.
    John Forsyth Sr. Papers.
Historic Mobile Preservation Society, Mobile, Alabama.
    John Forsyth Papers.
Library of Congress, Washington, D.C.
    F. W. Pickens Papers.
    George Washington Papers.

Mobile Municipal Archives, Mobile, Alabama.
   City of Mobile Alderman's Minute Books. Books 4 and 5, 1857–61.
Mobile Public Library, Mobile, Alabama.
   John Forsyth Papers.
National Archives, College Park, Maryland.
   RG 84. Records of Foreign Service Posts: Notes to Mexican Foreign Offices.
National Archives, Washington, D.C.
   M809 Records of the Bureau of Refugees, Freedmen, and Abandoned Lands.
   RG 59. Applications and Recommendations for Public Office, 1797–1924.
   RG 59. Despatches of United States Ministers to Mexico.
   RG 109. Compiled Service Records of Confederate Soldiers who Served in Organi-
      zations from Alabama.
   RG 109. Department of Alabama and West Florida: General and Special Orders,
      1861–65.
Perkins Library, Duke University, Durham, North Carolina.
   Braxton Bragg Papers.
   C. C. Clay Papers.
   Charles Augustus Ropes Dimon Papers.
   Stephen A. Douglas Papers.
   Historic American Sheet Music Collection.
   Richard Taylor Papers.
   John Darragh Wilkins Papers.
Probate Court of Mobile County, Alabama.
   Amnesty/Proclamation Oaths.
   Incorporation Records.
Regenstein Library, University of Chicago, Chicago, Illinois.
   Stephen A. Douglas Papers.
Southern Historical Collection, Wilson Library, University of North Carolina, Chapel
   Hill.
   Benjamin Fitzpatrick Papers.
   Levert Family Papers.
University of South Alabama Archives, Mobile, Alabama.
   Circuit Court Records, Mobile County, Alabama.
University of South Alabama Library, Mobile, Alabama.
   Records of the Assistant Commissioners for the State of Alabama, Bureau of Refu-
      gees, Freedmen, and Abandoned Lands, 1865–70 (microfilm).

Published Government Documents

Annals of the Congress of the United States, 1789–1824. 42 vols. Washington, D.C.:
   Government Printing Office, 1834–56.
Congressional Globe. 46 vols. Washington, D.C.: Government Printing Office, 1834–73.
Israel, Fred L., ed. *The State of the Union Messages of the Presidents.* 2 vols. New York:
   Chelsea House, 1966.

Journal of the Congress of the Confederate States of America, 1861–65. 7 vols. Washington, D.C.: Government Printing Office, 1904–5.

Manning, William R., ed. *Diplomatic Correspondence of the United States: Inter-American Affairs, 1831–1860.* 12 vols. Washington, D.C.: Carnegie Endowment for International Peace, 1932–39.

Official Records of the Confederate and Union Navies in the War of the Rebellion. 22 vols. Washington, D.C.: Government Printing Office, 1908.

Richardson, James D., ed. *A Compilation of the Messages and Papers of the Presidents, Vol. 3.* Washington: Bureau of National Literature and Art, 1897.

Transcriptions of City Documents: Mobile, Alabama, 1859–1869. Washington, D.C.: WPA Municipal and Court Records Project, 1939.

The War of the Rebellion: A Compilation of the Official Records of the Union and Confederate Armies. 127 vols. Washington, D.C.: Government Printing Office, 1880–1901.

Published Proceedings, Diaries, Memoirs, Letters, Pamphlets

Address of the Democracy of Alabama to the National Democratic Convention at Baltimore, June 18th, 1860. William S. Hoole Special Collections Library. Tuscaloosa, AL.

Brooks, R. P., ed. "Howell Cobb Papers." *Georgia Historical Quarterly* 5 (Sept. 1921): 1–42.

Buchanan, James. *Mr. Buchanan's Administration on the Eve of the Rebellion.* New York: D. Appleton, 1866.

Centennial Remembrance Book of Col. John Forsyth. Mobile, Alabama, 1912. John Forsyth Papers, Mobile Public Library.

Crawford, Samuel W. *The Genesis of the Civil War.* New York: F. P. Harper, 1887.

Davis, Jefferson. *The Rise and Fall of the Confederate Government,* 1881. Reprint, New York: Sagamore Press, 1958.

DeLeon, Thomas C. *Four Years in Rebel Capitals,* 1892. Reprint, Spartanburg: The Reprint Co., 1988.

Douglas' Doctrine of Popular Sovereignty in the Territories; Its Counterpart. By a Missourian. St. Louis: R. V. Kennedy & Company, 1860.

Forney, John W. *Eulogy Upon the Death of Hon. Stephen A. Douglas. Delivered at the Smithsonian Institute, Washington, July 3, 1861.* Philadelphia: Ringwalt and Brown, 1861.

Forsyth, Charles. *History of the Third Alabama Regiment, C.S.A.* Montgomery: Confederate Publishing Co., 1866.

Forsyth, John. *Address to the People of Georgia.* N.p.: 1840.

Hesseltine, William B., ed. *Three Against Lincoln: Murat Halstead Reports the Caucuses of 1860.* Baton Rouge: Louisiana State University Press, 1960.

Johnson, Donald B., ed. *National Party Platforms, 1840–1956.* Urbana: University of Illinois Press, 1978.

Letters of Hon. John Forsyth, of Alabama Late Minister to Mexico to Wm. F. Samford, Esq., In Defence of Stephen A. Douglas. Mobile: Lemuel Towers, 1859.

Letters, Speeches, and Addresses of August Belmont. Privately Published, 1890.

Longstreet, Augustus Baldwin. *A Voice from the South. Comprising Letters from Georgia to Massachusetts and to the Southern States.* Baltimore: Samuel E. Smith Printers, 1848.

McKee, Hudson, ed. *The National Conventions and Platforms of All Political Parties, 1789–1905.* 1906. Reprint, New York: AMS Press, 1971.

McMillan, Malcolm C., ed. *The Alabama Confederate Reader.* Tuscaloosa: University of Alabama Press, 1963.

Moore, John Bassett, ed. *The Works of James Buchanan.* 10 vols. New York: Antiquarian Press, 1960.

Phillips, Ulrich Bonnell, ed. "The Correspondence of Robert Toombs, Alexander Stephens, and Howell Cobb." *Annual Report of the American Historical Association* (1911): 123–47.

Proceedings of the Democratic State Convention Held in the City of Montgomery Commencing Wednesday, January 11, 1860. Montgomery: Shorter and Reid, 1860.

Russell, William H. *My Diary North and South.* 1863. Reprint, Philadelphia: Temple University Press, 1988.

Smith, William R. *The History and Debates of the Convention of the People of Alabama, Begun and Held in the City of Montgomery, on the Seventh Day of January, 1861.* 1861. Reprint, Spartanburg: The Reprint Co., 1975.

Speech of the Hon. John Forsyth of Georgia on the Subject of the Removal of the Public Deposits: Delivered in the Senate of the United States, January, 1834. Washington, D.C.: F. P. Blair, 1834.

The North and the South: A Lecture Before the Franklin Society of Mobile, May 2, 1854, By John Forsyth. Mobile: Thompson and Harris Printers, 1854.

Newspapers

Atlanta Constitution, 1877.
Augusta (Georgia) *Chronicle and Sentinel,* 1850.
Augusta (Georgia) *Constitutionalist,* 1850.
Baltimore American and Daily Commercial Advertiser, 1840–41.
Charleston Daily Courier, 1860.
Charleston Mercury, 1859–61.
Columbus (Georgia) *Times,* 1841, 1845–53.
Columbus (Georgia) *Enquirer,* 1842.
Harper's Weekly, 1867–68.
Memphis Appeal, 1862.
Mexican Extraordinary, 1856.
Mexico City El Heraldo, 1858.
Milledgeville (Georgia) *Southern Recorder,* 1843, 1847, 1850.
Milledgeville (Georgia) *Union Recorder,* 1846.
Mobile Advertiser and Register, 1861–68.
Mobile Daily Advertiser, 1860.

Mobile Daily Commercial Register, 1837–41; 1853–61.

Mobile Daily News, 1865.

Mobile Daily Register, 1868–77, 1895, 1907.

Mobile Evening News, 1865.

Mobile Register, 1999.

Mobile Nationalist, 1865–69.

Mobile Times, 1877.

Montgomery Daily Mail, 1860.

Montgomery Weekly Advertiser, 1858–60; 1872.

New York Evening Post, 1856.

New York Herald, 1857.

New York Times, 1859; 1863; 1874; 1877.

New York Tribune, 1850; 1872.

New York World, 1877.

Paducah Kentuckian, 1872.

Richmond Enquirer, 1837–40; 1862.

Richmond Whig, 1862.

Savannah Georgian, 1849.

St. Louis Republican, 1872.

Tuscaloosa Times, 1874.

Vicksburg Herald, 1872.

Washington Daily National Intelligencer, 1841.

Washington, D.C., Democratic Review, 1840.

Washington National Era, 1859.

Wetumpka [Alabama] Argus, 1840.

Wilmington Journal, 1860.

Secondary Sources

Books

Amos, Harriet E. *Cotton City: Urban Development in Antebellum Mobile.* Tuscaloosa: University of Alabama Press, 1985.

Anbinder, Tyler. *Nativism and Slavery: The Northern Know Nothings and the Politics of the 1850s.* New York: Oxford University Press, 1992.

Andrews, J. Cutler. *The South Reports the Civil War.* Princeton: Princeton University Press, 1970.

Aver, J. Jeffry, ed. *Anti-Slavery and Disunion, 1858–1861.* New York: Harper and Row, 1963.

Barney, William L. *The Secessionist Impulse: Alabama and Mississippi in 1860.* Princeton: Princeton University Press, 1974.

Bemis, Samuel Flagg, ed. *The American Secretaries of States and Their Diplomacy.* 18 vols. New York: Pageant Book Co., 1958–70.

Bergeron, Authur W. *Confederate Mobile.* Jackson: University of Mississippi Press, 1991.

Billington, Ray Allen. *The Protestant Crusade, 1800–1860.* New York: MacMillan Co., 1938.

Buchenau, Jürgen. *In The Shadow of the Giant: The Making of Mexico's Central American Policy, 1876–1930.* Tuscaloosa: University of Alabama Press, 1996.

Calcott, Wilfred Hardy. *Church and State in Mexico, 1827–1857.* New York: Octagon Books, 1965.

Callahan, James Morton. *American Foreign Policy in Mexican Relations.* New York: MacMillan, 1932.

Carey, Anthony Gene. *Politics, Slavery, and the Union in Antebellum Georgia.* Athens: University of Georgia Press, 1997.

Cole, Arthur C. *The Whig Party in the South.* 1913. Reprint, Gloucester, Mass.: Peter Smith, 1962.

Connelly, Thomas Lawrence. *Autumn of Glory: The Army of Tennessee, 1862–1865.* Baton Rouge: Louisiana State University Press, 1971.

Cook, James F. *Governors of Georgia.* Huntsville, Ala: Strode Publishing, 1979.

Cooper, William J., Jr. *Liberty and Slavery: Southern Politics to 1860.* New York: Alfred A. Knopf, 1983.

———. *The South and the Politics of Slavery, 1828–1856.* Baton Rouge: Louisiana State University Press, 1978.

Craven, Avery O. *The Growth of Southern Nationalism, 1848–1861.* Baton Rouge: Louisiana State University Press, 1953.

Crenshaw, Ollinger. *The Slave States in the Election of 1860.* Baltimore: Johns Hopkins University Press, 1945.

Donald, David. *Charles Sumner and the Coming of the Civil War.* New York: Alfred A. Knopf, 1960.

Donghi, Tulio Halperin. *The Contemporary History of Latin America.* Durham: Duke University Press, 1993.

Dorman, Lewy. *Party Politics in Alabama: From 1850 through 1860.* Wetumpka, Ala.: Wetumpka Printing Co., 1935.

Dubose, John Witherspoon. *The Life and Times of William Lowndes Yancey.* 2 vols. Birmingham, Ala.: Roberts and Son, 1892.

Duckett, Alvin Leroy. *John Forsyth, Political Tactician.* Athens: University of Georgia Press, 1962.

Dumond, Dwight Lowell, ed. *Southern Editorials on Secession.* Gloucester, Mass.: Peter Smith, 1964.

Dunning, William A. *Reconstruction: Political and Economic, 1865–1877.* 1907. Reprint, New York: Harper and Brothers, 1962.

Eaton, Clement. *A History of the Old South.* New York: MacMillan Co., 1949.

Ettinger, Amos Aschbach. *The Mission to Spain of Pierre Soulé, 1853–1855.* New Haven: Yale University Press, 1932.

Fehrenbacher, Donald E. *The South and Three Sectional Crises.* Baton Rouge: Louisiana State University Press, 1980.

Findling, John E. *Dictionary of American Diplomatic History.* Westport, Conn.: Greenwood Press, 1980.

Fitzgerald, Michael W. *Urban Emancipation. Popular Politics in Reconstruction Mobile, 1860–1890.* Baton Rouge: Louisiana State University Press, 2002.

Fleming, Walter L. *Civil War and Reconstruction in Alabama.* New York: Columbia University Press, 1905.

Flippin, Percy Scott. *Herschel V. Johnson of Georgia: States Right's Unionist.* Richmond: Dietz Printing Co., 1931.

Foner, Eric. *Reconstruction: America's Unfinished Revolution, 1863–1877.* New York: Harper and Row, 1988.

———. *Free Soil, Free Labor, Free Men: The Ideology of the Republican Party Before the Civil War.* Oxford: Oxford University Press, 1970.

Formisano, Ronald P. *The Birth of Mass Political Parties.* Princeton: Princeton University Press, 1971.

Franklin, John Hope. *Reconstruction After the Civil War.* Chicago: University of Chicago Press, 1964.

Gara, Larry. *The Presidency of Franklin Pierce.* Lawrence: University Press of Kansas, 1991.

Garber, Paul Neff. *The Gadsden Treaty.* Gloucester, Mass.: Peter Smith, 1959.

Gienapp, William E. *The Origins of the Republican Party, 1852–1856.* New York: Oxford University Press, 1987.

Gillette, William. *Retreat from Reconstruction, 1869–1879.* Baton Rouge: Louisiana State University Press, 1979.

Grabner, Norman A., ed. *Politics and the Crisis of 1860.* Urbana: University of Illinois Press, 1961.

Hale, Charles A. *Mexican Liberalism in the Age of Mora, 1821–1853.* New Haven: Yale University Press, 1968.

Hallock, Judith Lee. *Braxton Bragg and Confederate Defeat.* 2 Vols. Tuscaloosa: University of Alabama Press, 1991.

Hamilton, Holman. *Prologue to Conflict: The Crisis and Compromise of 1850.* Lexington: University of Kentucky Press, 1964.

Hammond, Bray. *Banks and Politics in America.* Princeton: Princeton University Press, 1957.

Hamnett, Brian. *Juárez.* New York: Longman Press, 1994.

Harris, Brayton. *Blue and Gray in Black and White. Newspapers in the Civil War.* Washington: Brasseys, 1999.

Hart, John Mason. *Revolutionary Mexico: The Coming and Process of the Mexican Revolution.* Berkeley: University of California Press, 1987.

Holt, Michael F. *The Political Crisis of the 1850s.* New York: W. W. Norton, 1978.

Horn, Stanley F. *The Army of Tennessee: A Military History.* New York: Bobbs-Merrill Co., 1941.

Jack, Theodore Henley. *Sectionalism and Party Politics in Alabama, 1819–1842.* Menasha, Wis.: George Banta, 1919.

Jeffries, Jeanie Forsyth. *A History of the Forsyth Family.* Indianapolis Ind.: William H. Burford, 1920.

Johannsen, Robert W. *Stephen A. Douglas.* New York: Oxford University Press, 1973.

Johnson, Allen, and Dumas Malone, eds. *Dictionary of American Biography.* 11 vols. New York: Charles Scribner's Sons, 1959.

Johnson, Richard A. *The Mexican Revolution of Ayutla, 1854–1855.* 1939. Reprint, Westport, Conn.: Greenwood Press, 1974.

Joseph, Gilbert M. and David Nugent, eds. *Everyday Forms of State Formation: Revolution and Negotiation of Rule in Modern Mexico.* Durham: Duke University Press, 1995.

Klien, Philip Shriver. *President James Buchanan: A Biography.* University Park, Penn.: Pennsylvania State University Press, 1962.

Knowlton, Robert J. *Church Property and the Mexican Reform, 1856–1910.* DeKalb: Northern Illinois University Press, 1976.

Kolchin, Peter. *First Freedom: The Response of Alabama Blacks to Emancipation and Reconstruction.* Westport, Conn.: Greenwood Press, 1972.

Lemly, James H. *The Gulf, Mobile, and Ohio.* Homewood, Illinois: Richard D. Irwin, Inc., 1953.

Logan, Andy. *The Man Who Robbed the Robber Barons. The Story of William D'Alton Mann: War Hero, Profiteer, Inventor, and Blackmailer Extraordinary.* New York: Norton, 1965.

Mallon, Florencia. *Peasant and Nation: The Making of Post-Colonial Mexico and Peru.* Berkeley: University of California Press, 1994.

Malin, James C. *The Nebraska Question, 1852–1854.* Ann Arbor: Edwards Brothers, 1953.

May, Robert E. *The Southern Dream of a Caribbean Empire: 1854–1861.* Baton Rouge: Louisiana State University Press, 1973.

McCormick, Richard L. *The Party Period and Public Policy: American Politics From the Age of Jackson to the Progressive Era.* New York: Oxford University Press, 1986.

———. *The Second American Party System: Party Formation in the Jacksonian Era.* Chapel Hill: University of North Carolina Press, 1966.

McKitrick, Eric L. *Andrew Johnson and Reconstruction.* Chicago: University of Chicago Press, 1960.

McPherson, James M. *Battle Cry of Freedom.* New York: Ballantine Books, 1988.

———. *Ordeal By Fire: The Civil War and Reconstruction.* New York: Alfred A. Knopf, 1982.

McWhiney, Grady. *Braxton Bragg and Confederate Defeat.* 2 Vols. Tuscaloosa: University of Alabama Press, 1969.

Meyer, Michael C., William L. Sherman, and Susan M. Deeds. *The Course of Mexican History.* New York: Oxford University Press, 1999.

Meyers, Marvin. *The Jacksonian Persuasion.* New York: Vintage Books, 1957.

Milton, George Fort. *The Eve of Conflict: Stephen A. Douglas and the Needless War,* 1934. Reprint, New York: Octagon Books, 1963.

Nevins, Allan. *Ordeal of the Union.* 2 vols. New York: Charles Schribners Sons, 1947.

Nichols, Roy Franklin. *Disruption of American Democracy.* New York: Collier Books, 1948.

―――. *The Democratic Machine, 1850–1854.* New York: AMS Press, 1967.

Olliff, Donathan C. *Reforma Mexico and the United States: A Search for Alternatives to Annexation, 1854–1861.* Tuscaloosa: University of Alabama Press, 1981.

Osthaus, Carl R. *Partisans of the Southern Press: Editorial Spokesmen of the Nineteenth Century.* Lexington: University of Kentucky Press, 1994.

Owen, Thomas M. *History of Alabama and Dictionary of Alabama Biography.* 4 vols. Chicago: S. J. Clark, 1921.

Perman, Michael. *The Road to Redemption: Southern Politics, 1869–1879.* Chapel Hill: University of North Carolina Press, 1984.

―――. *Reunion Without Compromise: The South and Reconstruction, 1865–1868.* Cambridge: Cambridge University Press, 1973.

Pessen, Edward. *Jacksonian America.* Urbana: University of Illinois Press, 1969.

Petrie, George, ed. *Studies in Southern and Alabama History.* Montgomery: Alabama Historical Society, 1904.

Potter, David M. *The Impending Crisis.* New York: Harper and Row, 1976.

Raat, W. Dirk. *Mexico and the United States: Ambivalent Vistas.* Athens: University of Georgia Press, 1992.

Remini, Robert. *Andrew Jackson and the Course of American Democracy, 1833–1845.* New York: Harper and Row, 1984.

Reynolds, Donald E. *Editors Make War: Southern Newspapers in the Secession Crisis.* Nashville: Vanderbilt University Press, 1970.

Ridley, Jasper. *Maximilian and Juárez.* New York: Ticknor and Fields, 1992.

Riley, B. F. *Makers and Romance of Alabama History.* N.p., n.d.

Rogers, William Warren, Robert David Ward, Leah Rawls Atkins, and Wayne Flint. *Alabama: The History of a Deep South State.* Tuscaloosa: University of Alabama Press, 1994.

Saunders, Robert Jr. *John Archibald Campbell, Southern Moderate, 1811–1889.* Tuscaloosa: University of Alabama Press, 1997.

Schlesinger, Arthur M., Jr., ed. *History of American Presidential Elections, 1789–1968.* 2 vols. New York: Chelsea House, 1971.

―――. *The Age of Jackson.* Boston: Little, Brown, and Co., 1945.

Schoonover, Thomas. *Dollars Over Diplomacy: The Triumph of Liberalism in Mexican-United States Relations, 1861–1867.* Baton Rouge: Louisiana State University Press, 1978.

Sharp, James Roger. *The Jacksonians Versus the Bank: Politics in the States After the Panic of 1837.* New York: Columbia University Press, 1970.

Shyrock, Richard Harrison. *Georgia and the Union in 1850.* Durham: Duke University Press, 1926.

Sifakis, Stewart. *Compendium of Confederate Armies: Alabama.* New York: Facts on File, Inc., 1992.

Sinkin, Richard N. *The Mexican Reform, 1855–1876: A Study in Liberal Nation Building.* Austin: Institute of Latin American Studies, 1979.

Smith, Gordon. *History of the Georgia Militia, 1783–1861. Vol 3: Counties and Commanders, Part 2.* Milledgeville, GA: Boyd Publishing, 2001.

Stampp, Kenneth. *America in 1857.* New York: Oxford University Press, 1990.

———. *The Era of Reconstruction, 1865–1877.* New York: Vintage Books, 1965.

Swanberg, W. A. *First Blood: The Story of Fort Sumter.* New York: Charles Scribner's Sons, 1957.

Thomas, Emory. *The Confederate Nation, 1861–1865.* New York: Harper and Row, 1970.

Thornton, J. Mills, III. *Politics and Power in a Slave Society.* Baton Rouge: Louisiana State University Press, 1978.

Wilson, Major L. *The Presidency of Martin Van Buren.* Lawrence: University Press of Kansas, 1984.

Woodward, C. Vann. *Origins of the New South, 1877–1913.* Baton Rouge: Louisiana State University Press, 1951.

Wooster, Ralph A. *The Secession Conventions of the South.* Princeton: Princeton University Press, 1962.

Articles

Alexander, Thomas, Kit C. Carter, Jack R. Lister, Jerry C. Oldshue, and Winfred G. Sandlin. "Who Were the Alabama Whigs?" *Alabama Review* 16 (January 1963): 5–19.

Amos, Harriet E. "Trials of a Unionist: Gustavus Horton, Military Mayor of Mobile During Reconstruction." *Gulf Coast Historical Review* 4 (spring 1989): 134–51.

Andrews, J. Cutler. "The Confederate Press and Public Morale." *Journal of Southern History* 32 (November 1966): 445–465.

Auchampaugh, Phillip G. "The Buchanan-Douglas Feud." *Illinois State Historical Society Journal* 35 (April 1932): 5–48.

Bailey, Hugh C. "Disloyalty in Early Confederate Alabama." *Journal of Southern History* 23 (November 1957): 522–528.

Bazant, Jan. "Mexico From Independence to 1867." In *The Cambridge History of Latin America,* edited by Leslie Bethel, 423–470. Cambridge: Cambridge University Press, 1985.

Bethel, Elizabeth. "The Freedmen's Bureau in Alabama." *Journal of Southern History* 14 (February 1948): 49–92.

Brading, David A. "Liberal Patriotism and the Mexican Reforma." *Journal of Latin American Studies* 20 (May 1988): 27–46.

Brantley, William H. "Alabama Secedes." *Alabama Review* 7 (July 1954): 165–185.

Brent, Joseph E. "No Compromise: The End of Presidential Reconstruction in Mobile, Alabama, January-May, 1867." *Gulf Coast Historical Review* 7 (fall 1991): 18–37.

Carey, Anthony Gene. "Two Southern to Be Americans: Proslavery Politics and the

Failure of the Know Nothing Party in Georgia, 1854–1856." *Civil War History* 41 (March 1995): 22–40.

Cox, John and LaWanda Cox. "General O. O. Howard and the Misrepresented Bureau." *Journal of Southern History* 19 (November 1953): 427–456.

Current, Richard N. "The Confederates and the First Shot." *Civil War History* 7 (December 1961): 357–369.

Dickett, A. L. "Slidell's Right Hand: Emile La Seré." *Louisiana History* 4 (summer 1963): 177–205.

Fitts, Albert N. "The Confederate Convention." *Alabama Review* 2 (April 1949): 83–99.

Fitzgerald, Michael W. "Railroad Subsidies and Black Aspirations: The Politics of Economic Development in Reconstruction Mobile, 1865–1879." *Civil War History* 39 (September 1993): 240–56.

———. "Wager Swayne, the Freedman's Bureau, and the Politics of Reconstruction in Alabama." *Alabama Review* 48 (July 1995): 188–218.

Folmer, John Kent. "Reaction to Reconstruction: John Forsyth and the *Mobile Advertiser and Register,* 1865–1867." *Alabama Historical Quarterly* 37 (winter 1975): 245–261.

Folsom, Burton W., II. "Party Formation and Development in Jacksonian America: The Old South." *Journal of American Studies* 7 (December 1993): 217–229.

Fornell, Earl W. "Mobile During the Blockade." *Alabama Historical Quarterly* 23 (spring 1961): 29–43.

Gienapp, William E. "The Crime Against Sumner: The Caning of Charles Sumner and the Rise of the Republican Party." *Civil War History* 25 (September 1979): 218–245.

Herndon, Dallas Tabor. "The Nashville Convention of 1850." *Publication of the Alabama Historical Society, Transactions* 5 (1904): 203–237.

Hinson, Billy G. "The Beginning of Military Reconstruction in Mobile, Alabama, May-November, 1867." *Gulf Coast Historical Review* 9 (fall 1993): 65–83.

Hodder, Frank Haywood. "The Railroad Background of the Kansas-Nebraska Act." *Mississippi Valley Historical Review* 12 (June 1925): 3–22.

Holt, Michael F. "The Politics of Impatience: The Origins of Know Nothingism." *Journal of American History* 60 (September 1973): 309–331.

Holt, Thad, Jr. "The Resignation of Mr. Justice Campbell." *Alabama Review* 12 (April 1959): 105–118.

Howard, Milo B., Jr. "The General Ticket." *Alabama Review* 19 (July 1966): 163–174.

Hume, Richard L. "The Freedmen's Bureau and the Freedman's Vote in the Reconstruction of Southern Alabama: An Account By Agent Samuel S. Gardner." *Alabama Historical Quarterly* 37 (fall 1975): 217–224.

Johannsen, Robert W. "Stephen A. Douglas, Harper's Magazine, and Popular Sovereignty." *Mississippi Valley Historical Review* 45 (March 1959): 606–631.

Johnson, Ludwell H. "Fort Sumter and Confederate Diplomacy." *Journal of Southern History* 26 (November 1960): 441–477.

Kurtz, Wilbur G. "The First Regiment of Georgia Volunteers in the Mexican War." *Georgia Historical Quarterly* 27 (December 1941): 301–323.

Long, Durwood. "Political Parties and Propaganda in the Presidential Election of 1860." *Alabama Historical Quarterly* 25 (spring 1963): 120–135.

McPherson, James M. "The Career of John Archibald Campbell: A Study of Politics and the Law." *Alabama Review* 19 (January 1966): 53–63.

———. "Grant or Greeley? The Abolitionist Dilemma in the Election of 1872." *Alabama Historical Review* 71 (October 1965): 43–61.

McWhiney, Grady. "Controversy in Kentucky: Braxton Bragg's Campaign of 1862." *Civil War History* 6 (March 1960): 5–42.

———. "Were the Whigs a Class Party in Alabama?" *Journal of Southern History* 23 (November 1957): 510–522.

Meyers, John B. "The Alabama Freedmen and the Economic Adjustments During Presidential Reconstruction, 1865–1867." *Alabama Review* 26 (October 1973): 252–266.

———. "The Freedman and the Law in Post-Bellum Alabama, 1865–1867." *Alabama Review* 23 (January 1970): 56–69.

Miller, Grace Lewis. "The Mobile and Ohio Railroad in Antebellum Times." *Alabama Historical Quarterly* 7 (spring 1945): 37–59.

Montgomery, Horace. "The Crisis of 1850 and Its Effect on Political Parties in Georgia." *Georgia Historical Quarterly* 24 (December 1940): 293–322.

Moore, John Preston. "Correspondence of Pierre Soule: The Louisiana Tehuantepec Company." *The Hispanic American Historical Review* 32 (February 1952): 59–72.

Nichols, James L. "Confederate Engineers and the Defense of Mobile." *Alabama Review* 12 (July 1959): 181–195.

Nichols, Roy Franklin. "The Kansas-Nebraska Act: A Century of Historiography." *Mississippi Valley Historical Review* 43 (June 1956): 187–212.

Nieman, Donald C. "Andrew Johnson, the Freedmen's Bureau, and the Problem of Equal Rights, 1865–1866." *Journal of Southern History* 44 (August 1978): 399–420.

Olliff, Donathan C. "Mexico's Mid-Nineteenth Century Drive For Material Development." *SECOLAS Annals* 8 (1977): 19–29.

Pierson, Michael D. "'All Southern Society is Assailed by the Foulest Charges': Charles Sumner's 'The Crime Against Kansas' and the Escalation of the Republican Anti-Slavery Rhetoric." *New England Quarterly* 58 (March 1995): 531–557.

Reid, Robert. "Changing Interpretations of the Reconstruction Period in Alabama History." *Alabama Review* 27 (October 1974): 263–281.

Scholes, Walter V. "A Revolution Falters: Mexico 1856–1857." *Hispanic American Historical Review* 32 (February 1952): 1–21.

Schweninger, Loren. "Alabama Blacks and the Congressional Reconstruction Acts of 1867." *Alabama Review* 31 (July 1978): 182–198.

———. "Black Citizenship and the Republican Party in Reconstruction Alabama." *Alabama Review* 29 (April 1976): 83–103.

Sellers, Charles Grier, Jr. "Who Were the Southern Whigs?" *Alabama Historical Review* 59 (January 1954): 335–346.

Steward, Luther N., Jr. "John Forsyth." *Alabama Review* 14 (April 1961): 98–123.

Walton, Brian G. "Georgia's Biennial Legislatures, 1840–1860, and the Elections to the U.S. Senate." *Georgia Historical Quarterly* 61 (Summer 1977): 140–155.

White, Kenneth B. "Wager Swayne: Racist or Realist?" *Alabama Review* 31 (April 1978): 92–109.

Wiggins, Sarah Woolfork. "The 'Pig-Iron' Kelley Riot in Mobile, May 14, 1867." *Alabama Review* 23 (January 1970): 45–55.

Wooster, Ralph A. "The Secession of the Lower South: An Examination of Changing Interpretations." *Civil War History* 7 (June 1961): 117–127.

Unpublished Secondary Sources

Chesnutt, David R. "John Forsyth: A Southern Partisan, 1865–1867." Master's thesis, Auburn University, 1967.

Lavanna, Elizabeth M. "South Alabama Newspapers in the Nineteenth Century." Master's thesis, University of Alabama, 1983.

Poore, Ralph. "Alabama's Enterprising Newspaper. The *Mobile Register* and Its Forbearers, 1813–1991." Unpublished manuscript, Mobile Public Library, Mobile, Alabama.

Robinson, Robert L. "Mobile in the 1850s: A Social, Cultural, and Economic History." Master's thesis, University of Alabama, 1982.

Steward, Luther Neal. "John Forsyth of Alabama, Southern Diplomat, Editor, and Politician." Master's thesis, Louisiana State University, 1954.

Thompson, Alan Smith. "Mobile, Alabama, 1850–1861: Economic, Political, Physical, and Population Characteristics." Ph.D. diss., University of Alabama, 1979.

Index